파고다 끝토익 1000제 LC

PAGODA Books

토익이란?

TOEIC(Test Of English for International Communication)은 영어가 모국어가 아닌 사람들을 대상으로 일상생활 또는 국제 업무 등에 필요한 실용 영어 능력을 평가하는 시험이다.

토익 시험은 언어의 본래 목적인 개인간의 '의사 소통(Communi-cation)'에 중점을 두고 있다. 영어에 대한 '지식'을 평가하는 것이 아니라 영어의 '사용법'에 대한 평가로 실용성과 기능성을 중시하는 시험이다.

따라서 TOEIC은 1979년 미국 ETS(Educational Testing Service)에 의해 개발된 이래 전 세계 150개 국가 14,000여 개의 기관에서 승진 또는 해외 파견 인원 선발 등의 목적으로 널리 활용되고 있으며 우리나라에는 1982년 도입되어 전 세계적으로 해마다 약 700만 명 이상이 응시하고 있다.

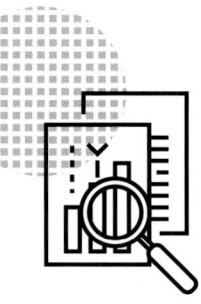

파고다 끝토익 1000제 LC

PAGODA Books

파고다
끝토익
1000제 LC

초판 1쇄 인쇄 2017년 8월 22일
초판 5쇄 발행 2019년 12월 13일

지 은 이	켈리 정, 에이프릴 김, 파고다교육그룹 언어교육연구소
펴 낸 이	고루다
펴 낸 곳	Wit&Wisdom 도서출판 위트앤위즈덤
임프린트	PAGODA Books
출판등록	2005년 5월 27일 제 300-2005-90호
주　　소	06614 서울특별시 서초구 강남대로 419, 19층(서초동, 파고다타워)
전　　화	(02) 6940-4070
팩　　스	(02) 536-0660
홈페이지	www.pagodabook.com
저작권자	ⓒ 2017 파고다아카데미, 위트앤위즈덤

이 책의 저작권은 저자와 출판사에 있습니다. 서면에 의한 저작권자와 출판사의 허락 없이
내용의 일부 혹은 전부를 인용 및 복제하거나 발췌하는 것을 금합니다.

Copyright ⓒ 2017 by PAGODA Academy, Wit&Wisdom

All rights reserved. No part of this publication may be reproduced, stored
in a retrieval system, or transmitted, in any form, or by any means, electronic,
mechanical, photocopying, recording or otherwise, without the prior written
permission of the copyright holder and the publisher.

ISBN 978-89-6281-805-5 (13740)

도서출판 위트앤위즈덤	www.pagodabook.com
파고다 어학원	www.pagoda21.com
파고다 인강	www.pagodastar.com
테스트 클리닉	www.testclinic.com

PAGODA Books는 도서출판 Wit&Wisdom의 성인 어학 전문 임프린트입니다.
낙장 및 파본은 구매처에서 교환해 드립니다.

토익에 관하여

시험 구성

구성	PART	PART별 내용		문항 수		시간	배점
Listening Comprehension	1	사진 묘사		6	100문항	45분	495점
	2	질의 응답		25			
	3	짧은 대화		39			
	4	짧은 담화		30			
Reading Comprehension	5	단문 빈칸 채우기(문법 / 어휘)		30	100문항	75분	495점
	6	장문 빈칸 메우기		16			
	7	독해	단일 지문	29			
			이중 지문	10			
			삼중 지문	15			
Total	7 PARTS			200문항		120분	990점

시험 준비물

1. **필기구:** 연필, 지우개
2. **신분증:** 주민등록증, 운전면허증, 기간 만료 전 여권, 공무원증, 청소년증, 사관생도 신분증
   * 학생증(대학,대학원), 사원증, 舊(구)주민등록증, 각종 자격증, 사진이 부착된 신용카드, 국제운전면허증, 유효기간이 지난 신분증은 절대 신분증으로 인정하지 않는다.

시험 시간

 오전 시험: 9시 20분 입실, 9시 50분 이후로 입실 불가   오후 시험: 2시 20분 입실, 2시 50분 이후로 입실 불가

시간		소요시간	내용
오전 9:30 ~ 9:45	오후 2:30 ~ 2:45	15분	답안지 작성 안내
오전 9:45 ~ 9:50	오후 2:45 ~ 2:50	5분	시험 시작 전 휴식 시간
오전 9:50 ~ 10:05	오후 2:50 ~ 3:05	15분	신분증 확인
오전 10:05 ~ 10:10	오후 3:05 ~ 3:10	5분	문제지 배부 및 파본 확인
오전 10:10 ~ 10:55	오후 3:10 ~ 3:55	45분	듣기 평가
오전 10:55 ~ 12:10	오후 3:55 ~ 5:10	75분	읽기 평가 및 2차 신분 확인 * 정확한 신분 확인 및 대리응시 등 부정행위 방지를 위해 독해 평가 시간에 2차 신분 확인 실시

파트별 토익 소개

PART 1　PHOTOGRAPHS
사진 묘사

PART 1은 제시한 사진을 올바르게 묘사한 문장을 찾는 문제로, 방송으로 사진에 대한 4개의 짧은 설명문을 한번 들려준다. 4개의 설명문은 문제지에 인쇄되어 있지 않으며 4개의 설명문을 잘 듣고 그 중에서 사진을 가장 정확하게 묘사하고 있는 문장을 답으로 선택한다.

문항 수	6문항 (1번 ~ 6번)
Direction 소요 시간	약 1분 30초
문제를 들려주는 시간	약 20초
다음 문제까지의 여유 시간	약 5초
문제 유형	유형 변경 없이 기존 유형의 문제 골고루 출제 1인 사진 2인 이상 사진 사물/풍경 사진

2인 이상 사진 »

(A) They're writing on a board.
(B) They're taking a file from a shelf.
(C) They're working at a desk.
(D) They're listening to a presentation.

PART 2

QUESTION-RESPONSE
질의 응답

PART 2는 질문에 대한 올바른 답을 찾는 문제로, 방송을 통해 질문과 질문에 대한 3개의 응답문을 각 한 번씩 들려준다. 질문과 응답문은 문제지에 인쇄가 되어 있지 않으며 질문에 대한 가장 어울리는 응답문을 답으로 선택한다.

문항 수	25문항 (7번 ~ 31번)
Direction 소요 시간	약 25초
문제를 들려주는 시간	약 15초
다음 문제까지의 여유 시간	약 5초
문제 유형	유형 변경 없이 기존 유형의 문제 골고루 출제 의문사 의문문(Who/When/Where/What/Which/How/Why) 부정의문문/부가의문문/ 평서문/선택의문문/ 제안·제공·요청의문문/Be동사/ 조동사 의문문/간접의문문

How 의문문 >> Mark your answer on your answer sheet. (A) (B) (C)

Q. How was the English test you took today?
A. (A) I took the bus home.
   (B) I thought it was too difficult.
   (C) I have two classes today.

PART 3

SHORT CONVERSATION
짧은 대화

PART 3은 짧은 대화문을 듣고 이에 대한 문제를 푸는 형식으로, 먼저 방송을 통해 짧은 대화를 들려준 뒤 이에 해당하는 질문을 들려 준다. 문제지에는 질문과 4개의 보기가 인쇄되어 있으며 문제를 들은 뒤 제시된 보기 중 가장 적당한 것을 답으로 선택한다.

문항 수	**13개 대화문, 39문항 (32번 ~ 70번)**
Direction 소요 시간	약 30초
문제를 들려주는 시간	약 30~40초
다음 문제까지의 여유 시간	약 8초
지문 유형	회사 생활, 일상생활, 공공 장소 및 서비스 기관 ➔ **3인 대화문 추가: 주고받는 대화 수 증가** ➔ **실생활에서 사용하는 회화 표현(구어체)의 증가**
질문 유형	- 전체 내용 관련 문제: 주제/목적, 인물, 장소 문제 - 세부사항 문제(문제점, 이유/방법, 핵심어 정보 찾기) - 제안·요청 문제 - 앞으로 할 일 문제 - **맥락상 화자의 의도 파악 문제** - **유추/추론 문제** - **시각 정보 연계 문제**

3인 대화 ≫
화자 의도 파악 ≫

Questions 32-34 refer to the following conversation with three speakers.

33. Why does the woman say, "There you go"?
    (A) She is happy to attend a meeting.
    (B) She is frustrated with a coworker.
    (C) She is offering encouragement.
    (D) She is handing over something.

유추/추론 문제 ≫

34. What do the men imply about the company?
    (A) It has launched new merchandise.
    (B) It is planning to relocate soon.
    (C) It has clients in several countries.
    (D) It is having financial difficulties.

Man 1 How have you two been doing with your sales lately?
Woman Um, not too bad. My clients have been ordering about the same amount of promotional merchandise as before.
Man 2 I haven't been doing so well. But I do have a meeting with a potential new client tomorrow.
Woman There you go. I'm sure things will turn around for you.
Man 1 Yeah, I hope it works out.
Woman It's probably just temporary due to the recession.
Man 2 Maybe, but I heard that the company may downsize to try to save money.
Man 1 Actually, I heard that, too.

PART 4

SHORT TALK
짧은 담화

PART 4는 짧은 담화를 듣고 이에 대한 문제를 푸는 형식으로, 먼저 방송을 통해 짧은 담화를 들려준 뒤 이에 해당하는 질문을 들려 준다. 문제지에는 질문과 4개의 보기가 인쇄되어 있으며 문제를 들은 뒤 제시된 보기 중 가장 적당한 것을 답으로 선택한다.

문항 수	**10개 지문, 30문항 (71번 ~ 100번)**
Direction 소요 시간	약 30초
문제를 들려주는 시간	약 30~40초
다음 문제까지의 여유 시간	약 8초
지문 유형	전화 · 녹음 메시지, 공지 · 안내, 인물 소개, 광고, 방송 · 보도 → **발음 생략, 군더더기 표현과 불완전한 문장이 포함된 지문의 실생활 영어(구어체)의 등장**
질문 유형	- 전체 내용 관련 문제: 주제/목적, 인물, 장소 문제 - 세부사항 문제(문제점, 이유/방법, 핵심어 정보 찾기) - 제안·요청 문제 - 앞으로 할 일 문제 - **맥락상 화자의 의도 파악 문제** - **시각 정보 연계 문제**

시각 정보 연계 문제 »

도표/그래픽 연관 문제 »

Questions 71-73 refer to the following talk and program.

Program	
Time	**Speaker**
14:00-14:55	Mr. Ward
15:00-15:55	Ms. Cornelio
15:55-16:10	**BREAK**
16:10-17:05	Ms. Turner
17:10-18:05	Mr. Roland

73. Look at the graphic. Who will be the final speaker?

(A) Mr. Ward
(B) Ms. Cornelio
(C) Ms. Turner
(D) Mr. Roland

Woman I'd like to welcome all of you to today's employee training and development seminar for business owners. I'll briefly go over a few details before we get started. There will be a 15 minute break for coffee and snacks half way through the program. This will be a good opportunity for you to mingle. If you need to leave the room during a talk, make sure to keep your wallet, phone, and …ah… any other valuable personal items with you. Also, please note that there will be a change in the order in the printed program. Um… Mr. Roland has to leave earlier than originally scheduled, so the last two speakers will be switched.

목차

토익이란?	4
토익에 관하여	5
파트별 토익 소개	6
목차	10
이 책의 구성과 특징	12
토익 점수 환산표	14
20일 학습 플랜	15

TEST 1	16
TEST 2	30
TEST 3	44
TEST 4	58
TEST 5	72

TEST 6 ～～～～～～～～～～～～ 86

TEST 7 ～～～～～～～～～～～～ 100

TEST 8 ～～～～～～～～～～～～ 114

TEST 9 ～～～～～～～～～～～～ 128

TEST 10 ～～～～～～～～～～～ 142

Scripts 156
Answers 234
Answer Sheets 241

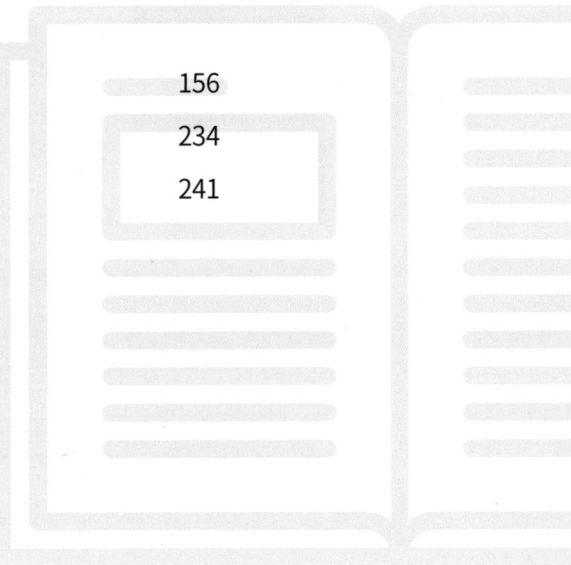

이 책의 구성과 특징

PART 1 사진의 유형을 이해하고 유형별 사진 공략법과 시제와 태 표현을 정확하게 구분한다.

PART 2 의문사 의문문, 비의문사 의문문에 따른 다양한 응답 표현 및 빈출 오답 유형을 익힌다.

PART 3 빠르게 전개되는 지문을 정확하게 파악하는 직청직해 능력, 문맥 파악 능력, 그리고 논리력을 기른다.

PART 4 출제되는 지문 유형을 익히고 해당 지문에 자주 나오는 빈출 어휘 및 표현을 학습한다.

1. 최신 경향을 반영한 실전 모의고사 10회분

최근 신토익 정기 토익 시험 문제들을 정밀하게 분석 및 반영하여, 실전 정기 토익과 가장 유사한 난이도로 실전 모의고사 10회분을 구성했다.

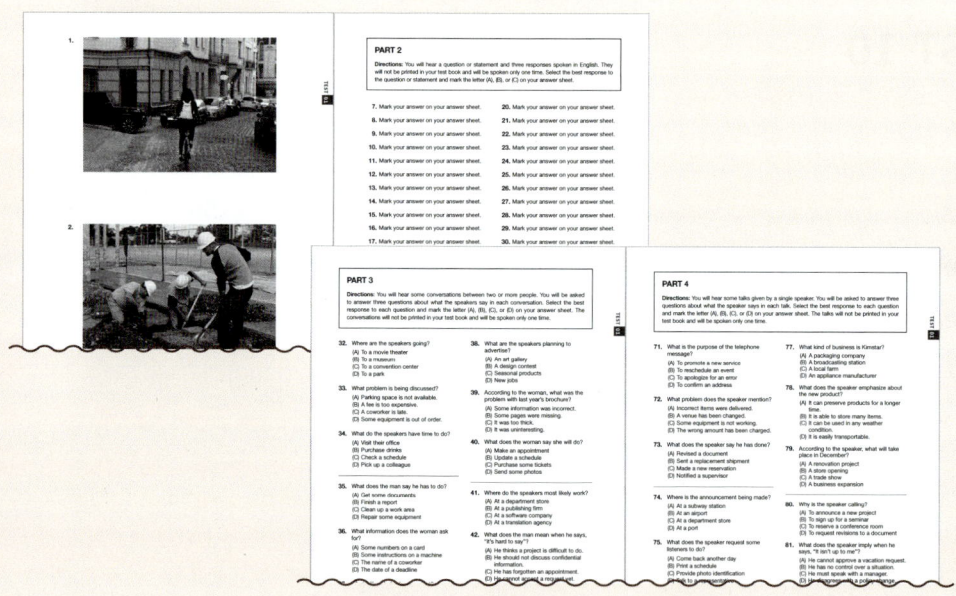

2. QR 코드 인증 음원 및 해석 제공

PART 1~4 모든 문제에 대한 음원과 해석을 QR 코드를 통해 제공하여, 학습자들이 언제 어디서든 편리하게 학습할 수 있도록 하였다.

3. 파고다 스타 강사진과 파고다 언어교육연구소의 문제풀이 노하우를 완벽히 담은 파트별 해설 (유료 3,000원)

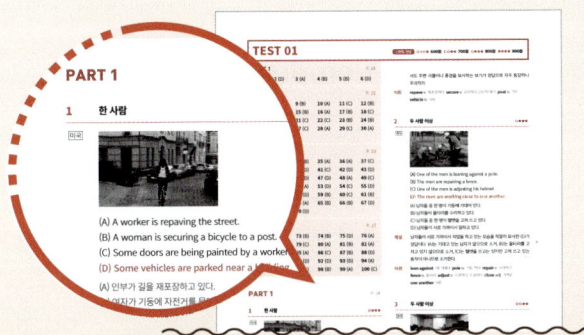

PART 1 사진을 기준으로 문제 유형을 분류하였고, 선택지의 상태, 동작, 위치 묘사 오류 파악을 통해 정·오답을 가려낼 수 있다.

PART 2 질문을 기준으로 문제 유형을 분류하여, 문제 유형별 정답을 파악하고 오답을 선별해 낼 수 있다.

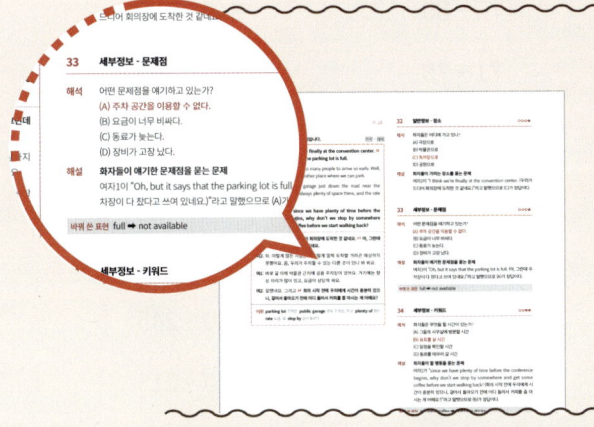

PART 3 문제의 키워드를 확인하고 지문 내 정답 힌트 찾기와 바꿔 쓴 표현 학습을 통해 고득점을 공략한다.

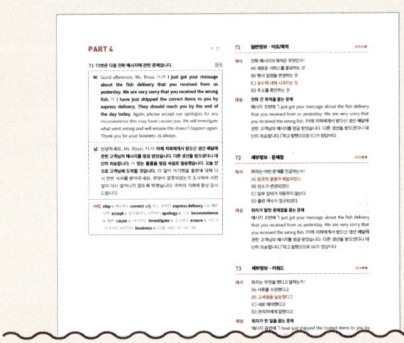

PART 4 문제의 키워드를 확인하고 지문 내 정답 힌트 찾기와 바꿔 쓴 표현 학습을 통해 고득점을 공략한다.

구매방법 1.

www.pagodastar.com으로 접속 후, 회원가입 및 로그인을 한다.

↓

홈페이지 메인 상단 메뉴의 과목선택 탭에서 "**교재/상품권**"을 클릭한다.

↓

파고다 끝토익 실전 1000제 **LC 해설서**를 구매한다.

구매방법 2.

www.pagodabook.com으로 접속 후, 왼쪽 메뉴에서 "**영어 > 토익**"을 클릭한다.

↓

파고다 끝토익 실전 1000제 **LC 도서**를 클릭한다.

↓

도서 정보 하단에 "**해설서 구매하기**"를 선택한다.

↓

연동된 파스타 홈페이지에서 회원가입 후 해설서를 구매한다.

온라인 해설서 구매 바로 가기

＊ 구매 후, 내 강의실 탭에서 "온라인 교재 다운로드"를 클릭한다.

토익 점수 환산표

Listening Comprehension	
정답 수	환산 점수대
96 ~ 100	480 ~ 495
91 ~ 95	470 ~ 495
86 ~ 90	440 ~ 490
81 ~ 85	410 ~ 460
76 ~ 80	390 ~ 430
71 ~ 75	360 ~ 400
66 ~ 70	330 ~ 370
61 ~ 65	300 ~ 345
56 ~ 60	270 ~ 315
51 ~ 55	240 ~ 285
46 ~ 50	210 ~ 255
41 ~ 45	180 ~ 225
36 ~ 40	150 ~ 195
31 ~ 35	120 ~ 165
26 ~ 30	90 ~ 135
21 ~ 25	60 ~ 105
16 ~ 20	40 ~ 75
11 ~ 15	10 ~ 45
6 ~ 10	5 ~ 20
1 ~ 5	5
0	0

Reading Comprehension	
정답 수	환산 점수대
96 ~ 100	450 ~ 495
91 ~ 95	420 ~ 465
86 ~ 90	400 ~ 435
81 ~ 85	370 ~ 410
76 ~ 80	340 ~ 380
71 ~ 75	310 ~ 355
66 ~ 70	280 ~ 325
61 ~ 65	260 ~ 300
56 ~ 60	230 ~ 270
51 ~ 55	200 ~ 245
46 ~ 50	170 ~ 215
41 ~ 45	140 ~ 185
36 ~ 40	120 ~ 160
31 ~ 35	90 ~ 130
26 ~ 30	60 ~ 105
21 ~ 25	30 ~ 75
16 ~ 20	10 ~ 50
11 ~ 15	5 ~ 20
6 ~ 10	5
1 ~ 5	5
0	0

20일 학습 플랜

DAY 1	DAY 2	DAY 3	DAY 4
TEST 01	TEST 01 복습	TEST 02	TEST 02 복습

DAY 5	DAY 6	DAY 7	DAY 8
TEST 03	TEST 03 복습	TEST 04	TEST 04 복습

DAY 9	DAY 10	DAY 11	DAY 12
TEST 05	TEST 05 복습	TEST 06	TEST 06 복습

DAY 13	DAY 14	DAY 15	DAY 16
TEST 07	TEST 07 복습	TEST 08	TEST 08 복습

DAY 17	DAY 18	DAY 19	DAY 20
TEST 09	TEST 09 복습	TEST 10	TEST 10 복습

Listening Comprehension

TEST 01

음원·해석

LISTENING TEST

In the Listening test, you will be asked to demonstrate how well you understand spoken English. The entire Listening test will last approximately 45 minutes. There are four parts, and directions are given for each part. You must mark your answers on the separate answer sheet. Do not write your answers in your test book.

PART 1

Directions: For each question in this part, you will hear four statements about a picture in your test book. When you hear the statements, you must select the one statement that best describes what you see in the picture. Then find the number of the question on your answer sheet and mark your answer. The statements will not be printed in your test book and will be spoken only one time.

Statement (B), "A man is pointing at a document," is the best description of the picture, so you should select answer (B) and mark it on your answer sheet.

1.

2.

3.

4.

5.

6.

PART 2

Directions: You will hear a question or statement and three responses spoken in English. They will not be printed in your test book and will be spoken only one time. Select the best response to the question or statement and mark the letter (A), (B), or (C) on your answer sheet.

7. Mark your answer on your answer sheet.
8. Mark your answer on your answer sheet.
9. Mark your answer on your answer sheet.
10. Mark your answer on your answer sheet.
11. Mark your answer on your answer sheet.
12. Mark your answer on your answer sheet.
13. Mark your answer on your answer sheet.
14. Mark your answer on your answer sheet.
15. Mark your answer on your answer sheet.
16. Mark your answer on your answer sheet.
17. Mark your answer on your answer sheet.
18. Mark your answer on your answer sheet.
19. Mark your answer on your answer sheet.
20. Mark your answer on your answer sheet.
21. Mark your answer on your answer sheet.
22. Mark your answer on your answer sheet.
23. Mark your answer on your answer sheet.
24. Mark your answer on your answer sheet.
25. Mark your answer on your answer sheet.
26. Mark your answer on your answer sheet.
27. Mark your answer on your answer sheet.
28. Mark your answer on your answer sheet.
29. Mark your answer on your answer sheet.
30. Mark your answer on your answer sheet.
31. Mark your answer on your answer sheet.

PART 3

Directions: You will hear some conversations between two or more people. You will be asked to answer three questions about what the speakers say in each conversation. Select the best response to each question and mark the letter (A), (B), (C), or (D) on your answer sheet. The conversations will not be printed in your test book and will be spoken only one time.

32. Where are the speakers going?
    (A) To a movie theater
    (B) To a museum
    (C) To a convention center
    (D) To a park

33. What problem is being discussed?
    (A) Parking space is not available.
    (B) A fee is too expensive.
    (C) A coworker is late.
    (D) Some equipment is out of order.

34. What do the speakers have time to do?
    (A) Visit their office
    (B) Purchase drinks
    (C) Check a schedule
    (D) Pick up a colleague

35. What does the man say he has to do?
    (A) Get some documents
    (B) Finish a report
    (C) Clean up a work area
    (D) Repair some equipment

36. What information does the woman ask for?
    (A) Some numbers on a card
    (B) Some instructions on a machine
    (C) The name of a coworker
    (D) The date of a deadline

37. What will probably happen next?
    (A) A package will be delivered.
    (B) A system will be tested.
    (C) The man will enter a building.
    (D) The woman will check an e-mail.

38. What are the speakers planning to advertise?
    (A) An art gallery
    (B) A design contest
    (C) Seasonal products
    (D) New jobs

39. According to the woman, what was the problem with last year's brochure?
    (A) Some information was incorrect.
    (B) Some pages were missing.
    (C) It was too thick.
    (D) It was uninteresting.

40. What does the woman say she will do?
    (A) Make an appointment
    (B) Update a schedule
    (C) Purchase some tickets
    (D) Send some photos

41. Where do the speakers most likely work?
    (A) At a department store
    (B) At a publishing firm
    (C) At a software company
    (D) At a translation agency

42. What does the man mean when he says, "it's hard to say"?
    (A) He thinks a project is difficult to do.
    (B) He should not discuss confidential information.
    (C) He has forgotten an appointment.
    (D) He cannot accept a request yet.

43. What does the woman propose?
    (A) Booking a flight
    (B) Printing some documents
    (C) Changing departments
    (D) Attending a meeting

GO ON TO THE NEXT PAGE

44. Where does the man most likely work?

(A) At an engineering firm
(B) At an office supplies store
(C) At a real estate agency
(D) At a moving company

45. What does the woman mention about her company's project?

(A) It will take place in the downtown area.
(B) It will be finished in one year.
(C) It requires a large budget.
(D) It needed a permit from the city government.

46. What information does the man ask for?

(A) The address of a building
(B) The price of some equipment
(C) The expected number of workers
(D) The dates of a stay

47. What are the speakers discussing?

(A) The date of a company trip
(B) The location of some offices
(C) Job openings at a firm
(D) Enrollment in upcoming workshops

48. What does the woman suggest doing?

(A) Making an additional session available
(B) Arranging for transportation
(C) Contacting an event organizer
(D) Hiring temporary workers

49. What does the man say he will do?

(A) Reserve a venue
(B) Print out a schedule
(C) Check with some colleagues
(D) Advertise some positions

50. What type of service does the woman's company provide?

(A) Commercial property management
(B) International delivery
(C) Interior design
(D) Large equipment storage

51. Why does the man say, "Tokyo is very far away"?

(A) To consider a job assignment
(B) To deny a request
(C) To express relief
(D) To show concern

52. What will the speakers most likely discuss next?

(A) A rental price
(B) Travel dates
(C) A shipping fee
(D) Potential customers

53. What is the woman preparing for?

(A) An anniversary celebration
(B) A business conference
(C) A grand opening
(D) A fundraising event

54. What does the woman request permission to do?

(A) Conduct a survey
(B) Put up a sign
(C) Sell food
(D) Take pictures

55. What will the man speak to his manager about?

(A) Reserving equipment
(B) Hiring a security officer
(C) Setting up a room
(D) Donating items

56. What problem is the company having?
(A) Many employees have left the company.
(B) Some shipments have been delayed.
(C) New competitors have entered the market.
(D) Its products have not been selling well.

57. What does the man recommend?
(A) Attending sports competitions
(B) Requesting more funds
(C) Updating some features
(D) Hiring temporary workers

58. What does the man ask Erin to do?
(A) Review a budget report
(B) Call some local businesses
(C) Schedule a video conference with clients
(D) Provide information at a future meeting

59. What problem does the woman mention?
(A) Customer complaints have been received.
(B) Business is slower than usual.
(C) A restaurant needs more workers.
(D) A permit has not been renewed.

60. What does the man suggest?
(A) Revising a policy
(B) Hiring additional kitchen staff
(C) Introducing a special offer
(D) Contacting an office

61. What does the woman ask the man to do?
(A) Interview some applicants
(B) Make food samples
(C) Prepare some documents
(D) Hold a workshop

Prices	
General	$17
Child	$10
Group (15+)	$13
Caldwell Members	$12

62. What kind of event is being discussed?
(A) A movie premiere
(B) A dance show
(C) A musical performance
(D) An art festival

63. Look at the graphic. What ticket price will the speakers most likely pay?
(A) $17
(B) $10
(C) $13
(D) $12

64. What does the man recommend the woman do?
(A) Speak to a coworker
(B) Work on the weekend
(C) Bring some cash
(D) Arrange a ride

GO ON TO THE NEXT PAGE

Bellanore Bistro
Chef's Special

Monday - Crab cakes

Tuesday - Pulled pork burgers

Wednesday - Shrimp pasta

Thursday - Eggplant parmesan

Friday - Roast chicken

---

http://www.arrowlines.com

Choose Your Car			
Select	Type	Availability	Car
▮	Regular	Seats open	A
▮	Regular	Seats open	B
▮	Regular	Seats open	C
▮	Business	Seats open	D
▮	Business	Full	E

65. Look at the graphic. Which day is the conversation taking place?

(A) Tuesday
(B) Wednesday
(C) Thursday
(D) Friday

66. What does the woman inquire about?

(A) Catering services
(B) Event space
(C) A corporate discount
(D) Parking fees

67. Why does the man apologize?

(A) A credit card cannot be processed.
(B) An ingredient was not fresh.
(C) A server was not available.
(D) A voucher cannot be accepted.

68. Why does the man dislike McGruder Terminal?

(A) It is located far away.
(B) It does not provide free Internet.
(C) It does not offer luggage storage.
(D) It is always crowded.

69. Look at the graphic. Which car will the speakers most likely select?

(A) Car A
(B) Car B
(C) Car C
(D) Car D

70. What does the man ask the woman about?

(A) Where he plans to visit
(B) Which document he will bring
(C) When the woman prefers to depart
(D) What payment method the woman will use

PART 4

Directions: You will hear some talks given by a single speaker. You will be asked to answer three questions about what the speaker says in each talk. Select the best response to each question and mark the letter (A), (B), (C), or (D) on your answer sheet. The talks will not be printed in your test book and will be spoken only one time.

71. What is the purpose of the telephone message?
(A) To promote a new service
(B) To reschedule an event
(C) To apologize for an error
(D) To confirm an address

72. What problem does the speaker mention?
(A) Incorrect items were delivered.
(B) A venue has been changed.
(C) Some equipment is not working.
(D) The wrong amount has been charged.

73. What does the speaker say he has done?
(A) Revised a document
(B) Sent a replacement shipment
(C) Made a new reservation
(D) Notified a supervisor

74. Where is the announcement being made?
(A) At a subway station
(B) At an airport
(C) At a department store
(D) At a port

75. What does the speaker request some listeners to do?
(A) Come back another day
(B) Print a schedule
(C) Provide photo identification
(D) Talk to a representative

76. According to the speaker, what will be offered?
(A) Food
(B) Brochures
(C) Timetables
(D) Coupons

77. What kind of business is Kimstar?
(A) A packaging company
(B) A broadcasting station
(C) A local farm
(D) An appliance manufacturer

78. What does the speaker emphasize about the new product?
(A) It can preserve products for a longer time.
(B) It is able to store many items.
(C) It can be used in any weather condition.
(D) It is easily transportable.

79. According to the speaker, what will take place in December?
(A) A renovation project
(B) A store opening
(C) A trade show
(D) A business expansion

80. Why is the speaker calling?
(A) To announce a new project
(B) To sign up for a seminar
(C) To reserve a conference room
(D) To request revisions to a document

81. What does the speaker imply when he says, "It isn't up to me"?
(A) He cannot approve a vacation request.
(B) He has no control over a situation.
(C) He must speak with a manager.
(D) He disagrees with a policy change.

82. What does the speaker ask the listener to do?
(A) Find out a price
(B) Submit an application
(C) Update a Web site
(D) Review a product

GO ON TO THE NEXT PAGE

83. What is the main topic of the announcement?
    (A) Redesigning the company logo
    (B) Permitting staff to work from home
    (C) Offering more educational opportunities
    (D) Allowing new workers more time off

84. According to the speaker, why is a change being made?
    (A) To improve product quality
    (B) To retain existing employees
    (C) To promote better communication
    (D) To ensure a safe working environment

85. What are the listeners told to do?
    (A) Inform staff of a policy
    (B) Update their personal information
    (C) Receive training regularly
    (D) Change schedules with team members

86. What is the subject of the talk?
    (A) A business relocation
    (B) New manufacturing equipment
    (C) Company security procedures
    (D) A product launch

87. What is implied about some files?
    (A) They are being transferred to another computer.
    (B) They cannot be accessed without a password.
    (C) They must be deleted every month.
    (D) They are currently being reviewed.

88. According to the speaker, what happens regularly?
    (A) Office supplies are purchased.
    (B) Computer software is checked.
    (C) Some employees are awarded.
    (D) Updated information is shared.

89. Why is the president coming for a visit?
    (A) A new product will be released.
    (B) A building has been purchased.
    (C) A store has been renovated.
    (D) A press conference will take place.

90. Why does the speaker say, "This won't be a formal inspection"?
    (A) To disagree with a plan
    (B) To confirm a deadline
    (C) To point out an accomplishment
    (D) To reassure staff

91. What event have the listeners been invited to?
    (A) An anniversary celebration
    (B) A corporate conference
    (C) A store sale
    (D) A welcome meal

92. What is Fitness Friend?
    (A) A social networking Web site
    (B) A health clinic
    (C) A radio show
    (D) An electronic device

93. What does the speaker mean when he says, "Why bother with all that"?
    (A) A store location is too far.
    (B) A product is not that popular.
    (C) A deadline has passed.
    (D) A task does not have to be inconvenient.

94. Why are listeners told to act soon?
    (A) A discount offer is temporary.
    (B) An application period is ending.
    (C) Some merchandise will sell out.
    (D) Some businesses will close next week.

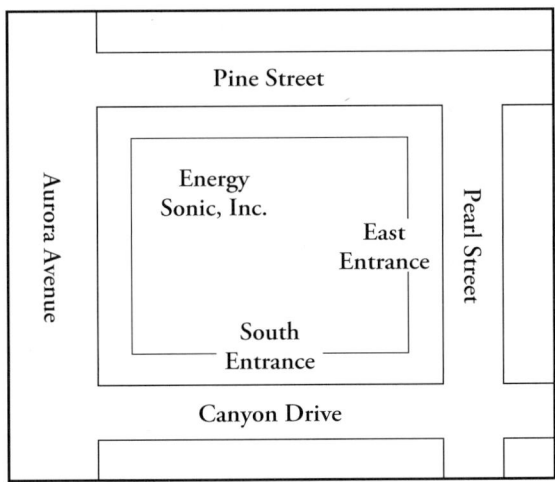

Procedure Checklist:
1. ___ Check code on packaging
2. ___ See that the items match the order
3. ___ Look for damaged merchandise
4. ___ Transfer items to storage

95. What will take place tomorrow?
(A) A race
(B) A parade
(C) A music festival
(D) An annual workshop

96. Look at the graphic. Which road will be closed?
(A) Pine Street
(B) Pearl Street
(C) Canyon Drive
(D) Aurora Avenue

97. What does the speaker suggest?
(A) Taking part in a local event
(B) Using public transportation
(C) Allowing more time to reach the office
(D) Working from home to avoid traffic

98. What does the speaker say she is worried about?
(A) Expensive shipping rates
(B) Wasted work time
(C) Slow customer service
(D) Defective merchandise

99. Look at the graphic. Which procedure does the speaker say requires extra attention?
(A) Procedure 1
(B) Procedure 2
(C) Procedure 3
(D) Procedure 4

100. What does the speaker say will happen on Saturday?
(A) A new delivery policy will be implemented.
(B) A retail store will relocate.
(C) A promotional event will start.
(D) A monthly report will be reviewed.

This is the end of the Listening test.

Listening Comprehension

TEST 02

음원·해석

LISTENING TEST

In the Listening test, you will be asked to demonstrate how well you understand spoken English. The entire Listening test will last approximately 45 minutes. There are four parts, and directions are given for each part. You must mark your answers on the separate answer sheet. Do not write your answers in your test book.

PART 1

Directions: For each question in this part, you will hear four statements about a picture in your test book. When you hear the statements, you must select the one statement that best describes what you see in the picture. Then find the number of the question on your answer sheet and mark your answer. The statements will not be printed in your test book and will be spoken only one time.

Statement (B), "A man is pointing at a document," is the best description of the picture, so you should select answer (B) and mark it on your answer sheet.

1.

2.

3.

4.

5.

6.

PART 2

Directions: You will hear a question or statement and three responses spoken in English. They will not be printed in your test book and will be spoken only one time. Select the best response to the question or statement and mark the letter (A), (B), or (C) on your answer sheet.

7. Mark your answer on your answer sheet.
8. Mark your answer on your answer sheet.
9. Mark your answer on your answer sheet.
10. Mark your answer on your answer sheet.
11. Mark your answer on your answer sheet.
12. Mark your answer on your answer sheet.
13. Mark your answer on your answer sheet.
14. Mark your answer on your answer sheet.
15. Mark your answer on your answer sheet.
16. Mark your answer on your answer sheet.
17. Mark your answer on your answer sheet.
18. Mark your answer on your answer sheet.
19. Mark your answer on your answer sheet.
20. Mark your answer on your answer sheet.
21. Mark your answer on your answer sheet.
22. Mark your answer on your answer sheet.
23. Mark your answer on your answer sheet.
24. Mark your answer on your answer sheet.
25. Mark your answer on your answer sheet.
26. Mark your answer on your answer sheet.
27. Mark your answer on your answer sheet.
28. Mark your answer on your answer sheet.
29. Mark your answer on your answer sheet.
30. Mark your answer on your answer sheet.
31. Mark your answer on your answer sheet.

PART 3

Directions: You will hear some conversations between two or more people. You will be asked to answer three questions about what the speakers say in each conversation. Select the best response to each question and mark the letter (A), (B), (C), or (D) on your answer sheet. The conversations will not be printed in your test book and will be spoken only one time.

32. What is the purpose of the call?
    (A) To order a software program
    (B) To sign up for an account
    (C) To inquire about a billing error
    (D) To hire a moving company

33. What does the man say happened?
    (A) An office was short on workers.
    (B) Some files were deleted.
    (C) A product was not available.
    (D) Some records were not correct.

34. What does the man suggest the woman do?
    (A) Ask for money off
    (B) Contact the company later
    (C) Talk to the manager of a department
    (D) Go to another location

35. Who most likely is the man?
    (A) An insurance agent
    (B) A construction worker
    (C) A delivery driver
    (D) A receptionist

36. What does the man want to change?
    (A) An appointment time
    (B) Some payment details
    (C) A meal preference
    (D) An order quantity

37. What will the woman do next?
    (A) Provide a credit card number
    (B) Look over a billing statement
    (C) Send her contact information
    (D) Update a planner

38. Where does the man most likely work?
    (A) At an insurance firm
    (B) At a legal office
    (C) At a software company
    (D) At a dental clinic

39. Why is the woman NOT available on Thursday?
    (A) She will be attending a seminar.
    (B) She will be on vacation.
    (C) She will be working in her office.
    (D) She will be visiting a client.

40. What does the man want the woman to do?
    (A) Complete an application
    (B) Visit a Web site
    (C) Take a test
    (D) Sign a contract

41. What does the woman ask the man to do?
    (A) Apply a discount
    (B) Exchange an item
    (C) Confirm an order
    (D) Suggest a product

42. What does the woman say she will do with the camcorder?
    (A) Record a wedding
    (B) Document her trip
    (C) Create an advertisement
    (D) Use it for presentations

43. What does the man say about the Tonika G56?
    (A) It is a new model.
    (B) It is easy to operate.
    (C) It is compatible with other devices.
    (D) It is cheaper than other models.

GO ON TO THE NEXT PAGE

44. Where do the interviewers most likely work?
(A) At a concert hall
(B) At a television station
(C) At a recruitment firm
(D) At a publishing company

45. What job requirement do the speakers discuss?
(A) Having a flexible schedule
(B) Using personal equipment
(C) Training staff members
(D) Working overseas

46. What will the man do next?
(A) Show a facility
(B) Give a phone number
(C) Play a video
(D) Introduce a coworker

47. What does the woman imply when she says, "Actually, I went last year"?
(A) She does not intend to attend the event.
(B) She did not enjoy doing the volunteer work.
(C) She will be able to leave the office on time.
(D) She will train other staff members.

48. What is the woman worried about?
(A) Leading a meeting
(B) Scheduling an event
(C) Dealing with customer complaints
(D) Working with new employees

49. What does the man suggest doing tomorrow?
(A) Conducting a survey
(B) Talking about an issue
(C) Making a special delivery
(D) Rescheduling a project

50. Where are the speakers?
(A) At a bookstore
(B) At a conference center
(C) At an airport
(D) At an office

51. Why did the woman decide not to attend the final presentation?
(A) She wanted to prepare for a meeting.
(B) She had heard the topic before.
(C) She had to visit a publisher.
(D) She wanted to avoid heavy traffic.

52. What does the woman suggest the man do?
(A) Make a reservation
(B) Write an article
(C) Check a schedule
(D) Guide a discussion

53. What type of business does the man probably work for?
(A) A moving company
(B) A newspaper publisher
(C) A Web design firm
(D) An electronics store

54. What does the man recommend doing?
(A) Signing up for an online service
(B) Rescheduling a delivery
(C) Returning an unused product
(D) Submitting a new mailing address

55. What does the woman ask about?
(A) An instruction manual
(B) A customer review
(C) An updated schedule
(D) A promotional offer

56. What does the man have tickets for?

(A) An overseas trip
(B) A music concert
(C) A sports match
(D) An art exhibition

57. According to the woman, why does she not need the tickets?

(A) She will be attending another event.
(B) She has to work late.
(C) She will be on vacation.
(D) She has already been to the event.

58. What will the man do next?

(A) Request a refund
(B) Go to lunch
(C) Watch a broadcast
(D) Post some information

59. What is the man preparing for?

(A) A job interview
(B) An orientation session
(C) A performance review
(D) A business conference

60. What does the woman imply when she says, "I completed my assignments early today"?

(A) She wants the man to review her work.
(B) She is going to leave the office early.
(C) She can help the man.
(D) She thinks a task is easy.

61. What will the woman most likely do next?

(A) Check on a request
(B) Examine some equipment
(C) Submit a report
(D) Revise some documents

Neherville Public Library Business Course Series	
Session A	Tuesdays, 10 A.M.
Session B	Wednesdays, 4 P.M.
Session C	Thursdays, 11 A.M.
Session D	Fridays, 7 P.M.

62. What was announced at today's meeting?

(A) An employee will be transferred.
(B) A business will expand.
(C) An office will be renovated.
(D) A board election will be held.

63. What is the man nervous about doing?

(A) Holding a press conference
(B) Writing a book
(C) Meeting with a client
(D) Applying for a position

64. Look at the graphic. What session will the man most likely attend?

(A) Session A
(B) Session B
(C) Session C
(D) Session D

GO ON TO THE NEXT PAGE

Orga's Global Bistro

Brunch Menu

Greek salad	$5.00
Potato pizza	$4.50
Shepherd's pie	$7.50
Mushroom sandwich	$6.00

65. Why did the woman's sister suggest the restaurant?

    (A) It is located in a popular area.
    (B) It provides excellent vegetarian options.
    (C) Its workers are very friendly.
    (D) Its prices are affordable.

66. What does the man say about the pumpkin soup?

    (A) It is prepared by the head chef.
    (B) It is being offered at a discount.
    (C) It is only sold with the main dish.
    (D) It is not available at the moment.

67. Look at the graphic. How much is the dish the woman ordered?

    (A) $5.00
    (B) $4.50
    (C) $7.50
    (D) $6.00

68. What would the man like to do?

    (A) Revise recruiting strategies
    (B) Visit a client
    (C) Teach a class
    (D) Go over some applications

69. Look at the graphic. Which method does the woman recommend using?

    (A) Referrals
    (B) Online submissions
    (C) Advertisements
    (D) College career expos

70. What does the man ask the woman to do?

    (A) Talk to a coworker
    (B) Conduct an interview
    (C) Extend a deadline
    (D) Reserve a room

PART 4

Directions: You will hear some talks given by a single speaker. You will be asked to answer three questions about what the speaker says in each talk. Select the best response to each question and mark the letter (A), (B), (C), or (D) on your answer sheet. The talks will not be printed in your test book and will be spoken only one time.

71. What is the speaker announcing?
(A) An upcoming inspection
(B) A business deal
(C) A company regulation
(D) A revised timetable

72. What has Wiztech requested?
(A) Wireless earphones
(B) Durable cases
(C) Additional data storage space
(D) Long-lasting batteries

73. What does the speaker ask listeners to do?
(A) Meet with their clients
(B) Contact some manufacturers
(C) Assign some tasks
(D) Create a presentation

74. What is the speaker's area of expertise?
(A) Event planning
(B) Information Technology
(C) Building maintenance
(D) Corporate accounting

75. What problem does the speaker mention?
(A) A Web site is not working.
(B) A coworker is not available.
(C) Some equipment was not set up properly.
(D) Some packages were shipped to the wrong address.

76. What does the speaker offer to do?
(A) Edit a video
(B) Contact board members
(C) Drop by a room
(D) Purchase some materials

77. What business is the speaker calling?
(A) A public transit service
(B) A travel agency
(C) An auto repair center
(D) A car dealership

78. Why did the speaker take a cab?
(A) A parking lot was full.
(B) He was late for a meeting.
(C) His car did not start.
(D) A vehicle did not arrive.

79. What does the speaker want to know?
(A) How long a trip will take
(B) Where to find a map
(C) If a schedule was changed
(D) When a model will be available

80. Who most likely is the speaker?
(A) A financial consultant
(B) A recruiting manager
(C) An airline employee
(D) A moving specialist

81. What does the speaker mean when he says, "it's already mid-December"?
(A) A deadline may need to be extended.
(B) Some travel arrangements should be confirmed.
(C) A report must be submitted soon.
(D) An alternative approach was taken.

82. What does the speaker want his department to do?
(A) Review some documents
(B) Give a presentation
(C) Attend a training session
(D) Conduct interviews

GO ON TO THE NEXT PAGE

83. Where is the announcement taking place?
(A) At a factory
(B) At a department store
(C) At a restaurant
(D) At a cooking school

84. What does the speaker say will happen after the event?
(A) A business owner will make a speech.
(B) A tour will be offered.
(C) Customers will complete a questionnaire.
(D) Some experts will give advice.

85. What does the speaker mention about Chickbee Appliances?
(A) It is hiring employees.
(B) It has changed its name.
(C) It recently started operating.
(D) It is moving to a different area.

86. Why has Bayville been popular with tourists?
(A) It has many shopping areas.
(B) Its mountains are attractive.
(C) It has a warm climate.
(D) Its food is unique.

87. According to the speaker, why has tourism declined in Bayville?
(A) Many historical sites in Bayville are closed.
(B) Bayville's weather has gotten cooler.
(C) Accommodation costs in Bayville are high.
(D) Bayville cannot be reached by train.

88. What will happen in April?
(A) A free bus service will begin.
(B) Discounted room rates will be offered.
(C) New entertainment venues will open.
(D) A City Council meeting will be held.

89. Where do the listeners most likely work?
(A) At a pharmaceutical company
(B) At a fitness club
(C) At a medical center
(D) At a health food store

90. What is the purpose of the meeting?
(A) To go over some safety practices
(B) To share information about a new product
(C) To discuss an upcoming event
(D) To explain changes to a schedule

91. Why does the speaker say, "We didn't have a lot of time to prepare the materials"?
(A) To compliment staff
(B) To offer an excuse
(C) To request assistance
(D) To delay a presentation

92. What course does the speaker teach?
(A) Cooking
(B) Woodwork
(C) Gardening
(D) Fitness

93. Why does the speaker say, "There's another class that uses this room"?
(A) To recommend taking an additional class
(B) To ask the listeners to provide their own tools
(C) To emphasize the need to finish on time
(D) To suggest the relocation of an event

94. What does the speaker remind the listeners to do before they leave?
(A) Pick up a brochure
(B) Complete a survey
(C) Submit a fee
(D) Log out of a computer

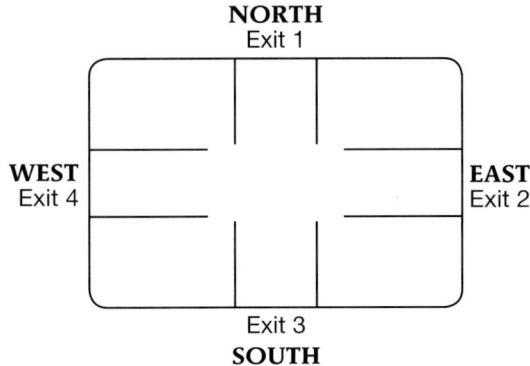

	Friday Schedule
09:00	
10:00	Monthly department meeting
11:00	
12:00	LUNCH
13:00	Senior managers' meeting
14:00	
15:00	Safety training session
16:00	
17:00	
18:00	

95. What is the speaker looking forward to?
  (A) Relocating to another city
  (B) Selling more tickets
  (C) Attending a performance
  (D) Launching a new product

96. Look at the graphic. Where will the logo be placed?
  (A) On the north side
  (B) On the south side
  (C) On the east side
  (D) On the west side

97. Who does the speaker want to advertise to?
  (A) International clients
  (B) Business owners
  (C) Local commuters
  (D) Popular artists

98. Where most likely does the speaker work?
  (A) At a Web design firm
  (B) At an accounting firm
  (C) At a marketing agency
  (D) At an employment agency

99. What does the speaker want to discuss with the listener?
  (A) Recent customer comments
  (B) A salary raise
  (C) Project expenses
  (D) A recruitment process

100. Look at the graphic. What time does the speaker want to meet?
  (A) At 11:00
  (B) At 14:00
  (C) At 16:00
  (D) At 18:00

This is the end of the Listening test.

Listening Comprehension

TEST 03

음원·해석

LISTENING TEST

In the Listening test, you will be asked to demonstrate how well you understand spoken English. The entire Listening test will last approximately 45 minutes. There are four parts, and directions are given for each part. You must mark your answers on the separate answer sheet. Do not write your answers in your test book.

PART 1

Directions: For each question in this part, you will hear four statements about a picture in your test book. When you hear the statements, you must select the one statement that best describes what you see in the picture. Then find the number of the question on your answer sheet and mark your answer. The statements will not be printed in your test book and will be spoken only one time.

Statement (B), "A man is pointing at a document," is the best description of the picture, so you should select answer (B) and mark it on your answer sheet.

1.

2.

3.

4.

5.

6.

GO ON TO THE NEXT PAGE

PART 2

Directions: You will hear a question or statement and three responses spoken in English. They will not be printed in your test book and will be spoken only one time. Select the best response to the question or statement and mark the letter (A), (B), or (C) on your answer sheet.

7. Mark your answer on your answer sheet.
8. Mark your answer on your answer sheet.
9. Mark your answer on your answer sheet.
10. Mark your answer on your answer sheet.
11. Mark your answer on your answer sheet.
12. Mark your answer on your answer sheet.
13. Mark your answer on your answer sheet.
14. Mark your answer on your answer sheet.
15. Mark your answer on your answer sheet.
16. Mark your answer on your answer sheet.
17. Mark your answer on your answer sheet.
18. Mark your answer on your answer sheet.
19. Mark your answer on your answer sheet.
20. Mark your answer on your answer sheet.
21. Mark your answer on your answer sheet.
22. Mark your answer on your answer sheet.
23. Mark your answer on your answer sheet.
24. Mark your answer on your answer sheet.
25. Mark your answer on your answer sheet.
26. Mark your answer on your answer sheet.
27. Mark your answer on your answer sheet.
28. Mark your answer on your answer sheet.
29. Mark your answer on your answer sheet.
30. Mark your answer on your answer sheet.
31. Mark your answer on your answer sheet.

PART 3

Directions: You will hear some conversations between two or more people. You will be asked to answer three questions about what the speakers say in each conversation. Select the best response to each question and mark the letter (A), (B), (C), or (D) on your answer sheet. The conversations will not be printed in your test book and will be spoken only one time.

32. What is being discussed?
    (A) A performance schedule
    (B) Room rates
    (C) Ticket availability
    (D) A seating assignment

33. Where are the speakers?
    (A) In an auditorium
    (B) At a hotel
    (C) In a parking lot
    (D) At a movie theater

34. What does the woman say she will do?
    (A) Pack up some equipment
    (B) Talk to a manager
    (C) Present her ID
    (D) Request a refund

35. What is the conversation mainly about?
    (A) A guest speaker
    (B) A meal preference
    (C) A photography session
    (D) A venue booking

36. What does the woman need to provide?
    (A) Her telephone number
    (B) Some identification
    (C) A payment
    (D) An application form

37. What do the visitors request?
    (A) Extra tables
    (B) A discount
    (C) Video equipment
    (D) A different menu

38. What is the man coordinating?
    (A) A client meeting
    (B) A retirement dinner
    (C) A sales conference
    (D) A staff orientation

39. What type of business do the speakers most likely work for?
    (A) An advertising agency
    (B) A computer store
    (C) A law firm
    (D) A photography studio

40. What does the man offer to do?
    (A) Make a reservation
    (B) Find a replacement speaker
    (C) Track a delivery
    (D) Review a business agreement

41. Why did the man call the woman?
    (A) To give her directions
    (B) To say he will not arrive on time
    (C) To turn down an invitation
    (D) To ask her to place an order

42. What does the woman suggest?
    (A) Changing a menu
    (B) Taking the subway
    (C) Hiring a marketing agency
    (D) Making a delivery arrangement

43. What does the man say he will do?
    (A) Check an e-mail
    (B) Stop by a store
    (C) Contact a coworker
    (D) Send a payment

GO ON TO THE NEXT PAGE

44. What is being printed?
(A) Instruction manuals
(B) Product catalogs
(C) Event calendars
(D) Promotional materials

45. What is the problem with the samples?
(A) An incorrect phone number is listed.
(B) Some details have been left out.
(C) The images are too blurry.
(D) They were printed in the wrong color.

46. What is the woman asked to do?
(A) Adjust a delivery date
(B) Cancel a service
(C) Give a discount
(D) Meet with a manager

47. Where do the speakers most likely work?
(A) In a supermarket
(B) In a factory
(C) At a hospital
(D) At a florist's

48. What problem does the woman mention?
(A) Some supplies were not available.
(B) A staff member did not come into work.
(C) Some equipment was broken.
(D) A door was locked.

49. According to the woman, what will happen at 11 A.M.?
(A) A store will open.
(B) A delivery will be made.
(C) An order will be placed.
(D) A technician will arrive.

50. Where most likely are the speakers?
(A) At a fundraising event
(B) At a stage play
(C) At a board meeting
(D) At a marketing seminar

51. Why does the man say, "Is that the best we can do"?
(A) He prefers to sit somewhere else.
(B) Some sales figures are low.
(C) He wants the woman to work harder.
(D) A presentation was disappointing.

52. What is mentioned about the screens?
(A) They were recently purchased.
(B) They need to undergo repairs.
(C) They are located at the stage.
(D) They display high-quality images.

53. Where does the man most likely work?
(A) At a software company
(B) At a courier company
(C) At a financial institution
(D) At an educational institution

54. What problem does the man mention?
(A) Some personal information was wrong.
(B) A document was not signed.
(C) An invoice has not been processed.
(D) Some equipment has been damaged.

55. What does the man say he will do?
(A) Send a file
(B) Reschedule a meeting
(C) Talk to a manager
(D) Issue a refund

56. Why is the woman calling the man?
  (A) To confirm a meeting
  (B) To report an equipment issue
  (C) To submit an order
  (D) To check a project deadline

57. What does the woman mean when she says, "I have a meeting here in ten minutes"?
  (A) She needs assistance within ten minutes.
  (B) She is not prepared for a presentation.
  (C) She wants the man to come by later.
  (D) She has decided not to attend the meeting.

58. What does the woman say is unusual about the meeting?
  (A) It will be held in the evening.
  (B) It will last a long time.
  (C) New video conferencing equipment will be used.
  (D) All of the attendees will meet in person.

59. Where most likely are the speakers?
  (A) At a department store
  (B) At an auto shop
  (C) At a city bank
  (D) At a parking lot

60. What does the woman decide to do?
  (A) Contact customer support
  (B) Make an online payment
  (C) Take an elevator
  (D) Withdraw some cash

61. What will the woman receive?
  (A) A text message
  (B) A coupon
  (C) A sample product
  (D) A refund

Woodwick Cabinet (List of Parts)	
Contents	**Quantity**
Casing nails (C392)	6
Box nails (B787)	4
Sinker nails (S109)	10
Finish nails (F453)	14

62. What is the woman trying to do?
  (A) Return a damaged product
  (B) Assemble a piece of furniture
  (C) Fix some equipment
  (D) Finish some remodeling work

63. Look at the graphic. What is the woman missing?
  (A) Casing nails
  (B) Box nails
  (C) Sinker nails
  (D) Finish nails

64. What does the man ask the woman to bring with her?
  (A) A warranty card
  (B) An instruction manual
  (C) A product box
  (D) An original receipt

GO ON TO THE NEXT PAGE

www.localbites.ca/review_section

Review of La Sorrento Bistro

Rating Area	Rating (out of 10)
Dining space	3
Menu choices	3
Pricing	8
Customer service	8

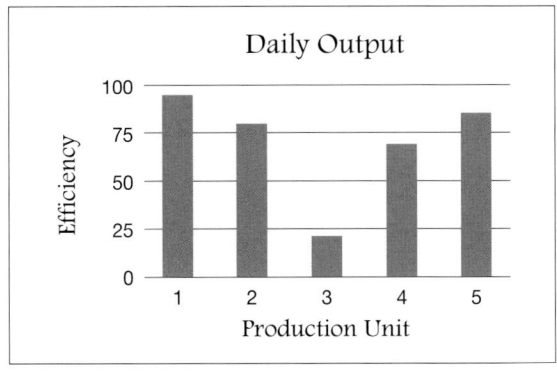

65. What is the man concerned about?
    (A) Losing customers
    (B) Increasing competition
    (C) Shortage of workers
    (D) High cost of food

66. Look at the graphic. Which area will be discussed at the next employee meeting?
    (A) Dining space
    (B) Menu choices
    (C) Pricing
    (D) Customer service

67. What does the woman recommend doing?
    (A) Employing a consultant
    (B) Holding a promotion
    (C) Rearranging some tables
    (D) Ordering more supplies

68. What industry do the speakers most likely work in?
    (A) Shipping and transportation
    (B) Computer software
    (C) Food and beverage
    (D) Textile manufacturing

69. Look at the graphic. Which unit is being discussed?
    (A) Unit 1
    (B) Unit 2
    (C) Unit 3
    (D) Unit 4

70. What will the man most likely do next?
    (A) Schedule maintenance work
    (B) Contact some customers
    (C) Revise an order
    (D) Prepare a new report

PART 4

Directions: You will hear some talks given by a single speaker. You will be asked to answer three questions about what the speaker says in each talk. Select the best response to each question and mark the letter (A), (B), (C), or (D) on your answer sheet. The talks will not be printed in your test book and will be spoken only one time.

71. What is the announcement mainly about?
    (A) Equipment maintenance
    (B) Recycling procedures
    (C) A training workshop
    (D) A construction project

72. Why is a change being made?
    (A) To expand office space
    (B) To improve sales figures
    (C) To provide a safer environment
    (D) To follow a new law

73. What does the speaker say will happen on Friday?
    (A) Some machines will be repaired.
    (B) Some items will be picked up.
    (C) New merchandise will arrive.
    (D) A seminar will be held.

74. What is the main subject of the broadcast?
    (A) Weather conditions
    (B) Traffic news
    (C) Volunteer opportunities
    (D) Road work

75. According to the speaker, what will happen today?
    (A) A gallery exhibition
    (B) An outdoor sale
    (C) A musical performance
    (D) A sports competition

76. What does the speaker advise listeners to do?
    (A) Bring their own drinks
    (B) Stay at home
    (C) Register for an event in advance
    (D) Purchase a parking permit

77. What product does Sana supply?
    (A) Clothing
    (B) Furniture
    (C) Jewelry
    (D) Stationery

78. Why does the speaker say, "Just check out all the different designs in their catalog"?
    (A) To praise some workers
    (B) To justify a choice
    (C) To suggest visiting some stores
    (D) To give an assignment

79. What will Marcella do?
    (A) Give manufacturing instructions
    (B) Present an award
    (C) Compare sales figures
    (D) Talk about promotional information

80. Where does the speaker work?
    (A) At a print shop
    (B) At a museum
    (C) At a travel agency
    (D) At a university

81. What will the listeners be doing today?
    (A) Picking up merchandise
    (B) Leading tours
    (C) Training interns
    (D) Distributing brochures

82. What has the speaker done for the listeners?
    (A) Indicated some areas on a map
    (B) Made arrangements for transportation
    (C) Prepared some food
    (D) Contacted local business owners

GO ON TO THE NEXT PAGE

83. What industry does Mr. Singh work in?
    (A) Technology
    (B) Travel
    (C) Finance
    (D) Landscaping

84. What will Mr. Singh talk about?
    (A) Employee management strategies
    (B) Coordinating an event
    (C) Garden care tips
    (D) Expanding a business

85. What does the speaker ask listeners to do?
    (A) Provide contact information
    (B) Find a partner
    (C) Read a brochure
    (D) Submit questions electronically

86. Where is the announcement taking place?
    (A) At an airport
    (B) At a hardware store
    (C) At a restaurant
    (D) At a supermarket

87. Why does the speaker say, "It will take just a few minutes of your time"?
    (A) To encourage the listeners to participate
    (B) To apologize for an error
    (C) To remind the listeners about a product
    (D) To provide a reason for a delay

88. What does the speaker say will be offered today?
    (A) Complimentary food
    (B) Expedited delivery
    (C) A seat upgrade
    (D) A discount voucher

89. What does the speaker remind the listeners about?
    (A) An office move
    (B) A performance review
    (C) A system update
    (D) A facility inspection

90. What are listeners required to do before leaving work?
    (A) Complete an updated form
    (B) Log out from their computers
    (C) Return an access card
    (D) Pack their personal belongings

91. What department does Ms. Kelley work in?
    (A) Shipping and receiving
    (B) Personnel
    (C) Technical support
    (D) Marketing

92. What is Master 2000?
    (A) A new type of credit card
    (B) A Web design application
    (C) An online payment system
    (D) An employee training program

93. What does the speaker mean when she says, "Don't you have better things to do"?
    (A) Passwords should be changed regularly.
    (B) Workers require additional training.
    (C) Security methods need to be improved.
    (D) Other applications are not efficient.

94. According to the speaker, what can listeners do on the Web site?
    (A) Compare prices
    (B) Watch a tutorial
    (C) Read product reviews
    (D) Submit a form

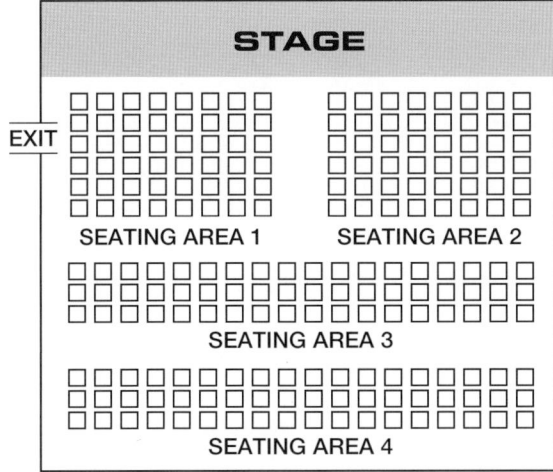

Request for Reimbursement	
Expenditure	Amount
Rental car	$835.00
Accommodation	$345.00
Meals	$380.00
Flight	$530.00

95. Who most likely are the listeners?

(A) Professional photographers
(B) Security staff
(C) Playwrights
(D) Contest participants

96. Look at the graphic. What seating area does the speaker want the listeners to sit in?

(A) Seating area 1
(B) Seating area 2
(C) Seating area 3
(D) Seating area 4

97. What are the listeners asked to do when the event ends?

(A) Attend a formal dinner
(B) Take part in a photo shoot
(C) Post some signs
(D) Meet with audience members

98. What did the listener do last week?

(A) She applied for a job.
(B) She toured an office building.
(C) She attended a function.
(D) She installed a program.

99. Look at the graphic. Which amount needs to be checked?

(A) $835.00
(B) $345.00
(C) $380.00
(D) $530.00

100. What does the speaker say was sent to the staff?

(A) A revised form
(B) A discount code
(C) A Web site address
(D) A new password

This is the end of the Listening test.

Listening Comprehension

TEST 04

음원·해석

LISTENING TEST

In the Listening test, you will be asked to demonstrate how well you understand spoken English. The entire Listening test will last approximately 45 minutes. There are four parts, and directions are given for each part. You must mark your answers on the separate answer sheet. Do not write your answers in your test book.

PART 1

Directions: For each question in this part, you will hear four statements about a picture in your test book. When you hear the statements, you must select the one statement that best describes what you see in the picture. Then find the number of the question on your answer sheet and mark your answer. The statements will not be printed in your test book and will be spoken only one time.

Statement (B), "A man is pointing at a document," is the best description of the picture, so you should select answer (B) and mark it on your answer sheet.

1.

2.

3.

4.

5.

6.

PART 2

Directions: You will hear a question or statement and three responses spoken in English. They will not be printed in your test book and will be spoken only one time. Select the best response to the question or statement and mark the letter (A), (B), or (C) on your answer sheet.

7. Mark your answer on your answer sheet.
8. Mark your answer on your answer sheet.
9. Mark your answer on your answer sheet.
10. Mark your answer on your answer sheet.
11. Mark your answer on your answer sheet.
12. Mark your answer on your answer sheet.
13. Mark your answer on your answer sheet.
14. Mark your answer on your answer sheet.
15. Mark your answer on your answer sheet.
16. Mark your answer on your answer sheet.
17. Mark your answer on your answer sheet.
18. Mark your answer on your answer sheet.
19. Mark your answer on your answer sheet.
20. Mark your answer on your answer sheet.
21. Mark your answer on your answer sheet.
22. Mark your answer on your answer sheet.
23. Mark your answer on your answer sheet.
24. Mark your answer on your answer sheet.
25. Mark your answer on your answer sheet.
26. Mark your answer on your answer sheet.
27. Mark your answer on your answer sheet.
28. Mark your answer on your answer sheet.
29. Mark your answer on your answer sheet.
30. Mark your answer on your answer sheet.
31. Mark your answer on your answer sheet.

PART 3

Directions: You will hear some conversations between two or more people. You will be asked to answer three questions about what the speakers say in each conversation. Select the best response to each question and mark the letter (A), (B), (C), or (D) on your answer sheet. The conversations will not be printed in your test book and will be spoken only one time.

32. In which department does the man work?
    (A) Accounting
    (B) Technical Support
    (C) Sales
    (D) Customer Service

33. What does the man suggest doing?
    (A) Checking an order
    (B) Sending a report
    (C) Restarting a machine
    (D) Finding a coworker

34. What does the man say he can do?
    (A) Reschedule a meeting
    (B) Contact another department
    (C) Accept a payment
    (D) Go to the woman's work area

35. What are the speakers discussing?
    (A) A product design
    (B) A medical prescription
    (C) A building address
    (D) An appointment time

36. Why is the man behind schedule?
    (A) A business has been busy.
    (B) A doctor is away from the office.
    (C) A computer is not working properly.
    (D) A staff member made a mistake.

37. What does the woman say she will do?
    (A) Print a receipt
    (B) Come back tomorrow
    (C) Visit a nearby store
    (D) Return some items

38. Why is the man calling?
    (A) To set up a repair service
    (B) To promote a special deal
    (C) To confirm order details
    (D) To ask survey questions

39. What type of products does the man's business sell?
    (A) Computer parts
    (B) Home appliances
    (C) Office supplies
    (D) Restaurant furniture

40. What does the man offer to do for the woman?
    (A) Send an invoice by e-mail
    (B) Give her a replacement item
    (C) Reduce a price
    (D) Put her name on a list

41. Where do the speakers most likely work?
    (A) At a fitness center
    (B) At a research facility
    (C) At an art school
    (D) At a grocery store

42. What is the main topic of the conversation?
    (A) A budget proposal
    (B) Membership fees
    (C) Questionnaire responses
    (D) A training video

43. What does the man imply when he says, "That might cause conflicts with our schedules"?
    (A) He anticipates that customers will not like a policy.
    (B) He is unsure a suggestion could be implemented.
    (C) He is not happy about his work hours.
    (D) He wants additional time to make a decision.

GO ON TO THE NEXT PAGE

44. What field does Carl work in?

(A) Accounting
(B) Environment
(C) Communications
(D) Engineering

45. What does the woman want to go over with Carl?

(A) Supervising a project
(B) Recording time worked
(C) Claiming business expenses
(D) Revising a floor plan

46. Why has a meeting been moved?

(A) A computer system is down.
(B) Some documents are not ready.
(C) Some employees arrived late.
(D) A facility is closed.

47. Where do the speakers most likely work?

(A) At a caterer
(B) At a dental office
(C) At a factory
(D) At an office supply store

48. Why does the man say, "This isn't their first time you know"?

(A) He would like employees to be more careful.
(B) He discovered a new problem.
(C) He is upset with a situation.
(D) He does not agree with the woman.

49. What will the man probably do next?

(A) Take inventory
(B) Contact a client
(C) Visit a store
(D) Make a reservation

50. What problem does the man mention?

(A) An event has been cancelled.
(B) Some equipment is not working.
(C) Inclement weather is expected.
(D) Important news has been delayed.

51. What does the woman say she will decide tomorrow?

(A) When to start a promotion
(B) If a business should be closed
(C) When to sign a contract
(D) If extra workers should be hired

52. What does the man offer to do?

(A) Contact staff members
(B) Lead a training session
(C) Review a schedule
(D) Work longer hours

53. Why is the woman calling?

(A) To point out inaccurate information in an article
(B) To place an advertisement in a newspaper
(C) To ask for a discounted rate
(D) To inquire about missed deliveries

54. What does the man offer to do for the woman?

(A) Contact a journalist
(B) Send a free copy
(C) Renew her subscription
(D) Make a correction

55. What information does the man want to confirm?

(A) The details of a payment
(B) A delivery address
(C) The password for an account
(D) A birth date

56. Why is the woman calling?

(A) To submit a work request
(B) To check an order's status
(C) To ask about a charge
(D) To purchase a new part

57. What problem does the man mention?

(A) Some information was wrong.
(B) A vehicle had to be repaired.
(C) Some merchandise has sold out.
(D) A bank account number is missing.

58. What does the man offer to do?

(A) Transfer a call
(B) Speak with a manager
(C) Extend a warranty
(D) Provide a reimbursement

59. What most likely is the woman's job?

(A) A building inspector
(B) A customer service agent
(C) A pharmacy manager
(D) A Web site designer

60. What problem does the woman mention?

(A) A flight has been delayed.
(B) A complaint has been received.
(C) A project cannot be finished on time.
(D) A supervisor will not be at work.

61. What does the man say he will do?

(A) Sign a form
(B) Give a refund
(C) Extend a deadline
(D) Postpone a meeting

ITEM	AMOUNT
Hotel X 6 Nights	$480
Room Service	$ 90
Business Lunch	$120
Airfare	$620

62. Who most likely is the woman?

(A) A hotel receptionist
(B) A sales manager
(C) An accounting employee
(D) A tour guide

63. What is the man's problem?

(A) He cannot find some documents.
(B) He cannot be reimbursed for any expenses.
(C) There are no more rooms available.
(D) There are some problems with his report.

64. Look at the graphic. How much will Mr. Moore NOT get back?

(A) $480
(B) $90
(C) $120
(D) $620

GO ON TO THE NEXT PAGE

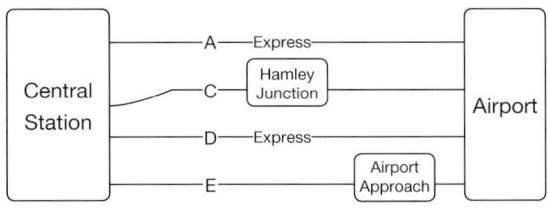

Play	Starting Time
The Village Riot	6:30 P.M.
Harkin's Past	7:00 P.M.
The Roof Peddler	8:00 P.M.
Children of One	9:30 P.M.

65. Where does the conversation take place?

(A) At a conference center
(B) At a subway station
(C) At an airport
(D) At a hotel

66. Look at the graphic. Which line does the man suggest the woman take?

(A) Line A
(B) Line C
(C) Line D
(D) Line E

67. Why is the woman going to Miami?

(A) To inspect a facility
(B) To meet a friend
(C) To attend a convention
(D) To purchase a property

68. What does the woman ask the man about?

(A) A theater schedule
(B) A television program
(C) His favorite actor
(D) His evening plans

69. Look at the graphic. What time will the man probably watch a play?

(A) At 6:30 P.M.
(B) At 7:00 P.M.
(C) At 8:00 P.M.
(D) At 9:30 P.M.

70. What is the woman doing on the weekend?

(A) Working in her office
(B) Remodeling her home
(C) Watching a movie
(D) Attending a convention

PART 4

Directions: You will hear some talks given by a single speaker. You will be asked to answer three questions about what the speaker says in each talk. Select the best response to each question and mark the letter (A), (B), (C), or (D) on your answer sheet. The talks will not be printed in your test book and will be spoken only one time.

71. What is the purpose of the talk?
    (A) To promote a charity event
    (B) To introduce some artwork
    (C) To announce a drawing contest
    (D) To explain a policy

72. What will the speaker give to the listeners?
    (A) A voucher
    (B) A notebook
    (C) An audio device
    (D) A building map

73. According to the speaker, what will begin at 2 o'clock?
    (A) A banquet
    (B) A tour
    (C) A film
    (D) A competition

74. What is the broadcast about?
    (A) An upcoming performance
    (B) The opening of a theater
    (C) Registration for music classes
    (D) A famous author

75. According to the speaker, what did Anna Rethom do recently?
    (A) She wrote a play.
    (B) She attended a ceremony.
    (C) She changed her career.
    (D) She won an award.

76. What will listeners most likely hear next?
    (A) A song
    (B) An advertisement
    (C) A news report
    (D) A traffic update

77. What is the speaker mainly discussing?
    (A) Changing project deadlines
    (B) Posting job openings
    (C) Using video conferencing
    (D) Reserving meeting rooms

78. What does the speaker say will take place at the company next Thursday?
    (A) A job interview
    (B) A training session
    (C) An office move
    (D) A client meeting

79. Why will some employees be unavailable next week?
    (A) They will be on vacation.
    (B) They will be giving a tour.
    (C) They will be attending a conference.
    (D) They will be installing some equipment.

80. What did City Life Magazine recently do?
    (A) It hired a new chief editor.
    (B) It held a special promotion.
    (C) It acquired a publishing company.
    (D) It recognized a business establishment.

81. What does the speaker mean when she says, "another new gym just opened up down the street"?
    (A) More customers will sign up for a membership.
    (B) A business has moved to a new location.
    (C) The local competition has increased.
    (D) A company's sales have grown.

82. What does the speaker's company intend to do?
    (A) Offer free classes
    (B) Renovate its facilities
    (C) Expand to another city
    (D) Purchase more exercise equipment

GO ON TO THE NEXT PAGE

83. What is the man waiting for?
(A) The departure of his flight
(B) The delivery of some food
(C) The return of his luggage
(D) The arrival of his clients

84. What is scheduled for Wednesday?
(A) A contract signing
(B) A facility tour
(C) A company dinner
(D) A product presentation

85. Why does the man say, "I realize it's a long trip"?
(A) To tell the listener to cancel a flight
(B) To advise the listener to bring some food
(C) To complain to the listener about a schedule
(D) To apologize to the listener for an inconvenience

86. Who is the advertisement intended for?
(A) News journalists
(B) Office assistants
(C) Business owners
(D) Computer programmers

87. What is being described?
(A) A mobile phone
(B) A training video
(C) A recruiting service
(D) A software program

88. What are the listeners encouraged to do?
(A) Download an application
(B) Visit a store
(C) Purchase a subscription
(D) Call a number

89. What has the speaker been asked to do?
(A) Coordinate an event
(B) Revise a document
(C) Give a lecture
(D) Participate in a study

90. What does the speaker mean when she says, "the data will not be published for a while"?
(A) She would like a deadline extension.
(B) She is unable to talk about a subject.
(C) She made an error during an experiment.
(D) She thinks a process is too slow.

91. What does the speaker say is available on her Web site?
(A) A schedule of events
(B) Online reviews
(C) Video demonstrations
(D) A list of fees

92. What does the speaker remind the listeners about?
(A) A workshop for managers
(B) A visit from students
(C) A change in safety procedures
(D) An inspection of machines

93. What may factory workers be asked to do tomorrow?
(A) Demonstrate some equipment
(B) Attend a training session
(C) Present a report
(D) Work additional hours

94. What do listeners need to do after the meeting?
(A) Send an e-mail
(B) Examine some machinery
(C) Talk to staff members
(D) Fill out a survey

Order List	
Item	Quantity
Highlighter	20
Poster paper	35
Toner cartridge	170
Envelope	200

95. Look at the graphic. Which quantity on the order list might be changed?
    (A) 20
    (B) 35
    (C) 170
    (D) 200

96. What is the speaker planning to do tomorrow?
    (A) Interview an applicant
    (B) Return Ms. Wright's call
    (C) Ship some supplies
    (D) Go on a business trip

97. What does the speaker say about Danica?
    (A) She will attend a conference.
    (B) She will charge a credit card.
    (C) She is going to look after some customers.
    (D) She is going to be training some workers.

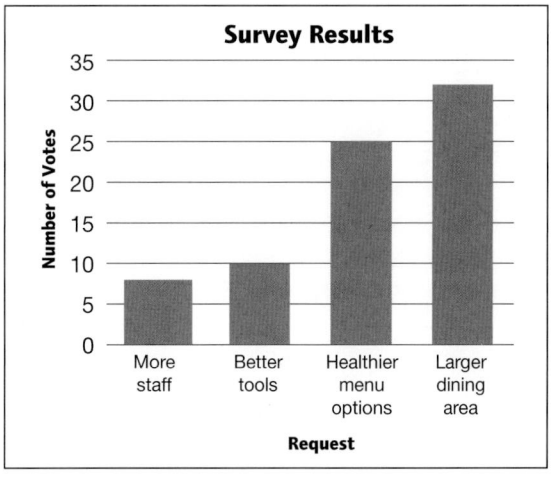

98. Where do the listeners most likely work?
    (A) At a coffee shop
    (B) At a library
    (C) At a grocery store
    (D) At a plant

99. Look at the graphic. Which request will the company start working on?
    (A) More staff
    (B) Better tools
    (C) Healthier menu options
    (D) A larger dining area

100. What will the employees receive for completing the survey?
    (A) Gift certificates
    (B) Free beverages
    (C) A t-shirt
    (D) A signed book

This is the end of the Listening test.

Listening Comprehension

TEST 05

음원·해석

LISTENING TEST

In the Listening test, you will be asked to demonstrate how well you understand spoken English. The entire Listening test will last approximately 45 minutes. There are four parts, and directions are given for each part. You must mark your answers on the separate answer sheet. Do not write your answers in your test book.

PART 1

Directions: For each question in this part, you will hear four statements about a picture in your test book. When you hear the statements, you must select the one statement that best describes what you see in the picture. Then find the number of the question on your answer sheet and mark your answer. The statements will not be printed in your test book and will be spoken only one time.

Statement (B), "A man is pointing at a document," is the best description of the picture, so you should select answer (B) and mark it on your answer sheet.

1.

2.

3.

4.

5.

6.

PART 2

Directions: You will hear a question or statement and three responses spoken in English. They will not be printed in your test book and will be spoken only one time. Select the best response to the question or statement and mark the letter (A), (B), or (C) on your answer sheet.

7. Mark your answer on your answer sheet.
8. Mark your answer on your answer sheet.
9. Mark your answer on your answer sheet.
10. Mark your answer on your answer sheet.
11. Mark your answer on your answer sheet.
12. Mark your answer on your answer sheet.
13. Mark your answer on your answer sheet.
14. Mark your answer on your answer sheet.
15. Mark your answer on your answer sheet.
16. Mark your answer on your answer sheet.
17. Mark your answer on your answer sheet.
18. Mark your answer on your answer sheet.
19. Mark your answer on your answer sheet.
20. Mark your answer on your answer sheet.
21. Mark your answer on your answer sheet.
22. Mark your answer on your answer sheet.
23. Mark your answer on your answer sheet.
24. Mark your answer on your answer sheet.
25. Mark your answer on your answer sheet.
26. Mark your answer on your answer sheet.
27. Mark your answer on your answer sheet.
28. Mark your answer on your answer sheet.
29. Mark your answer on your answer sheet.
30. Mark your answer on your answer sheet.
31. Mark your answer on your answer sheet.

PART 3

Directions: You will hear some conversations between two or more people. You will be asked to answer three questions about what the speakers say in each conversation. Select the best response to each question and mark the letter (A), (B), (C), or (D) on your answer sheet. The conversations will not be printed in your test book and will be spoken only one time.

32. What did the man do on his vacation?
    (A) He went shopping.
    (B) He went bike riding.
    (C) He went hiking.
    (D) He went skiing.

33. What does the man say about the place he visited?
    (A) It was hot.
    (B) It is well-known.
    (C) It was crowded.
    (D) It is nearby.

34. According to the woman, what did the company do recently?
    (A) It renovated an office.
    (B) It approved a budget.
    (C) It held a press conference.
    (D) It started a new project.

35. What does the man request that the woman do?
    (A) Review a report
    (B) Process an application
    (C) Issue a refund
    (D) Extend a deadline

36. What problem does the man mention?
    (A) He cannot attend a meeting.
    (B) He lost some receipts.
    (C) He damaged an item.
    (D) He miscalculated some numbers.

37. What does the woman say she will do?
    (A) Send a payment
    (B) Order some equipment
    (C) Check with a manager
    (D) Email an invoice

38. Where do the speakers probably work?
    (A) At a restaurant
    (B) At a movie theater
    (C) At a museum
    (D) At a tour company

39. What does the man inform the woman about?
    (A) A new movie
    (B) A special offer
    (C) An art show
    (D) A schedule change

40. What will the woman do after her meeting?
    (A) Go to the man's desk
    (B) Review a proposal
    (C) Send out an e-mail
    (D) Visit another business

41. What are the speakers mainly discussing?
    (A) A corporate Web site
    (B) A new staff member
    (C) An advertising campaign
    (D) A revised policy

42. What does the man say should be emphasized?
    (A) Lowering a budget
    (B) Hiring more qualified employees
    (C) Developing a better product
    (D) Targeting a specific age group

43. What is the man asked to do tomorrow?
    (A) Attend a meeting
    (B) Send a document
    (C) Visit a manufacturing facility
    (D) Contact a company representative

GO ON TO THE NEXT PAGE

44. What are the speakers mainly discussing?
    (A) Designing a company logo
    (B) Acquiring more clients
    (C) Holding training workshops
    (D) Updating a Web site

45. What problem has the woman identified?
    (A) A name is not written correctly.
    (B) A license has expired.
    (C) The size of an image is too small.
    (D) Some figures are inaccurate.

46. Why does the woman say, "I get confused sometimes, too"?
    (A) To review a process with the man
    (B) To make sure a deadline is met
    (C) To show she understands a mistake
    (D) To give driving directions to the man

47. Who is the man?
    (A) A journalist
    (B) A physician
    (C) A computer programmer
    (D) A financial consultant

48. What did the woman's company recently do?
    (A) Remodeled an office
    (B) Designed a new logo
    (C) Employed a fitness instructor
    (D) Participated in a convention

49. What does the man say about the program?
    (A) It is probably expensive.
    (B) It will be implemented soon.
    (C) It was advertised in a newspaper.
    (D) It needs to be improved.

50. Who most likely are Mary and Joe?
    (A) Construction workers
    (B) Prospective home buyers
    (C) Real estate agents
    (D) Building inspectors

51. What are Mary and Joe concerned about?
    (A) The location of a home
    (B) Access to public transportation
    (C) The lease period
    (D) Renovation costs

52. What is suggested about the owner?
    (A) She is available only in the morning.
    (B) She owns more than one property.
    (C) She will be working in a different city.
    (D) She manages a landscaping company.

53. What are the speakers organizing?
    (A) A job fair
    (B) A business trip
    (C) An orchestra concert
    (D) An awards ceremony

54. What problem does the woman mention?
    (A) An employee will be late.
    (B) A speaker is no longer available.
    (C) An order has not been made.
    (D) A venue is under construction.

55. What most likely will the man do next?
    (A) Review an application
    (B) Buy a flight ticket
    (C) Print a document
    (D) Talk to a colleague

56. Where does the woman work?
    (A) At a health center
    (B) At a transportation company
    (C) At a law office
    (D) At an employment agency

57. What does the man say he will be doing next week?
    (A) Attending a conference
    (B) Interviewing job applicants
    (C) Working in another country
    (D) Taking a vacation

58. What does the man imply when he says, "I work until 2 o'clock on Wednesdays"?
    (A) He wants to work full-time.
    (B) He will be leaving earlier than scheduled.
    (C) He is only available on weekends.
    (D) He requires a later appointment.

59. What are the speakers discussing?
    (A) Renovating an office building
    (B) Holding a seasonal sale
    (C) Using an employment service
    (D) Organizing a company trip

60. What type of business does the man operate?
    (A) A restaurant
    (B) A travel agency
    (C) A supermarket
    (D) A cleaning company

61. What does the woman suggest?
    (A) Conducting a survey
    (B) Looking for another company
    (C) Placing an advertisement
    (D) Reviewing some applications

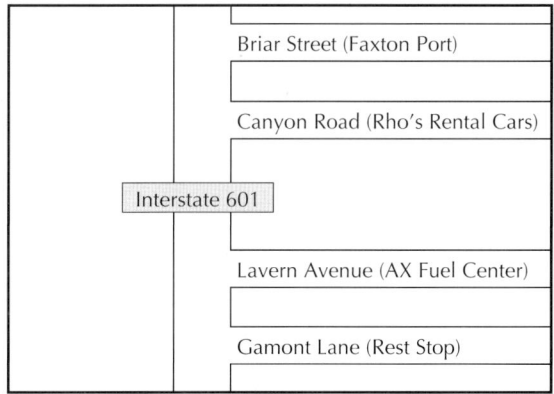

62. What are the speakers worried about?
    (A) Missing a ferry ride
    (B) Paying extra money
    (C) Experiencing traffic congestion
    (D) Finding a parking spot

63. Look at the graphic. Which street does the man tell the woman to take?
    (A) Garmont Lane
    (B) Lavern Avenue
    (C) Canyon Road
    (D) Briar Street

64. What does the woman say she hopes to do?
    (A) Take photos
    (B) Buy a gift
    (C) Purchase food
    (D) Check a map

GO ON TO THE NEXT PAGE

License Level	Annual Cost
Basic	$1,600
Professional	$2,800
Team	$4,000
Enterprise	$6,500

Name	Arriving from
Reeya Singh	Houston
Chris Walker	Sydney
Bill Keen	Sydney
Nicole Brunski	San Diego

65. What is the purpose of the phone call?

(A) To propose a business plan
(B) To reschedule an event
(C) To sign up for a workshop
(D) To ask about a product

66. What information does the man ask for?

(A) The names of guests
(B) The number of users
(C) The location of a building
(D) The length of a session

67. Look at the graphic. How much will the woman likely pay?

(A) $1,600
(B) $2,800
(C) $4,000
(D) $6,500

68. What is the purpose of the woman's trip?

(A) To tour a facility
(B) To attend a conference
(C) To visit some clients
(D) To train some workers

69. Look at the graphic. Who will arrive next?

(A) Reeya Singh
(B) Chris Walker
(C) Bill Keen
(D) Nicole Brunski

70. What does the man offer to do?

(A) Contact a hotel
(B) Purchase some beverages
(C) Return to the airport
(D) Speak with an airline worker

PART 4

Directions: You will hear some talks given by a single speaker. You will be asked to answer three questions about what the speaker says in each talk. Select the best response to each question and mark the letter (A), (B), (C), or (D) on your answer sheet. The talks will not be printed in your test book and will be spoken only one time.

71. Where most likely is this announcement being made?
    (A) At a theme park
    (B) At an international airport
    (C) At a train station
    (D) At a bus terminal

72. What does the speaker say is now available?
    (A) Automated ticketing machines
    (B) A remodeled waiting area
    (C) A new cafeteria menu
    (D) Free wireless Internet

73. What is mentioned about the instructions?
    (A) They can be found inside the product packaging.
    (B) They can be downloaded from the Web site.
    (C) They are printed on the tickets.
    (D) They are offered in different languages.

74. What is the purpose of the message?
    (A) To set up a payment plan
    (B) To advertise a service
    (C) To provide some instructions
    (D) To request contact information

75. What does the speaker's business specialize in?
    (A) Equipment installation
    (B) Online marketing
    (C) Office design
    (D) Energy conservation

76. What does the speaker offer to send?
    (A) Customer recommendations
    (B) A work contract
    (C) Warranty details
    (D) A sample product

77. What is the subject of the news report?
    (A) The demand for skilled employees
    (B) The high cost of production
    (C) Manufacturing plants that have closed
    (D) Employees searching for better jobs

78. What does the speaker say Lowerton Technical School has done?
    (A) It has moved to another city.
    (B) It has started an annual career fair.
    (C) It has awarded scholarships to students.
    (D) It has increased its course offerings.

79. What does the speaker mean when she says, "they're getting applications on a daily basis"?
    (A) An application deadline is approaching.
    (B) A strategy is working.
    (C) A salary package is attractive.
    (D) A news article is wrong.

80. What does the speaker say the company is considering?
    (A) Purchasing more furniture
    (B) Changing lunch hours
    (C) Expanding a cafeteria
    (D) Changing food vendors

81. What can the listeners receive for free tomorrow?
    (A) A shopping bag
    (B) A coffee mug
    (C) Some snacks
    (D) Some pens

82. Why should the listeners go to Andrew's desk?
    (A) To drop off a form
    (B) To register for training
    (C) To enter a contest
    (D) To pick up a catalog

GO ON TO THE NEXT PAGE

83. What is the speaker mainly discussing?
  (A) Some vacation plans
  (B) Some visiting investors
  (C) A retirement dinner
  (D) A convention schedule

84. What change does the speaker mention?
  (A) The date of a meeting
  (B) The price of a flight
  (C) The length of a presentation
  (D) The number of guests

85. What does the speaker imply when she says, "That performance got poor reviews"?
  (A) She believes an itinerary should be revised.
  (B) She does not agree with a critic's review.
  (C) She would like to get a refund.
  (D) She thinks that a venue will not have many people.

86. What event was held last weekend?
  (A) An art exhibition
  (B) An anniversary celebration
  (C) A stage play
  (D) An outdoor festival

87. Why is the town raising money?
  (A) To renovate a public library
  (B) To create a school program
  (C) To expand a park
  (D) To develop a shopping center

88. According to the speaker, why was the event rescheduled?
  (A) The weather was inclement.
  (B) A keynote speaker could not attend.
  (C) A venue was already booked.
  (D) Some supplies were not available.

89. What is the speaker calling about?
  (A) A business consultation
  (B) A newspaper article
  (C) A cost estimate
  (D) An upcoming inspection

90. Why does the speaker say, "Not many people can do that"?
  (A) To explain a policy
  (B) To refuse a request
  (C) To express gratitude
  (D) To provide encouragement

91. What does the speaker recommend that the listener do in May?
  (A) Renovate a store
  (B) Hire more workers
  (C) Move to another city
  (D) Participate in a seminar

92. According to the speaker, what is going to change at the company?
  (A) How work hours are recorded
  (B) How deliveries are tracked
  (C) How clients are contacted
  (D) How shipments are packaged

93. What will the company be able to do for its clients?
  (A) Provide a wider range of products
  (B) Offer lower service fees
  (C) Reply to inquiries faster
  (D) Give more accurate updates

94. What will Mr. Benfer do?
  (A) Hold training sessions
  (B) Inspect some machines
  (C) Manage a new branch
  (D) Revise a work schedule

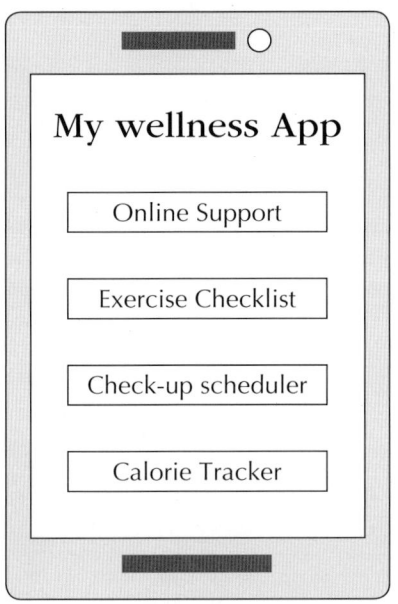

Satisfaction Survey	
Category	Rating (Out of 5)
Equipment	4
Pricing	3
Cleanliness	4
Customer service	5

95. Where is the talk most likely taking place?

(A) At a nutrition store
(B) At a call center
(C) At a health clinic
(D) At a sporting goods retailer

96. What are the listeners asked to do?

(A) Register for a class
(B) Test some new software
(C) Fill out a survey form
(D) Watch a video demonstration

97. Look at the graphic. What feature does the speaker think is most useful?

(A) Online Support
(B) Exercise Checklist
(C) Check-up Scheduler
(D) Calorie Tracker

98. Who is the message most likely intended for?

(A) A fitness club member
(B) An advertising specialist
(C) A personal trainer
(D) A maintenance worker

99. What does the speaker say she has mailed to the listener?

(A) A restaurant guide
(B) A course schedule
(C) A discount coupon
(D) A business directory

100. Look at the graphic. Which category would the speaker like to discuss further?

(A) Equipment
(B) Pricing
(C) Cleanliness
(D) Customer service

This is the end of the Listening test.

Listening Comprehension

TEST 06

음원·해석

LISTENING TEST

In the Listening test, you will be asked to demonstrate how well you understand spoken English. The entire Listening test will last approximately 45 minutes. There are four parts, and directions are given for each part. You must mark your answers on the separate answer sheet. Do not write your answers in your test book.

PART 1

Directions: For each question in this part, you will hear four statements about a picture in your test book. When you hear the statements, you must select the one statement that best describes what you see in the picture. Then find the number of the question on your answer sheet and mark your answer. The statements will not be printed in your test book and will be spoken only one time.

Statement (B), "A man is pointing at a document," is the best description of the picture, so you should select answer (B) and mark it on your answer sheet.

1.

2.

3.

4.

5.

6.

PART 2

Directions: You will hear a question or statement and three responses spoken in English. They will not be printed in your test book and will be spoken only one time. Select the best response to the question or statement and mark the letter (A), (B), or (C) on your answer sheet.

7. Mark your answer on your answer sheet.
8. Mark your answer on your answer sheet.
9. Mark your answer on your answer sheet.
10. Mark your answer on your answer sheet.
11. Mark your answer on your answer sheet.
12. Mark your answer on your answer sheet.
13. Mark your answer on your answer sheet.
14. Mark your answer on your answer sheet.
15. Mark your answer on your answer sheet.
16. Mark your answer on your answer sheet.
17. Mark your answer on your answer sheet.
18. Mark your answer on your answer sheet.
19. Mark your answer on your answer sheet.
20. Mark your answer on your answer sheet.
21. Mark your answer on your answer sheet.
22. Mark your answer on your answer sheet.
23. Mark your answer on your answer sheet.
24. Mark your answer on your answer sheet.
25. Mark your answer on your answer sheet.
26. Mark your answer on your answer sheet.
27. Mark your answer on your answer sheet.
28. Mark your answer on your answer sheet.
29. Mark your answer on your answer sheet.
30. Mark your answer on your answer sheet.
31. Mark your answer on your answer sheet.

PART 3

Directions: You will hear some conversations between two or more people. You will be asked to answer three questions about what the speakers say in each conversation. Select the best response to each question and mark the letter (A), (B), (C), or (D) on your answer sheet. The conversations will not be printed in your test book and will be spoken only one time.

32. Where does the conversation most likely take place?
(A) At a gallery
(B) At a train station
(C) At a convention center
(D) At a theater

33. Why does the man apologize?
(A) Some fees have been raised.
(B) Some seats are sold out.
(C) A refund cannot be issued.
(D) A venue is not available.

34. What will the woman do next?
(A) Sign up for a membership
(B) Make a phone call
(C) Visit another location
(D) Fill out a questionnaire

35. What is the conversation mainly about?
(A) Launching a new product
(B) Designing a user manual
(C) Attending a press conference
(D) Preparing a business presentation

36. What does the woman recommend doing?
(A) Renovating a Web site
(B) Producing a video
(C) Contacting a different supplier
(D) Training an employee

37. What does the man say he is worried about?
(A) High costs
(B) A defective item
(C) Customer complaints
(D) A tight schedule

38. Why does the woman say, "I need the marketing team's budget proposal"?
(A) To justify changes to a schedule
(B) To inform the man of a new project
(C) To request more time for an assignment
(D) To ask for a document from the man

39. What does the man say about the advertising cost estimate?
(A) It is not accurate.
(B) It will be higher than before.
(C) It was prepared by a director.
(D) It has been sent by e-mail.

40. What will the woman discuss at today's meeting?
(A) Designing new products
(B) Holding seasonal sales
(C) Promotions for employees
(D) Negotiations with local businesses

41. What does the man want to purchase?
(A) A mattress
(B) A desk
(C) A chair
(D) A table

42. Why does the woman apologize?
(A) An item is sold out.
(B) A payment was not processed.
(C) A supervisor is unavailable.
(D) An offer has ended.

43. What does the man ask for?
(A) An instruction manual
(B) A discount
(C) A free delivery service
(D) A product catalog

GO ON TO THE NEXT PAGE

44. What industry do the speakers most likely work in?
(A) Banking
(B) Tourism
(C) Marketing
(D) Pharmaceutical

45. What does the woman say will happen this year?
(A) A corporate merger will be finalized.
(B) An annual conference will be held.
(C) A new product will be launched.
(D) An advertising campaign will be run.

46. What does the woman imply when she says, "Didn't Dr. Chen take part in the project"?
(A) Some information is missing.
(B) She did not know about an event.
(C) The man should help with a project.
(D) Another person will make a presentation.

47. Why does the woman want to save money?
(A) To expand a business
(B) To go on a trip
(C) To purchase a home
(D) To renovate an office

48. What does the man recommend?
(A) Working more hours
(B) Using an online software
(C) Contacting travel agencies
(D) Borrowing some money

49. What is the woman concerned about?
(A) The price of a product
(B) The quality of a service
(C) The length of a warranty
(D) The time of a flight

50. Who most likely is the woman?
(A) A business owner
(B) A tour guide
(C) A journalist
(D) An interior designer

51. What is the woman pleased about?
(A) The cost of a service
(B) An advertisement design
(C) The location of a store
(D) A newspaper article

52. What does the man ask about?
(A) Making an appointment
(B) Viewing a property
(C) Submitting a receipt
(D) Changing a layout

53. Why does the woman call the man?
(A) To check the price of a service
(B) To change an appointment time
(C) To request directions to a business
(D) To reply to a message

54. What problem does the man mention?
(A) He lost his credit card.
(B) He did not receive some information.
(C) He is late for a meeting.
(D) He cannot access a Web site.

55. What does the man say he will do at lunchtime?
(A) Meet a client
(B) Order some food
(C) Visit a bank
(D) Send e-mails

56. Where does the conversation take place?
   (A) At a hotel
   (B) At a car rental company
   (C) In a bus terminal
   (D) In a railway station

57. According to the man, what will the women receive?
   (A) A travel bag
   (B) A discount coupon
   (C) A city map
   (D) A parking permit

58. What will the women most likely do next?
   (A) Go to a restaurant
   (B) Review a presentation
   (C) Make a phone call
   (D) Cancel a reservation

59. What type of event are the speakers discussing?
   (A) A summer party
   (B) An awards ceremony
   (C) A birthday celebration
   (D) A store opening

60. What does the man suggest?
   (A) Changing a venue
   (B) Advertising an event online
   (C) Playing live music
   (D) Bringing food

61. What will the speakers do tomorrow?
   (A) Send out invitations
   (B) Look at menus
   (C) Attend a meeting
   (D) Make a payment

Stumerick Building Directory	
Business	Suite #
Haxwell Eyewear	105
Stuvesant Associates	107
Maycare Health Clinic	202
Ranz Publishing	205

62. What is the purpose of the man's visit?
   (A) He has a dentist appointment.
   (B) He has to purchase some medicine.
   (C) He is interviewing for a position.
   (D) He is going to repair some equipment.

63. What does the woman mention about parking?
   (A) It has limited space during the mornings.
   (B) It will be expanded next week.
   (C) It is complimentary for a certain amount of time.
   (D) It is only offered to workers in the building.

64. Look at the graphic. Which business name should be updated on the building directory?
   (A) Haxwell Eyewear
   (B) Stuvesant Associates
   (C) Maycare Health Clinic
   (D) Ranz Publishing

GO ON TO THE NEXT PAGE

Project Plan	
Stage 1	Construct porch, decks, and patio
Stage 2	Prepare soil
Stage 3	Plant trees and flowers
Stage 4	Repave driveway

PRODUCT	COST
Mobile phone	$280
Extended warranty	$68
Monthly global roaming plan	$30
Leather case	$25
Total	$403

65. What most likely is the man's profession?

(A) Landscape architect
(B) Real estate agent
(C) Electrical engineer
(D) Interior designer

66. Look at the graphic. What stage of the project will begin next week?

(A) Stage 1
(B) Stage 2
(C) Stage 3
(D) Stage 4

67. What does the woman ask the man to send?

(A) An event invitation
(B) A delivery address
(C) A cost estimate
(D) A construction blueprint

68. Who most likely is the woman?

(A) A tour guide
(B) A software developer
(C) A salesperson
(D) A repair technician

69. What does the man ask about?

(A) A contract extension
(B) An application update
(C) Travel accessories
(D) Online billing

70. Look at the graphic. How much money will be removed from the bill?

(A) $280
(B) $68
(C) $30
(D) $25

PART 4

Directions: You will hear some talks given by a single speaker. You will be asked to answer three questions about what the speaker says in each talk. Select the best response to each question and mark the letter (A), (B), (C), or (D) on your answer sheet. The talks will not be printed in your test book and will be spoken only one time.

71. Where does the speaker work?
    (A) At a business school
    (B) At a radio station
    (C) At a publishing company
    (D) At a financial institution

72. What will Professor Murray be discussing?
    (A) Finding jobs
    (B) Authoring books
    (C) Presentation techniques
    (D) Money management

73. What does the speaker encourage listeners to do?
    (A) Purchase a book
    (B) Ask questions by phone
    (C) Sign up for a membership
    (D) Invite other people

74. According to the speaker, what is being changed?
    (A) The deadline for requesting vacation time
    (B) The process for acquiring parking passes
    (C) The procedure for entering a building
    (D) The code for accessing a Web site

75. What must employees do before the change takes place?
    (A) Have a permit renewed
    (B) Have their photos taken
    (C) Attend a training workshop
    (D) Update their contact information

76. What does the speaker say was sent in an e-mail?
    (A) An appointment time
    (B) A revised schedule
    (C) A new passcode
    (D) An application form

77. What type of business does the speaker work for?
    (A) A cosmetics company
    (B) A staffing agency
    (C) A clothing retailer
    (D) An electronics manufacturer

78. What does the speaker imply when he says, "you might have to wait a bit"?
    (A) He is indicating that a meeting may be postponed.
    (B) He recommends making an appointment.
    (C) He is suggesting that the listeners get some food.
    (D) He wants the listeners to be patient.

79. What does the speaker encourage the listeners to do?
    (A) Have their meetings rescheduled
    (B) Have their orders confirmed
    (C) Have their résumés checked
    (D) Have their parking passes validated

80. Where does the speaker most likely work?
    (A) At an employment agency
    (B) At a medical supplies company
    (C) At a furniture store
    (D) At a charity organization

81. Why does the speaker say, "We actually already have enough volunteers signed up"?
    (A) To invite more workers
    (B) To decline an offer
    (C) To praise an event organizer
    (D) To request detailed information

82. What does the speaker ask the listener to do?
    (A) Meet with an employee
    (B) Send a payment
    (C) Choose a different date
    (D) Fill out a form online

GO ON TO THE NEXT PAGE

83. According to the message, why is the diner closed?
(A) It has moved to another location.
(B) It is holding a private party.
(C) It has changed its business hours.
(D) It is remodeling.

84. What new item is the diner offering?
(A) Vegetarian dishes
(B) Chocolate cakes
(C) Gourmet coffees
(D) Fresh seafood

85. How can customers obtain a coupon for a free dessert?
(A) By visiting a Web site
(B) By filling out a survey
(C) By purchasing a magazine
(D) By bringing a guest

86. Why does the speaker say, "Six weeks is quite a while to receive an order"?
(A) To request a deadline extension
(B) To express concern about a supplier
(C) To acknowledge customer complaints
(D) To negotiate a lower price

87. According to the speaker, what will happen this week?
(A) A report will be submitted.
(B) Some contracts will be signed.
(C) A product will be tested.
(D) New staff will start work.

88. What does the speaker request help with?
(A) Training some employees
(B) Transporting some equipment
(C) Making a sales presentation
(D) Supervising a manufacturing process

89. What is the talk mainly about?
(A) Organizing a sports event
(B) Electing a mayor
(C) Creating a playground
(D) Implementing a new law

90. What problem does the speaker mention?
(A) An expired permit
(B) Damaged equipment
(C) A lack of funding
(D) Resident complaints

91. What are the listeners asked to do?
(A) Teach a class
(B) Hire some architects
(C) Make a donation
(D) Contact business owners

92. What kind of company does the speaker most likely work at?
(A) A real estate agency
(B) A marketing firm
(C) A clothing store
(D) A hotel

93. According to the speaker, what is the problem?
(A) A price is higher than expected.
(B) A room is smaller than requested.
(C) A manager is not available.
(D) A document is not valid.

94. What does the speaker ask the listener to do?
(A) Provide contact information
(B) Make a payment
(C) Visit a Web site
(D) Respond to a message

| Georgetown Port Ferry ||
Departure	Arrival
7:45 A.M.	8:30 A.M.
11:30 A.M.	12:15 P.M.
4:00 P.M.	4:45 P.M.
8:00 P.M.	8:45 P.M.

95. What is the cause of the cancellation?
    (A) A damaged boat
    (B) Poor weather conditions
    (C) Lack of visitors
    (D) A port renovation project

96. Look at the graphic. What time will the ferry leave?
    (A) At 7:45 A.M
    (B) At 11:30 A.M
    (C) At 4:00 P.M
    (D) At 8:00 P.M

97. What does the speaker advise the listeners to do?
    (A) Request a refund
    (B) Show a receipt
    (C) Wear warm clothes
    (D) Bring some food

98. Where is the talk most likely taking place?
    (A) At a client meeting
    (B) At a staff training session
    (C) At a marketing class
    (D) At a computer skills workshop

99. Look at the graphic. Which part of the letterhead does the speaker discuss first?
    (A) Logo
    (B) Company name
    (C) Contact information
    (D) Slogan

100. What will the listeners most likely do next?
    (A) Write some ideas
    (B) Find a partner
    (C) Take a break
    (D) Submit a form

This is the end of the Listening test.

Listening Comprehension

TEST 07

음원·해석

LISTENING TEST

In the Listening test, you will be asked to demonstrate how well you understand spoken English. The entire Listening test will last approximately 45 minutes. There are four parts, and directions are given for each part. You must mark your answers on the separate answer sheet. Do not write your answers in your test book.

PART 1

Directions: For each question in this part, you will hear four statements about a picture in your test book. When you hear the statements, you must select the one statement that best describes what you see in the picture. Then find the number of the question on your answer sheet and mark your answer. The statements will not be printed in your test book and will be spoken only one time.

Statement (B), "A man is pointing at a document," is the best description of the picture, so you should select answer (B) and mark it on your answer sheet.

1.

2.

3.

4.

5.

6.

PART 2

Directions: You will hear a question or statement and three responses spoken in English. They will not be printed in your test book and will be spoken only one time. Select the best response to the question or statement and mark the letter (A), (B), or (C) on your answer sheet.

7. Mark your answer on your answer sheet.
8. Mark your answer on your answer sheet.
9. Mark your answer on your answer sheet.
10. Mark your answer on your answer sheet.
11. Mark your answer on your answer sheet.
12. Mark your answer on your answer sheet.
13. Mark your answer on your answer sheet.
14. Mark your answer on your answer sheet.
15. Mark your answer on your answer sheet.
16. Mark your answer on your answer sheet.
17. Mark your answer on your answer sheet.
18. Mark your answer on your answer sheet.
19. Mark your answer on your answer sheet.
20. Mark your answer on your answer sheet.
21. Mark your answer on your answer sheet.
22. Mark your answer on your answer sheet.
23. Mark your answer on your answer sheet.
24. Mark your answer on your answer sheet.
25. Mark your answer on your answer sheet.
26. Mark your answer on your answer sheet.
27. Mark your answer on your answer sheet.
28. Mark your answer on your answer sheet.
29. Mark your answer on your answer sheet.
30. Mark your answer on your answer sheet.
31. Mark your answer on your answer sheet.

PART 3

Directions: You will hear some conversations between two or more people. You will be asked to answer three questions about what the speakers say in each conversation. Select the best response to each question and mark the letter (A), (B), (C), or (D) on your answer sheet. The conversations will not be printed in your test book and will be spoken only one time.

32. Why did the man decide to shop at the store?
    (A) He saw an advertisement on the Internet.
    (B) His lunch break is longer than usual.
    (C) The employees are very knowledgeable.
    (D) The store is near his office.

33. What does the woman say the man needs?
    (A) An online receipt
    (B) A photo identification
    (C) An item number
    (D) A discount voucher

34. Why does the man say he will return later?
    (A) He wants to get some cash.
    (B) He has to print something at his work.
    (C) He has to attend a meeting.
    (D) He wants to compare prices.

35. Where is the conversation most likely taking place?
    (A) At a restaurant
    (B) At a department store
    (C) At a dry cleaner's
    (D) At a conference center

36. What is the man doing on Wednesday?
    (A) Making a speech
    (B) Training an employee
    (C) Visiting a client
    (D) Attending a banquet

37. What does the woman offer to do?
    (A) Give a refund
    (B) Set aside an item
    (C) Provide a faster service
    (D) Reserve a different room

38. What does the man want to do?
    (A) Apply for a job
    (B) Register for an event
    (C) Change an order
    (D) Test a product

39. What problem is mentioned?
    (A) Tickets are not available.
    (B) A schedule has changed.
    (C) A Web site is not operating properly.
    (D) Some fees have increased.

40. What information does the woman ask for?
    (A) A model number
    (B) An e-mail address
    (C) A name
    (D) A password

41. Who most likely is the man?
    (A) A hotel receptionist
    (B) A restaurant server
    (C) A store cashier
    (D) A bank employee

42. What does the man inquire about?
    (A) A training workshop
    (B) A job opening
    (C) A work schedule
    (D) A room reservation

43. What does the woman mean when she says, "I don't know"?
    (A) She is unable to fulfill the man's request.
    (B) She thinks more workers are not needed.
    (C) She has to speak with a manager first.
    (D) She is not sure about the time of an event.

GO ON TO THE NEXT PAGE

44. What does the man request the woman do?
   (A) Perform a colleague's task
   (B) Reschedule a meeting
   (C) Find a document
   (D) Visit a coworker

45. What does the woman say she needs?
   (A) An e-mail address
   (B) Tools for a project
   (C) Directions to an office
   (D) A phone number

46. What does the man remind the woman to do?
   (A) Obtain a signature
   (B) Take inventory
   (C) Place an order
   (D) Notify a supervisor

47. What is the purpose of the woman's call?
   (A) To postpone a meeting at work
   (B) To ask about a charge
   (C) To make a reservation
   (D) To invite an acquaintance to a trip

48. What will the woman do on Thursday?
   (A) Watch a performance
   (B) Attend a conference
   (C) Participate in a tour
   (D) Receive a treatment

49. What does the man offer to do?
   (A) Order some supplies
   (B) Talk to a coworker
   (C) Update an invoice
   (D) Contact another branch

50. What does the man say he will do soon?
   (A) Teach at a college
   (B) Relocate to another country
   (C) Have his eyes examined
   (D) Start his own business

51. According to the conversation, what did Paula do already?
   (A) She printed a document.
   (B) She changed a prescription.
   (C) She rescheduled an appointment.
   (D) She made an order.

52. What does Paula ask the man to do?
   (A) Pay a bill
   (B) Wait for a doctor
   (C) Sign a form
   (D) Try out an item

53. What does the woman say is special about the handbags?
   (A) It is limited in quantity.
   (B) It is discounted.
   (C) It is locally produced.
   (D) It is handmade.

54. What does the man imply when he says, "payday is still weeks away"?
   (A) He can't afford to make a purchase.
   (B) He gets paid more than once a month.
   (C) He has to wait longer than usual for his paycheck.
   (D) He needs a pay increase.

55. What does the woman say about her handbag?
   (A) She sold it to a coworker.
   (B) She returned it for a refund.
   (C) She exchanged it for a different one.
   (D) She gave it to a family member.

56. What problem does the man mention?
    (A) Some work is not complete.
    (B) A project requires additional funding.
    (C) Some supplies are missing.
    (D) A payment has not been processed.

57. According to the woman, what caused the problem?
    (A) Unclear instructions
    (B) Poor quality materials
    (C) Staffing changes
    (D) Inclement weather

58. What does the woman say she will do now?
    (A) Revise a schedule
    (B) File a complaint
    (C) Inspect a machine
    (D) Call a specialist

59. Why is the woman contacting the man?
    (A) To discuss a contract
    (B) To visit some building sites
    (C) To inquire about a meeting room
    (D) To purchase some equipment

60. What information does the man request?
    (A) The construction work period
    (B) The woman's phone number
    (C) The name of a supervisor
    (D) The number of participants

61. What does the man say he will do?
    (A) Revise a guest list
    (B) Expedite a delivery
    (C) Send a photograph
    (D) Provide a Web site address

20F Large Conference Room [Monday]	
9:00 A.M.	Quarterly financial review
10:00 A.M.	Sales planning
11:00 A.M.	New product education
12:00 P.M.	Employee safety training

62. What type of business do the speakers most likely work for?
    (A) A film production company
    (B) A construction company
    (C) A financial services firm
    (D) A legal consulting firm

63. Look at the graphic. Which event is Alexandra responsible for?
    (A) Quarterly financial review
    (B) Sales planning
    (C) New product education
    (D) Employee safety training

64. What does the man say he will do?
    (A) Ask that a file be sent to a client
    (B) Request that a colleague switch rooms
    (C) Check some work guidelines
    (D) Oversee a training workshop

GO ON TO THE NEXT PAGE

Review of Haochi Chinese Grill

Food quality: 5
Table service: 3
Restaurant location: 1
Interior layout: 2

Destination	Gate	Time	Status
Detroit	A21	13:25	Canceled
Seattle	C19	13:45	On time
Pittsburgh	B16	13:55	On time
Los Angeles	C23	14:00	Delayed

65. Who most likely is the woman?
   (A) A magazine editor
   (B) A food critic
   (C) A chef
   (D) A designer

66. Look at the graphic. Which area does the man think the Haochi Chinese Grill can improve in?
   (A) Food quality
   (B) Table service
   (C) Restaurant location
   (D) Interior layout

67. What does the woman suggest?
   (A) Meeting with staff members
   (B) Getting feedback from customers
   (C) Moving to a larger building
   (D) Offering special menus

68. What type of event are the speakers traveling to?
   (A) A product launch
   (B) A concert
   (C) An art exhibition
   (D) A conference

69. Why is the man staying just a short time?
   (A) He is moving to another branch.
   (B) He is going on vacation.
   (C) He has to return for a meeting.
   (D) He has to finish a project.

70. Look at the graphic. What city are the speakers flying to?
   (A) Detroit
   (B) Seattle
   (C) Pittsburgh
   (D) Los Angeles

PART 4

Directions: You will hear some talks given by a single speaker. You will be asked to answer three questions about what the speaker says in each talk. Select the best response to each question and mark the letter (A), (B), (C), or (D) on your answer sheet. The talks will not be printed in your test book and will be spoken only one time.

71. What service is being advertised?
    (A) A recycling program
    (B) A payment plan
    (C) Machine repair
    (D) Free shipping

72. How can listeners get a voucher?
    (A) By writing a review
    (B) By completing a survey
    (C) By spending a certain amount
    (D) By bringing an item

73. What is available on the Web site?
    (A) A user manual
    (B) A product catalog
    (C) Directions to a store
    (D) Information about a warranty

74. Where most likely is this announcement being made?
    (A) At a furniture store
    (B) At a train station
    (C) At a manufacturing plant
    (D) At a call center

75. What problem does the speaker mention?
    (A) A deadline has not been met.
    (B) A customer complaint has been received.
    (C) Some equipment is out of order.
    (D) Some documents are missing.

76. What might employees be informed about tonight?
    (A) Survey results
    (B) Revised work schedules
    (C) An upcoming sale
    (D) A facility inspection

77. What has the company done this year?
    (A) It has purchased another company.
    (B) It has achieved a sales goal.
    (C) It has won an award.
    (D) It has increased its staff.

78. According to the woman, what will be available?
    (A) A conference room
    (B) A redesigned Web site
    (C) A managing position
    (D) A new cafeteria

79. What does the woman mean when she says, "why not give it a try"?
    (A) Invest some money
    (B) Submit an article
    (C) Train new workers
    (D) Apply for a transfer

80. What is the main purpose of the talk?
    (A) To announce an award winner
    (B) To promote a new product
    (C) To introduce some colleagues
    (D) To discuss sales figures

81. What is said about the advertisements?
    (A) They were created with a low budget.
    (B) They feature various celebrities.
    (C) They focus on environmental protection.
    (D) They are being shown worldwide.

82. What does Mazak Advertising plan to do?
    (A) Expand into overseas markets
    (B) Increase production efficiency
    (C) Hire more employees
    (D) Contribute money to an organization

GO ON TO THE NEXT PAGE

83. What type of business is the speaker calling?

    (A) A real estate agency
    (B) A paint manufacturing company
    (C) A hair design salon
    (D) An interior decorating firm

84. How did the speaker learn about the company?

    (A) She read a flyer in a boutique.
    (B) She got a recommendation from an acquaintance.
    (C) She saw an advertisement in a newspaper.
    (D) She watched a commercial on television.

85. What is the speaker mostly concerned about?

    (A) The location of an office
    (B) The time of a meeting
    (C) The size of a space
    (D) The cost of a service

86. What is the main topic of the meeting?

    (A) A production deadline
    (B) A company policy
    (C) Sales figures
    (D) Customer comments

87. What feature of the product does the speaker talk about?

    (A) Internet access
    (B) Detachable battery
    (C) Wireless charging
    (D) Slim design

88. What does the speaker imply when she says, "the online demo video is now 30 minutes long"?

    (A) The video should be edited.
    (B) The demonstration is difficult to understand.
    (C) Users can download the video.
    (D) Employees should watch the demonstration carefully.

89. What type of job is being advertised?

    (A) Delivery worker
    (B) Packaging production supervisor
    (C) Teaching assistant
    (D) Tow truck driver

90. According to the speaker, what will Bondra Limited provide?

    (A) Free accommodations
    (B) End-of-year bonuses
    (C) On-the-job training
    (D) Health insurance

91. How should people apply for the job?

    (A) By visiting a company's Web site
    (B) By going to an office
    (C) By attending a job fair
    (D) By emailing a résumé

92. What is the speaker calling about?

    (A) A vacant position
    (B) A work payment
    (C) An apartment deposit
    (D) A recent bank transaction

93. What does the speaker say has changed?

    (A) A credit card number
    (B) A delivery time
    (C) A home address
    (D) A meeting location

94. Why does the speaker say, "I need to pay my bills"?

    (A) He wants a reply quickly.
    (B) He is sorry about an error.
    (C) He is offering reassurance.
    (D) He prefers another option.

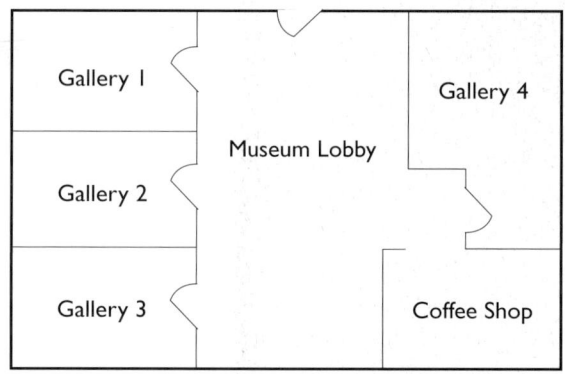

Survey Responses

Bigger discounts – 38%
Fresher fruits and vegetables – 18%
More foreign foods – 17%
Longer Sunday hours – 27%

95. What did the listeners probably see on the tour?
(A) Photos
(B) Drawings
(C) Artifacts
(D) Sculptures

96. What does the guide suggest the listeners do to get more information about the exhibit?
(A) Go to a Web site
(B) Buy a book
(C) Take a class
(D) View a video

97. Look at the graphic. In which room is the Chinese jewelry exhibit?
(A) Gallery 1
(B) Gallery 2
(C) Gallery 3
(D) Gallery 4

98. According to the speaker, what is the business's main goal?
(A) Promoting products
(B) Lowering costs
(C) Environment protection
(D) Customer satisfaction

99. Look at the graphic. Which survey response does the speaker want to address?
(A) Bigger discounts
(B) Fresher fruits and vegetables
(C) More foreign foods
(D) Longer Sunday hours

100. What solution does the speaker suggest?
(A) Making bulk orders
(B) Hiring additional workers
(C) Recycling more
(D) Advertising online

This is the end of the Listening test.

Listening Comprehension

TEST 08

음원 · 해석

LISTENING TEST

In the Listening test, you will be asked to demonstrate how well you understand spoken English. The entire Listening test will last approximately 45 minutes. There are four parts, and directions are given for each part. You must mark your answers on the separate answer sheet. Do not write your answers in your test book.

PART 1

Directions: For each question in this part, you will hear four statements about a picture in your test book. When you hear the statements, you must select the one statement that best describes what you see in the picture. Then find the number of the question on your answer sheet and mark your answer. The statements will not be printed in your test book and will be spoken only one time.

Statement (B), "A man is pointing at a document," is the best description of the picture, so you should select answer (B) and mark it on your answer sheet.

1.

2.

3.

4.

5.

6.

PART 2

Directions: You will hear a question or statement and three responses spoken in English. They will not be printed in your test book and will be spoken only one time. Select the best response to the question or statement and mark the letter (A), (B), or (C) on your answer sheet.

7. Mark your answer on your answer sheet.
8. Mark your answer on your answer sheet.
9. Mark your answer on your answer sheet.
10. Mark your answer on your answer sheet.
11. Mark your answer on your answer sheet.
12. Mark your answer on your answer sheet.
13. Mark your answer on your answer sheet.
14. Mark your answer on your answer sheet.
15. Mark your answer on your answer sheet.
16. Mark your answer on your answer sheet.
17. Mark your answer on your answer sheet.
18. Mark your answer on your answer sheet.
19. Mark your answer on your answer sheet.
20. Mark your answer on your answer sheet.
21. Mark your answer on your answer sheet.
22. Mark your answer on your answer sheet.
23. Mark your answer on your answer sheet.
24. Mark your answer on your answer sheet.
25. Mark your answer on your answer sheet.
26. Mark your answer on your answer sheet.
27. Mark your answer on your answer sheet.
28. Mark your answer on your answer sheet.
29. Mark your answer on your answer sheet.
30. Mark your answer on your answer sheet.
31. Mark your answer on your answer sheet.

PART 3

Directions: You will hear some conversations between two or more people. You will be asked to answer three questions about what the speakers say in each conversation. Select the best response to each question and mark the letter (A), (B), (C), or (D) on your answer sheet. The conversations will not be printed in your test book and will be spoken only one time.

32. What are the speakers discussing?
    (A) A smartphone
    (B) A desktop computer
    (C) A washing machine
    (D) A cooking appliance

33. What does the woman want to know?
    (A) The color choices
    (B) The size options
    (C) The delivery date
    (D) The warranty period

34. What will the man most likely do next?
    (A) Process a payment
    (B) Demonstrate a product
    (C) Explain a policy
    (D) Contact a manufacturer

35. Why is the woman calling?
    (A) To order some office equipment
    (B) To receive details about a moving service
    (C) To check the status of a delivery
    (D) To discuss the sale of a commercial property

36. What event does the woman mention?
    (A) A store reopening
    (B) A trade show
    (C) A building tour
    (D) A seasonal sale

37. What additional information does the man request?
    (A) The dimensions of items
    (B) A corporate membership number
    (C) A shipping address
    (D) The name of the woman's supervisor

38. Why is the man calling?
    (A) To make an order
    (B) To offer employment
    (C) To discuss relocation costs
    (D) To arrange an interview

39. What is the woman concerned about?
    (A) An increase in price
    (B) A delay in production
    (C) The lack of transportation options
    (D) The availability of staff members

40. What does the man say he will do next?
    (A) Meet with coworkers
    (B) Visit an office
    (C) Call a train station
    (D) Provide detailed information

41. What are the speakers discussing?
    (A) A staff workshop
    (B) A vacation policy
    (C) A company relocation
    (D) A contract negotiation

42. Why does the man say that he is happy?
    (A) A budget has been approved.
    (B) A consultant is available.
    (C) A deadline has been extended.
    (D) A room is large enough.

43. What does the woman offer to do?
    (A) Request more chairs
    (B) Select another date
    (C) Interview an employee
    (D) Contact department heads

GO ON TO THE NEXT PAGE

44. What does the man inquire about?

(A) The cost of an item
(B) The length of a sale
(C) The business hours
(D) The refund policy

45. Why does the man say, "I really like them"?

(A) To compliment a friend's fashion style
(B) To thank a store employee for a suggestion
(C) To recommend an item to a colleague
(D) To express interest in purchasing an item

46. What does the woman say she will do?

(A) Search a database
(B) Talk to a manager
(C) Reserve a product
(D) Give a discount

47. Where most likely do the speakers work?

(A) At a bookstore
(B) At a job placement agency
(C) At a computer repair shop
(D) At a university

48. What task have the women been doing?

(A) Inspecting some machines
(B) Putting information into a database
(C) Creating invitations for an event
(D) Reviewing some applications

49. What does the man propose?

(A) Organizing a training workshop
(B) Extending a project deadline
(C) Recruiting more employees
(D) Purchasing new equipment

50. What are the speakers mainly discussing?

(A) Building renovations
(B) Accounting needs
(C) A new software program
(D) An advertising campaign

51. What suggestion does the man make?

(A) Hiring an outside consultant
(B) Moving to another location
(C) Purchasing new equipment
(D) Opening a different account

52. What does the woman want the man to provide?

(A) A budget proposal
(B) A client list
(C) Contact information
(D) Product samples

53. What is the man unable to do?

(A) Reserve a room
(B) Access a system
(C) Download a file
(D) Find a device

54. What happened last night?

(A) Some orders were shipped.
(B) Some workers were hired.
(C) An office building was remodeled.
(D) An equipment update was performed.

55. What does the woman offer to do?

(A) Contact a client
(B) Submit a form
(C) Train a worker
(D) Repair a computer

56. What are the speakers mainly discussing?
    (A) An upcoming assignment
    (B) An overseas trip
    (C) A job applicant
    (D) A corporate gathering

57. What is mentioned about the Rogan Gallery?
    (A) It has been renovated.
    (B) Its curator is retiring soon.
    (C) It provides discounts to residents.
    (D) Some of its sections are closed.

58. What is Maya asked to do?
    (A) Provide training
    (B) Contact a business
    (C) Reserve a room
    (D) Take photos

59. What are the speakers working on?
    (A) A building design
    (B) A product survey
    (C) A user guide
    (D) An annual budget

60. What does the woman say about the city orchestra group?
    (A) Its members will be receiving new instruments.
    (B) Its members will be performing soon.
    (C) Its members will be departing for a trip.
    (D) Its members will be receiving prizes.

61. Why does the man say, "I think Ryan should be able to assist us on Friday"?
    (A) To propose a different solution
    (B) To remind the woman of a deadline
    (C) To show frustration with a coworker
    (D) To approve the woman's request

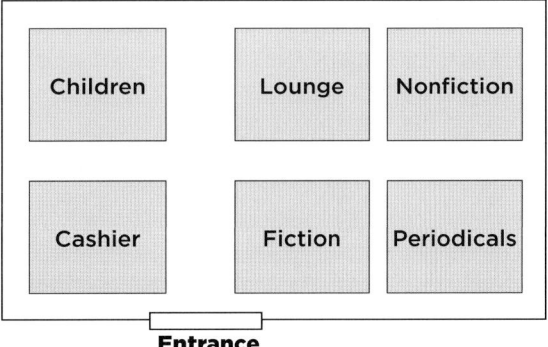

62. Who most likely is the woman?
    (A) A delivery driver
    (B) A sales associate
    (C) A journalist
    (D) A teacher

63. What does the man say he has heard about the book?
    (A) It is available in an electronic format.
    (B) It was written for adults.
    (C) It will create opportunities for conversation.
    (D) It is the most recent book by the author.

64. Look at the graphic. In which section is the book the man is looking for located?
    (A) Nonfiction
    (B) Periodicals
    (C) Fiction
    (D) Children

Oriental Lily Flowers Size Chart			
Type 1	Type 2	Type 3	Type 4
3 feet tall	4 feet tall	5 feet tall	6 feet tall

65. Why does the man want some flowers?

(A) To enhance the appearance of an outdoor area
(B) To hand them out as gifts to some staff members
(C) To use them in a scientific experiment
(D) To attract more customers to a store

66. Look at the graphic. What size flowers will the man most likely choose?

(A) 3 feet
(B) 4 feet
(C) 5 feet
(D) 6 feet

67. What additional service does the woman offer the man?

(A) Lawn cutting
(B) Expedited shipping
(C) Balcony cleaning
(D) Flower planting

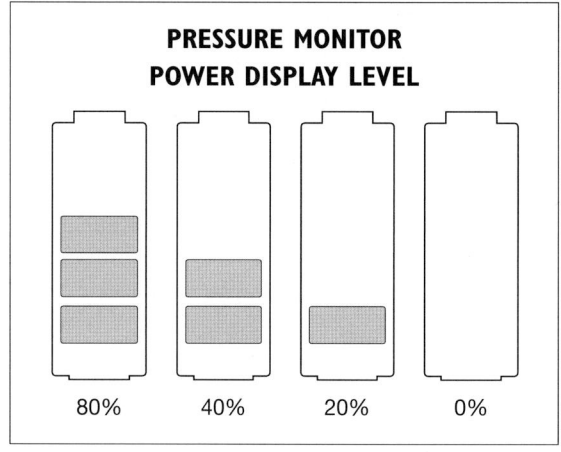

68. What event is taking place?

(A) A factory inspection
(B) A guided tour
(C) A training session
(D) A client meeting

69. What does the woman ask about?

(A) Survey responses
(B) New machine models
(C) Other power sources
(D) Extra supply orders

70. Look at the graphic. According to the man, how many bars will be displayed when the battery should be replaced?

(A) Three bars
(B) Two bars
(C) One bar
(D) Zero bars

PART 4

Directions: You will hear some talks given by a single speaker. You will be asked to answer three questions about what the speaker says in each talk. Select the best response to each question and mark the letter (A), (B), (C), or (D) on your answer sheet. The talks will not be printed in your test book and will be spoken only one time.

71. What is expected to happen tomorrow?
(A) Traffic delays will occur.
(B) New subway lines will open.
(C) The weather will clear up.
(D) A workers' strike will start.

72. What are people advised to do?
(A) Visit a city department
(B) Use public transportation
(C) Call a hotline
(D) Stay away from the sun

73. How long are the weather conditions expected to last?
(A) One day
(B) Two days
(C) One week
(D) Two weeks

74. Why is the speaker calling Jeremy?
(A) To provide new contact information
(B) To discuss plans for staff training
(C) To reschedule a meeting with a client
(D) To check on a financial report

75. What does the speaker mean when he says, "there will be a department meeting in the afternoon today"?
(A) An employee will be busy.
(B) He will not be able to attend a conference.
(C) An assignment is almost finished.
(D) He has to create a presentation.

76. What will the speaker do tomorrow?
(A) Review job applications
(B) Demonstrate a product
(C) Go to a company dinner
(D) Speak with Lester

77. Who is Justin Mills?
(A) A radio host
(B) A financial advisor
(C) A newspaper editor
(D) A computer programmer

78. What will Justin Mills be doing next month?
(A) Managing a company
(B) Traveling overseas
(C) Creating a Web site
(D) Leading some seminars

79. What does the speaker tell the listeners to do?
(A) Write articles
(B) Post questions online
(C) Register for an event
(D) Look at photos

80. What is available by the entrance?
(A) A schedule
(B) A sign-up sheet
(C) Beverages
(D) Protective equipment

81. What does the speaker suggest when she says, "Space is limited"?
(A) Listeners should move to another room.
(B) Listeners must make a decision soon.
(C) A new class will be added.
(D) An error has to be corrected.

82. What will the listeners do next?
(A) Watch a demonstration
(B) Speak with a famous athlete
(C) Make a payment
(D) Complete a form

GO ON TO THE NEXT PAGE

83. What kind of business does the speaker work for?
 (A) An electronics retailer
 (B) An accounting agency
 (C) A marketing firm
 (D) A clothing manufacturer

84. What does the speaker announce?
 (A) A job vacancy
 (B) An acquisition of an company
 (C) A revised policy
 (D) An award nomination

85. What does the speaker mention about Raj Singh's project?
 (A) It involved working with different teams.
 (B) It helped improve a client's sales.
 (C) It did not require a large budget.
 (D) It was completed last year.

86. What is the report about?
 (A) Popular local restaurants
 (B) Consuming healthy food
 (C) Exercise tips
 (D) Cooking classes

87. What does John Umunna encourage listeners to do?
 (A) Take vitamin supplements
 (B) Register for a fitness class
 (C) Make food at home
 (D) Subscribe to a magazine

88. According to the speaker, what can listeners find on a Web site?
 (A) Reviews about businesses
 (B) Information about a study
 (C) Product prices
 (D) Cooking instructions

89. Why has the bus stopped?
 (A) To pay for parking
 (B) To fill up on gas
 (C) To give tourists an opportunity to shop
 (D) To let passengers enjoy a view

90. According to the speaker, why was Slatington important in the past?
 (A) It was the first city to use agricultural machinery.
 (B) It was a center for mining activities.
 (C) A major power plant was built there.
 (D) A famous company was started there.

91. What will the tour group do next?
 (A) Have a meal
 (B) Take some photos
 (C) Purchase souvenirs
 (D) Watch a video

92. What type of business does the speaker work for?
 (A) A computer manufacturer
 (B) An office supply store
 (C) An electronics recycling company
 (D) A commercial relocation firm

93. What does the speaker mean when he says, "Many companies are signing up"?
 (A) The listeners may qualify for a discount.
 (B) The listeners should hire his business.
 (C) He is thinking about expanding some services.
 (D) He believes that an industry's trends will begin to change.

94. What will the listeners see in a video?
 (A) An award acceptance speech
 (B) A product demonstration
 (C) Client testimonials
 (D) Facility tours

Time	Presenter
First presentation	Nadia Wong
Second presentation	Gary Almont
Third presentation	Lewis Walton
Fourth presentation	Mayumi Kosaka

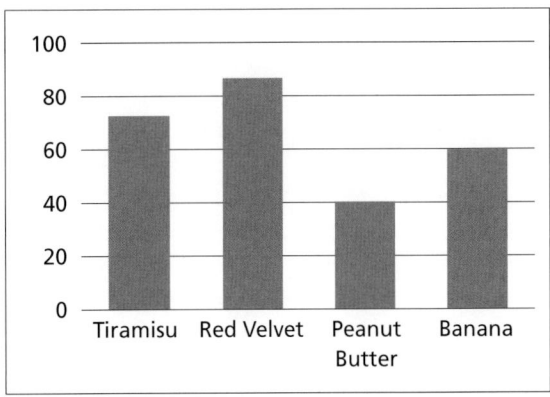

95. Who most likely is the talk intended for?

(A) Medical professionals
(B) Jewelry designers
(C) Travel agents
(D) Fashion magazine writers

96. Look at the graph. Which presentation has been changed?

(A) The first presentation
(B) The second presentation
(C) The third presentation
(D) The fourth presentation

97. How can listeners enter a raffle?

(A) By registering for a membership
(B) By testing a product
(C) By submitting some comments
(D) By volunteering at an event

98. Look at the graphic. Which cake flavor will be discounted this week?

(A) Tiramisu
(B) Red Velvet
(C) Peanut Butter
(D) Banana

99. Why does the speaker thank Michelle?

(A) She recommended a promotional event.
(B) She created new cake flavors.
(C) She supervised a renovation project.
(D) She worked over the weekend.

100. What does the speaker encourage the listeners to do?

(A) Analyze some data
(B) Register for a workshop
(C) Share suggestions
(D) Invite guests

This is the end of the Listening test.

Listening Comprehension

TEST 09

음원·해석

LISTENING TEST

In the Listening test, you will be asked to demonstrate how well you understand spoken English. The entire Listening test will last approximately 45 minutes. There are four parts, and directions are given for each part. You must mark your answers on the separate answer sheet. Do not write your answers in your test book.

PART 1

Directions: For each question in this part, you will hear four statements about a picture in your test book. When you hear the statements, you must select the one statement that best describes what you see in the picture. Then find the number of the question on your answer sheet and mark your answer. The statements will not be printed in your test book and will be spoken only one time.

Statement (B), "A man is pointing at a document," is the best description of the picture, so you should select answer (B) and mark it on your answer sheet.

1.

2.

3.

4.

5.

6.

PART 2

Directions: You will hear a question or statement and three responses spoken in English. They will not be printed in your test book and will be spoken only one time. Select the best response to the question or statement and mark the letter (A), (B), or (C) on your answer sheet.

7. Mark your answer on your answer sheet.
8. Mark your answer on your answer sheet.
9. Mark your answer on your answer sheet.
10. Mark your answer on your answer sheet.
11. Mark your answer on your answer sheet.
12. Mark your answer on your answer sheet.
13. Mark your answer on your answer sheet.
14. Mark your answer on your answer sheet.
15. Mark your answer on your answer sheet.
16. Mark your answer on your answer sheet.
17. Mark your answer on your answer sheet.
18. Mark your answer on your answer sheet.
19. Mark your answer on your answer sheet.
20. Mark your answer on your answer sheet.
21. Mark your answer on your answer sheet.
22. Mark your answer on your answer sheet.
23. Mark your answer on your answer sheet.
24. Mark your answer on your answer sheet.
25. Mark your answer on your answer sheet.
26. Mark your answer on your answer sheet.
27. Mark your answer on your answer sheet.
28. Mark your answer on your answer sheet.
29. Mark your answer on your answer sheet.
30. Mark your answer on your answer sheet.
31. Mark your answer on your answer sheet.

PART 3

Directions: You will hear some conversations between two or more people. You will be asked to answer three questions about what the speakers say in each conversation. Select the best response to each question and mark the letter (A), (B), (C), or (D) on your answer sheet. The conversations will not be printed in your test book and will be spoken only one time.

32. Where most likely are the speakers?
    (A) At an appliance store
    (B) At a computer repair shop
    (C) At an auto center
    (D) At a food packaging plant

33. What problem does the man mention?
    (A) A shipment has been delayed.
    (B) A product is not working properly.
    (C) A manager is not available.
    (D) A price has gone up.

34. What would the man like to do?
    (A) Get his money back
    (B) Look at a catalog
    (C) Visit another location
    (D) Bring a document

35. What did the man recently do?
    (A) He organized some events.
    (B) He looked over some comments.
    (C) He revised a work schedule.
    (D) He applied for a position.

36. Why does the woman say, "the remodeling project has been taking up all my time"?
    (A) To extend a deadline
    (B) To request more workers
    (C) To give an excuse
    (D) To seek advice

37. What will the man suggest at next week's meeting?
    (A) Offering reduced rates
    (B) Providing a shuttle service
    (C) Extending a facility's operating hours
    (D) Adding more parking spaces

38. Why will the man visit the woman's office?
    (A) To sell a product
    (B) To collect a package
    (C) To fix a machine
    (D) To make a payment

39. What does the woman say she will do?
    (A) Finish a project
    (B) Notify a security guard
    (C) Leave a door open
    (D) Receive a delivery

40. What does the woman ask the man to email her?
    (A) A brochure
    (B) A contract
    (C) A warranty
    (D) An invoice

41. What is the woman shopping for?
    (A) Toys
    (B) Children's clothes
    (C) Books
    (D) Sports equipment

42. What does Rodrigo say about some items?
    (A) They're no longer available.
    (B) They've recently arrived.
    (C) They've been used before.
    (D) They're located on another floor.

43. What service does Rodrigo mention?
    (A) Gift wrapping
    (B) In-store consultation
    (C) Free shipping
    (D) Online reservation

GO ON TO THE NEXT PAGE

44. What suggestion does the woman provide?
(A) Prioritizing everyday tasks
(B) Reducing workloads
(C) Getting to the office early
(D) Tracking time spent on assignments

45. What does the woman intend to do?
(A) Change careers
(B) Travel overseas
(C) Register for a class
(D) Publish a book

46. What does the woman mean when she says, "That's tough to say"?
(A) She thinks a word is hard to pronounce.
(B) She cannot provide an answer at the moment.
(C) She has many difficult jobs to do.
(D) She does not wish to answer a question.

47. Where is the man calling from?
(A) A warehouse
(B) A furniture store
(C) His work
(D) His home

48. What does the woman say was entered incorrectly?
(A) An item code
(B) An address
(C) A credit card number
(D) A shipping date

49. What does the woman say she will do?
(A) Talk to a manager
(B) Send an e-mail
(C) Give a refund
(D) Rush a delivery

50. What are the speakers mainly discussing?
(A) Moving offices
(B) Preparing some data
(C) Training employees
(D) Upgrading some equipment

51. Why was the man unable to finish a task?
(A) A system was not working.
(B) A room was not available.
(C) A document had errors.
(D) A coworker arrived late.

52. What does the woman say she will do tomorrow?
(A) Meet a client
(B) Pick up a shipment
(C) Call a technician
(D) Email a file

53. What service does Vidia Business Solutions provide?
(A) Financial planning
(B) Graphic design
(C) Product advertisement
(D) Client management

54. What did the woman's company do three months ago?
(A) It acquired a business.
(B) It received an award.
(C) It moved to a different city.
(D) It launched a marketing campaign.

55. What does Kenneth offer to do?
(A) Go over some service options
(B) Update an invoice
(C) Negotiate some prices
(D) Drop off a package

56. What did the woman do in Germany?
(A) Speak at a convention
(B) Demonstrate a product
(C) Meet with some distributors
(D) Conduct job interviews

57. What problem is mentioned?
(A) An item is sold out.
(B) A service is expensive.
(C) A room is not available.
(D) A client is dissatisfied.

58. What does the man suggest?
(A) Extending a deadline
(B) Placing an advertisement
(C) Signing a short-term agreement
(D) Modifying a production process

59. What is the man's problem?
(A) He did not receive a delivery.
(B) He is unable to find a product.
(C) He was overcharged for an item.
(D) He cannot carry some merchandise.

60. What does the woman explain?
(A) A technical issue
(B) A new service
(C) A business policy
(D) A staff shortage

61. What does the woman ask the man to do?
(A) Speak to a manager
(B) Visit another store
(C) Bring a receipt
(D) Participate in a survey

File	Created by
The World Economy	Rex Kamata
Investment Portfolio	Brian McCurdie
Weekly Sales Report	Tom Avery
Employee Evaluation Form	Jeong-Seok Ok

62. Why is the woman unable to check the company's files?
(A) She did not update a program.
(B) Her password has been changed.
(C) Her computer will not turn on.
(D) She cannot connect to a server.

63. Look at the graphic. Who created the file the speakers are referring to?
(A) Rex Kamata
(B) Brian McCurdie
(C) Tom Avery
(D) Jeong-Seok Ok

64. What does the woman ask the man to do?
(A) Print a document
(B) Submit a presentation
(C) Revise a report
(D) Contact technical support

GO ON TO THE NEXT PAGE

Lounge		Restrooms 👫
Room 304		
Room 303		
Room 302	Room 301	Media Room

65. What will the man be doing later today?
  (A) Evaluating team members
  (B) Visiting a main office
  (C) Picking up a client
  (D) Delivering furniture

66. Look at the graphic. What room has been assigned to the man?
  (A) Room 301
  (B) Room 302
  (C) Room 303
  (D) Room 304

67. What will take place tomorrow morning?
  (A) A corporate banquet
  (B) A branch opening
  (C) A facility tour
  (D) A staff meeting

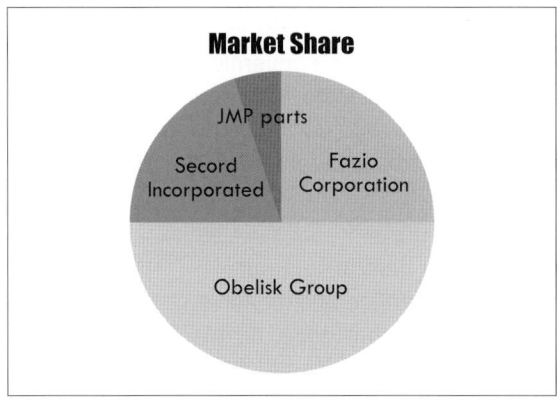

68. What are the speakers mainly discussing?
  (A) A corporate merger
  (B) An advertising campaign
  (C) A newspaper subscription
  (D) A quarterly budget

69. Look at the graphic. Where do the speakers work?
  (A) At Obelisk Group
  (B) At Secord Incorporated
  (C) At JMP Parts
  (D) At Fazio Corporation

70. Why does the woman say she is unsure?
  (A) She is new to the industry.
  (B) A company has been losing profits.
  (C) The man has a busy schedule.
  (D) Some numbers may be inaccurate.

PART 4

Directions: You will hear some talks given by a single speaker. You will be asked to answer three questions about what the speaker says in each talk. Select the best response to each question and mark the letter (A), (B), (C), or (D) on your answer sheet. The talks will not be printed in your test book and will be spoken only one time.

71. What kind of event is being held?
    (A) A film festival
    (B) A photo contest
    (C) A music performance
    (D) A theater opening

72. According to Catalina Murphy, why was the event changed?
    (A) To give participants more time to prepare
    (B) To lower operating expenses
    (C) To appeal to a younger audience
    (D) To allow for more submissions

73. How can listeners obtain more information about the event?
    (A) By calling a radio station
    (B) By joining a club
    (C) By visiting a museum
    (D) By going to a Web site

74. Where does the announcement most likely take place?
    (A) On a cruise ship
    (B) On a train
    (C) In an airplane
    (D) On a bus

75. What is the reason for the delay?
    (A) A worker is unavailable.
    (B) Maintenance is being performed.
    (C) Some passengers are late.
    (D) Some bags are missing.

76. What does the speaker say he expects will happen?
    (A) Traffic will get worse in the evening.
    (B) The weather will be better than anticipated.
    (C) A different route will be taken to reach a city.
    (D) The listeners will arrive at their destination as scheduled.

77. Why did the listener cancel his membership?
    (A) Storage space wasn't available.
    (B) Membership was too expensive.
    (C) Some equipment was not working.
    (D) The fitness center was unclean.

78. What does the speaker offer the listener?
    (A) Personal exercise equipment
    (B) Reserved parking
    (C) 24-hour spa access
    (D) Complimentary training sessions

79. How long does the special offer last?
    (A) One week
    (B) Two weeks
    (C) One month
    (D) Two months

80. Who is the message intended for?
    (A) An executive officer
    (B) A new worker
    (C) A guest speaker
    (D) A potential client

81. What is the speaker requesting?
    (A) An introductory statement
    (B) A budget proposal
    (C) A reference letter
    (D) A signed contract

82. What does the speaker mean when he says, "We're planning to put it in our newsletter for next week"?
    (A) An article needs to be reviewed.
    (B) An editor will not be available next week.
    (C) He would like a task to be finished soon.
    (D) He will extend a project deadline.

GO ON TO THE NEXT PAGE

83. Who is the speaker addressing?
    (A) Library staff members
    (B) School teachers
    (C) Corporate sponsors
    (D) Local newspaper reporters

84. What news does the speaker announce?
    (A) A building will be undergoing renovation.
    (B) An event will be rescheduled.
    (C) A new manager has been hired.
    (D) A donation has been received.

85. What does the speaker ask listeners to do?
    (A) Complete a survey
    (B) Distribute some instructions
    (C) Reorganize some books
    (D) Attend a training workshop

86. Who most likely are the listeners?
    (A) Potential customers
    (B) Convention participants
    (C) Event organizers
    (D) New staff members

87. What does the speaker mean when he says, "Each office has a security system"?
    (A) A renovation project will start soon.
    (B) A system is advanced.
    (C) The listeners may have to use their IDs.
    (D) The listeners should be prepared to wait.

88. What does the speaker say has recently changed?
    (A) A company Web site
    (B) A building map
    (C) A cafeteria menu
    (D) A computer database

89. What is the topic of the workshop?
    (A) Creating business plans
    (B) Producing advertisements
    (C) Finding employment
    (D) Developing presentation skills

90. According to the speaker, why is it important to make a good first impression?
    (A) To entertain an audience
    (B) To get investors' support
    (C) To attract more customers
    (D) To gain colleagues' respect

91. What does the speaker ask members of the group to do?
    (A) Prepare some questions
    (B) Make a group presentation
    (C) Complete a survey
    (D) Describe previous work experience

92. What is the main purpose of the message?
    (A) To inquire about a product
    (B) To set up a meeting
    (C) To recommend a business
    (D) To check on an order

93. What does the speaker imply when she says, "We have less than three months until the grand opening"?
    (A) She cannot attend the grand opening.
    (B) She wants more time to finish a project.
    (C) A decision needs to be made soon.
    (D) A venue should be reserved in advance.

94. What most likely will the speaker do next?
    (A) Call a restaurant
    (B) Visit a Web site
    (C) Interview some candidates
    (D) Send some documents

Late Fees

3 days late	€50
7 days late	€100
14 days late	€150
21 days late	€200

95. Where most likely does the speaker work?
    (A) At a wireless communication company
    (B) At a property management office
    (C) At a construction firm
    (D) At a bank

96. Look at the graphic. How much is the listener's late fee?
    (A) €50
    (B) €100
    (C) €150
    (D) €200

97. What should the listener provide to register for a service?
    (A) A mailing address
    (B) A telephone number
    (C) Some financial information
    (D) Some employment details

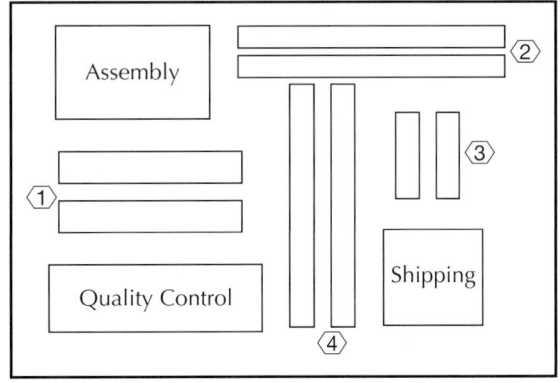

98. Why is a change being made?
    (A) To increase safety
    (B) To save money
    (C) To make a process more efficient
    (D) To create additional space

99. Look at the graphic. Where are the new storage cases located?
    (A) Area 1
    (B) Area 2
    (C) Area 3
    (D) Area 4

100. What does the man say listeners can find at his desk?
    (A) An inventory list
    (B) A sign-up sheet
    (C) Machine operating manuals
    (D) Employee IDs

This is the end of the Listening test.

Listening Comprehension

TEST 10

음원·해석

LISTENING TEST

In the Listening test, you will be asked to demonstrate how well you understand spoken English. The entire Listening test will last approximately 45 minutes. There are four parts, and directions are given for each part. You must mark your answers on the separate answer sheet. Do not write your answers in your test book.

PART 1

Directions: For each question in this part, you will hear four statements about a picture in your test book. When you hear the statements, you must select the one statement that best describes what you see in the picture. Then find the number of the question on your answer sheet and mark your answer. The statements will not be printed in your test book and will be spoken only one time.

Statement (B), "A man is pointing at a document," is the best description of the picture, so you should select answer (B) and mark it on your answer sheet.

1.

2.

3.

4.

5.

6.

PART 2

Directions: You will hear a question or statement and three responses spoken in English. They will not be printed in your test book and will be spoken only one time. Select the best response to the question or statement and mark the letter (A), (B), or (C) on your answer sheet.

7. Mark your answer on your answer sheet.
8. Mark your answer on your answer sheet.
9. Mark your answer on your answer sheet.
10. Mark your answer on your answer sheet.
11. Mark your answer on your answer sheet.
12. Mark your answer on your answer sheet.
13. Mark your answer on your answer sheet.
14. Mark your answer on your answer sheet.
15. Mark your answer on your answer sheet.
16. Mark your answer on your answer sheet.
17. Mark your answer on your answer sheet.
18. Mark your answer on your answer sheet.
19. Mark your answer on your answer sheet.
20. Mark your answer on your answer sheet.
21. Mark your answer on your answer sheet.
22. Mark your answer on your answer sheet.
23. Mark your answer on your answer sheet.
24. Mark your answer on your answer sheet.
25. Mark your answer on your answer sheet.
26. Mark your answer on your answer sheet.
27. Mark your answer on your answer sheet.
28. Mark your answer on your answer sheet.
29. Mark your answer on your answer sheet.
30. Mark your answer on your answer sheet.
31. Mark your answer on your answer sheet.

PART 3

Directions: You will hear some conversations between two or more people. You will be asked to answer three questions about what the speakers say in each conversation. Select the best response to each question and mark the letter (A), (B), (C), or (D) on your answer sheet. The conversations will not be printed in your test book and will be spoken only one time.

32. Why is the woman calling?
    (A) To inquire about tourist attractions
    (B) To report a malfunctioning television
    (C) To ask for another room
    (D) To complain about loud noise

33. What does the man say about the other hotel guests?
    (A) They're going to have a meal.
    (B) They're taking a bus.
    (C) They're watching a movie.
    (D) They're leaving for a conference.

34. What does the woman ask the man to do?
    (A) Contact a manager
    (B) Send an employee to a room
    (C) Recommend a tour
    (D) Make a reservation at a restaurant

35. Where do the speakers most likely work?
    (A) At an electronics company
    (B) At an advertising agency
    (C) At a printing center
    (D) At an office supplies store

36. What does the client want the speakers to do?
    (A) Replace some appliances
    (B) Cancel an online order
    (C) Send some catalogs
    (D) Change a color scheme

37. Why will the speakers have to wait to complete a task?
    (A) Some supplies have not arrived.
    (B) A document is missing.
    (C) Some equipment is being repaired.
    (D) A manager is not available.

38. Who most likely is the woman?
    (A) A plant manager
    (B) An online customer
    (C) A clothing store employee
    (D) A call center agent

39. What does the man ask the woman to do?
    (A) Provide contact information
    (B) Adjust a schedule
    (C) Choose another product
    (D) Give an order number

40. What does the man say he will arrange?
    (A) An automated payment
    (B) A personal consultation
    (C) An overnight delivery
    (D) A refund

41. What is Vanessa trying to do?
    (A) Renew her passport
    (B) Fix her vehicle
    (C) Get another job
    (D) Find a new home

42. What is Vanessa worried about?
    (A) Driving time
    (B) A registration deadline
    (C) Work hours
    (D) A late payment

43. What will the man do next?
    (A) Update a program
    (B) Transfer some money
    (C) Provide directions
    (D) Print a document

GO ON TO THE NEXT PAGE

44. What kind of business does the man most likely work for?

(A) A moving company
(B) A furniture store
(C) A travel agency
(D) An interior design firm

45. Why is the woman pleased?

(A) A proposal has been approved.
(B) She has been given a discount.
(C) A job has been completed quickly.
(D) She has received a free item.

46. What detail does the woman remember?

(A) The name of an employee
(B) The number of items she purchased
(C) The location of a business
(D) The contents of some boxes

47. What are the speakers discussing?

(A) A recent business merger
(B) An upcoming seminar
(C) A fitness program
(D) A building renovation project

48. What does the man imply when he says, "How could anyone do that"?

(A) He wants someone to help him with a job.
(B) He can't understand a coworker's behavior.
(C) He doesn't know how to use some equipment.
(D) He believes a task is not possible to do.

49. What does the woman say she will do?

(A) Arrange transportation
(B) Send e-mails
(C) Revise a schedule
(D) Visit an office

50. Where most likely are the speakers?

(A) At a sporting goods store
(B) At a library
(C) At a gym
(D) At a medical center

51. Why does the woman need to show her employee ID card?

(A) To receive a free item
(B) To enter a building
(C) To access a computer
(D) To get a discount

52. What will the woman most likely do next?

(A) Visit another business
(B) Talk to a supervisor
(C) Fill out some documents
(D) Pay a bill online

53. Where do the speakers work?

(A) At a restaurant
(B) At a fitness center
(C) At a pharmacy
(D) At a job agency

54. Why will the man miss work today?

(A) He has a client meeting.
(B) He has no transportation.
(C) He is going on vacation.
(D) He is not feeling well.

55. What do the speakers say about Juan?

(A) He needs some additional training.
(B) He is always on time.
(C) He will hold a staff meeting.
(D) He does not want to work late.

56. What does the man ask about?

(A) Conducting a customer survey
(B) Exchanging a defective item
(C) Testing out a product
(D) Setting up a display

57. What does the woman say about the store's customers?

(A) They prefer to pay by cash.
(B) They may be interested in products for children.
(C) They want the business hours to be longer.
(D) They use coupons regularly.

58. According to the man, what is special about the products?

(A) They have a handle that is easy to grip.
(B) They come in many shapes and sizes.
(C) They are made of materials that are recycled.
(D) They are made by local companies.

59. Where most likely is the woman?

(A) At an exit of a subway station
(B) At an entrance of a building
(C) In a computer laboratory
(D) In a hotel room

60. What information does the man request?

(A) The location of a meeting
(B) The name of an employee
(C) An identification number
(D) A reservation date

61. What does the man mean when he says, "That's against company policy"?

(A) He will review some guidelines.
(B) He wants to explain some errors.
(C) He does not agree with a policy.
(D) He has to reject a request.

			↑ Front			
25 A	25 B	25 C		25 D	25 E	25 F
26 A	26 B	26 C	Rear ↓	26 D	26 E	26 F

62. What is the conversation mainly about?

(A) Resolving an issue
(B) Selecting a product
(C) Contacting a supervisor
(D) Attending a conference

63. Look at the graphic. Which seat was the woman originally assigned to?

(A) 25 D
(B) 25 E
(C) 26 D
(D) 26 E

64. What does the man recommend doing?

(A) Using a voucher
(B) Informing a flight attendant
(C) Watching a film
(D) Ordering a special meal

GO ON TO THE NEXT PAGE

Model	Price
White Birch Wood	$399
Mahogany Wood	$499
Industrial Steel	$399
Antique Steel	$599

Printing Firm	Location
Vercom	Seattle
Satex	Tacoma
Medio	Everett
Gomca	Bellingham

65. What does the client want?

(A) A cheaper price
(B) An earlier delivery
(C) A different material
(D) A unique design

66. Look at the graphic. What will the client receive?

(A) White Birch Wood
(B) Mahogany Wood
(C) Industrial Steel
(D) Antique Steel

67. What will the man most likely do next?

(A) Ship an item
(B) Make a phone call
(C) Go to another department
(D) Provide a discount

68. What kind of event is the company organizing?

(A) A music show
(B) An art exhibition
(C) A sports festival
(D) A dance contest

69. What is the woman concerned about?

(A) Poor reviews
(B) A reduced budget
(C) The number of attendees
(D) A schedule change

70. Look at the graphic. Which firm will the speakers most likely choose?

(A) Vercom
(B) Satex
(C) Medio
(D) Gomca

PART 4

Directions: You will hear some talks given by a single speaker. You will be asked to answer three questions about what the speaker says in each talk. Select the best response to each question and mark the letter (A), (B), (C), or (D) on your answer sheet. The talks will not be printed in your test book and will be spoken only one time.

71. What did the library recently receive?
 (A) A monetary donation
 (B) New office furniture
 (C) A construction permit
 (D) Some new books

72. According to the speaker, what will start in the second week of July?
 (A) Hiring of new library employees
 (B) Meeting of the Library Committee
 (C) Repairing of some shelves
 (D) Building of a Web site

73. What does the woman ask the staff to do?
 (A) Work additional hours
 (B) Attend a seminar
 (C) Train summer interns
 (D) Help with a project

74. Why did Ms. Jones meet with the speaker?
 (A) To sign an agreement
 (B) To inspect a store
 (C) To make a video
 (D) To discuss a design

75. What does the speaker offer Ms. Jones?
 (A) A full-time job
 (B) A reduced price
 (C) A gift card
 (D) A magazine subscription

76. What does the speaker say Ms. Jones must do before next Tuesday?
 (A) Send a registration fee
 (B) Inform the speaker of a decision
 (C) Complete a survey on a Web site
 (D) Visit an agency

77. What event are the listeners attending?
 (A) An awards ceremony
 (B) A sales convention
 (C) A job fair
 (D) A financial seminar

78. What did CLA, Inc. recently do?
 (A) Increased its profits
 (B) Expanded overseas
 (C) Reorganized a department
 (D) Promoted an employee

79. According to the speaker, why should listeners speak to Mr. Witte after the event?
 (A) To receive information about a talk
 (B) To get a book signed
 (C) To apply for a job opening
 (D) To order a product in advance

80. According to the speaker, what is the company trying to do?
 (A) Protect the environment
 (B) Host a fundraising event
 (C) Lower operation costs
 (D) Increase its sales

81. What does the speaker mean when he says, "I know what you may be thinking"?
 (A) He is pleased with some suggestions.
 (B) He understands a possible concern.
 (C) He is familiar with a product.
 (D) He expects to see more customers.

82. What will the listeners receive if they participate?
 (A) A cash bonus
 (B) An extra day off
 (C) A complimentary meal
 (D) An employee award

GO ON TO THE NEXT PAGE

83. What does the plant produce?
    (A) Clothing
    (B) Smart phones
    (C) Office supplies
    (D) Furniture

84. What does the woman imply when she says, "1,500 is a huge order"?
    (A) A mistake may have been made.
    (B) A sales target has been met.
    (C) She will need additional workers.
    (D) She will give a special discount.

85. What does the woman tell the listener about the plant?
    (A) Its production capacity is limited.
    (B) It has recently purchased new machines.
    (C) Its facilities are currently closed.
    (D) It will be moving to a different location.

86. Where does this announcement most likely take place?
    (A) At a software company
    (B) At a city college
    (C) At a medical center
    (D) At an advertising agency

87. What change does the speaker mention?
    (A) The internship will be longer this year.
    (B) The students will work in a different building.
    (C) Some staff members will do additional assessments.
    (D) A project will involve more members.

88. Why is the change being made?
    (A) To improve the quality of products
    (B) To offer training more frequently
    (C) To provide a safer work environment
    (D) To identify potential employees

89. According to the speaker, what service will the company be providing?
    (A) Online ordering
    (B) Nationwide delivery
    (C) Free consultations
    (D) 24-hour customer support

90. Why did the company increase its services?
    (A) Some complaints have been received.
    (B) More competitors have entered the market.
    (C) Shipping costs have dropped.
    (D) There has been a greater demand.

91. What will the speaker do over the next quarter?
    (A) Collect customer feedback
    (B) Check the company's sales
    (C) Sells products overseas
    (D) Search for a larger facility

92. What type of business is being discussed?
    (A) A supermarket
    (B) An ice cream shop
    (C) A restaurant
    (D) A catering company

93. What will some customers receive this morning?
    (A) A shopping bag
    (B) A promotional mug
    (C) A complimentary beverage
    (D) A discount coupon

94. Why does the speaker say, "the store has been open for almost two hours now"?
    (A) To point out that the employees are busy
    (B) To imply that an offer will not last long
    (C) To advise customers to return later
    (D) To suggest making an order in advance

Business Expense Report		
ITEM	AMOUNT	DATE
Taxi	$23.15	August 7
Hotel	$270	August 8
Sales luncheon	$217.10	August 9
Airport shuttle	$27.50	August 10

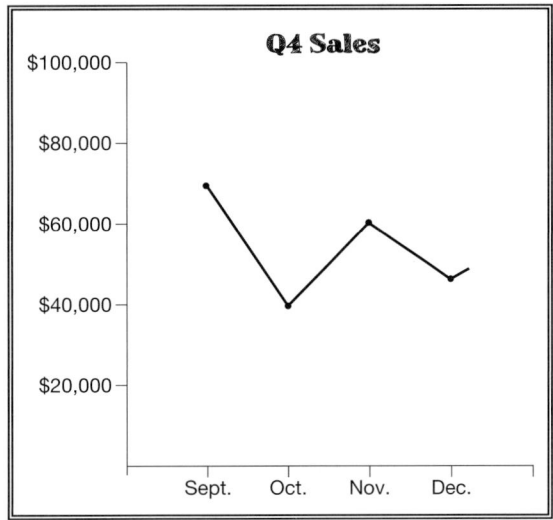

95. Why is the speaker calling?

    (A) A hotel has been overbooked.
    (B) A deposit was not made.
    (C) A meeting has been cancelled.
    (D) A receipt was not included.

96. Look at the graphic, which expense needs to be confirmed?

    (A) Taxi
    (B) Hotel
    (C) Sales luncheon
    (D) Airport shuttle

97. What does speaker say she can do?

    (A) Make a reservation
    (B) Contact a manager
    (C) Send a payment
    (D) Explain a procedure

98. Where most likely is the talk taking place?

    (A) At a clothing store
    (B) At a bookstore
    (C) At a grocery store
    (D) At a hardware store

99. Look at the graphic. When was the discount event held?

    (A) In September
    (B) In October
    (C) In November
    (D) In December

100. According to the speaker, what does the business plan to do next year?

    (A) Improve a catalog
    (B) Redesign a Web site
    (C) Expand an office space
    (D) Find a new supplier

This is the end of the Listening test.

Listening Comprehension

Scripts

TEST 01

PART 1 P. 18

1 한 사람

(A) A worker is repaving the street.
(B) A woman is securing a bicycle to a post.
(C) Some doors are being painted by a worker.
(D) Some vehicles are parked near a building.

2 두 사람 이상

(A) One of the men is leaning against a pole.
(B) The men are repairing a fence.
(C) One of the men is adjusting his helmet.
(D) The men are working close to one another.

3 두 사람 이상

(A) An audience is listening to a presenter.
(B) Some chairs are being rearranged in rows.
(C) A whiteboard is being installed on a wall.
(D) Some people are setting up a workstation.

4 한 사람

(A) Windows have been opened in a store.
(B) Garments are hanging on racks.
(C) A man is trying on a shirt.
(D) A man is checking his reflection in the mirror.

5 두 사람 이상

(A) Passengers are lining up at a ticket counter.
(B) Passengers are going up some stairs.
(C) Passengers are putting bags in overhead compartments.
(D) Passengers are disembarking from an airplane.

6 사물/풍경

(A) All of the chairs are occupied.
(B) Some books have been piled on the floor.
(C) A desk has been placed next to an entrance.
(D) Reading materials are arranged on shelves.

PART 2 P. 22

7 Who 의문문

Who was promoted to the position of senior editor?
(A) I'll revise the article.
(B) It was a promotional sale.
(C) Ichiro got the job.

8 When 의문문

When should I print out the handouts?
(A) The training has been canceled.
(B) Print in color, please.
(C) Thirty copies should be plenty.

9 부가 의문문

The stationery cabinet isn't locked, is it?
(A) It's the next station.
(B) Yes, but Mike can open it for you.
(C) We need more office supplies.

10 제안/청유문

Would you like to have dinner with us?
(A) Sorry, I have to work late.
(B) Be careful - It's hot.
(C) Sure, they'll be there.

11 Do 의문문

Did Tahera relocate to the city branch?
(A) The location is really convenient.
(B) I need to trim some branches.
(C) Yes, I met her there last week.

12 Which 의문문

Which musical performance did you enjoy the most?
(A) My performance review went very well.
(B) I liked them all.
(C) I sat in the first row.

13 부가 의문문

Mr. Lopez has the original copy of the lease agreement, right?
(A) It should be in his office.
(B) The rent is 150 dollars a week.
(C) A one-bedroom apartment.

14 When 의문문

When does the new office assistant start?
(A) Not very often.
(B) Ryan's looking after the new hires this time.
(C) He had three references.

15 제안/청유문

Could you lend me your scissors when you're done with them?
(A) I have some paper here.
(B) Actually, they're Brian's.
(C) At a hardware store.

16 How 의문문

How much do you think it will cost to repair my phone?
(A) Did you get a warranty with it?
(B) It won't take too long.
(C) Fix one of those buttons.

17 부정 의문문

Won't Anthony be leading the training session next Monday?
(A) Our train leaves at six.
(B) No, he'll be at a conference.
(C) It was very well-organized.

18 Where 의문문

Where are the discounted coats?
(A) Sure, I'll count them.
(B) In a smaller size.
(C) They're no longer on sale.

19 Do 의문문

Do I need a microphone for my presentation?
(A) You'll be talking to a small group.
(B) Just before the coffee break.
(C) The slides were well-prepared.

20 When 의문문

When were those expenses authorized?
(A) Our manager should know.
(B) She'll arrive next week.
(C) By a famous author.

21 평서문

This memo from Ms. Holmes is not very clear.
(A) A group e-mail sent to everyone.
(B) Just this morning.
(C) I'm not sure what it's about, either.

22 부가 의문문

This year's film festival wasn't well-attended, was it?
(A) A 9 o'clock movie.
(B) It's playing in theater 3.
(C) There was another event on that day.

23 제안/청유문

Can we recruit additional interns?
(A) A large number of applications.
(B) No, our budget's a bit tight this year.
(C) It's the revised edition.

24 Which 의문문

Which of the software training sessions should I attend this week?
(A) All staff members must attend.
(B) They've been rescheduled to next week.
(C) Ms. Kim led them.

25 제안/청유문

I'd like you to pick up the clients from the airport.
(A) OK. When should I go?
(B) Yes, it's quite heavy.
(C) Sure, any connecting flight is fine.

26 선택 의문문

Would you like to dine inside or outside?
(A) Isn't it supposed to rain?
(B) We live on the south side of town.
(C) The menu is on your table.

27 평서문

I finished going over the financial report.
(A) She's an experienced accountant.
(B) I have a degree in banking and finance.
(C) The sales figures were very disappointing.

28 선택 의문문

Should we rent one car or two?
(A) One won't fit all of us.
(B) You can borrow it.
(C) Where's your license?

29 Have 의문문

Have you received your new access key card for the building?
(A) No, it's 13 digits.
(B) He works in the Security Department.
(C) I just returned today from a business trip.

30 Why 의문문

Why are they vacuuming the floors now?
(A) Is it hard for you to concentrate?
(B) Of course. I cleaned them already.
(C) I'm on the second floor.

31 Have 의문문

Has the building manager replaced the old lights at the rear entrance?
(A) How much did it cost?
(B) The request was for the front entrance.
(C) Energy-saving bulbs.

PART 3

32-34번은 다음 대화에 관한 문제입니다.

W1: Sarah, I think we're finally at the convention center. Oh, but it says that the parking lot is full.

W2: Wow. I didn't expect so many people to arrive so early. Well, let's see if there is another place where we can park.

W1: There is a public garage just down the road near the museum. There's always plenty of space there, and the rate is quite cheap.

W2: Great. And since we have plenty of time before the conference begins, why don't we stop by somewhere and get some coffee before we start walking back?

35-37번은 다음 대화에 관한 문제입니다.

M: Hello, this is Bernie Hrudey, and I'm an employee at Silverthorne Technologies. I forgot to take some documents from my office yesterday. But I can't enter the building with my access card now because it's after-hours. Could someone from security let me in?

W: I have to first verify that you work here. Could you read the identification number on your access card to me?

M: Okay. It's 82141. Is there any other information that you need?

W: No, that's fine, Mr. Hrudey. I've checked your name in our system. Just wait there, and a security guard will be there to open the entrance for you in a minute.

신유형 38-40번은 다음 세 화자의 대화에 관한 문제입니다.

M1: Hey Rashid. Hi Frieda. I could use your help creating the brochure for our spring products. It needs to be ready by the end of this month.

M2: OK. Why don't we use last year's as a model?

W: Actually, I think last year's brochure was too plain. To be honest, it was quite boring to look through.

M1: Hmm. I have to agree. It should have more eye-catching colors and designs.

W: Right. I'll try to find photos of attractive brochures online and email them to you tonight. Maybe we can use them to get ideas for what features to include in ours.

신유형 41-43번은 다음 대화에 관한 문제입니다.

W: Hey, Fahed, I've just been reviewing the software you designed for Milagro Publishing, and I'm really impressed.

M: Oh, thank you—it was a challenging project!

W: Would you be interested in doing some similar work for our new client Ito-Trans? They're a major translation firm in Osaka, and they are hoping to upgrade their systems with some customized software.

M: That sounds great, but for now, it's hard to say. I'll know more after today's meeting with my supervisor, though.

W: Hmm, do you think it would be OK if I joined that meeting to discuss the project with the two of you? That way, your supervisor will be aware of all the details.

M: No problem—I'll be sure to let him know.

44-46번은 다음 대화에 관한 문제입니다.

W: Good afternoon. I'm interested in renting some office space from your company. My engineering team will be in Beijing working on a business assignment for six months, so we need a proper office.

M: Certainly. Could you give me a few more details?

W: Yes—we will be working in the downtown area, near Wanfujing Street, so we want to be fairly close by. We need an office that can easily fit 10 people and has one large conference room. Do you think that's possible?

M: We have a few places for rent in that part of town, but I'm not sure when they would be available. Could you let me know exactly when you are planning to arrive and leave?

47-49번은 다음 대화에 관한 문제입니다.

W: John. I was doing the room assignments for next week's professional development workshops, and I saw that your session on public speaking is full already.

M: Yes, I was surprised at how quickly the seats filled up. I even had to turn away some people.

W: Wow. We should consider adding another session for people who weren't able to sign up. Would you be able to fit a second workshop into your schedule?

M: I'm afraid I won't have time. But I'll talk to Sung-kyu and Rumi to see if they have some room in their schedules.

신유형 50-52번은 다음 대화에 관한 문제입니다.

W: Thank you for calling Elmont Property Management. How may I be of assistance?

M: Hello, I have a small office building here in Los Angeles, and I'd like to lease it out. I'll be working in Tokyo for the next five years.

W: Alright, that's definitely our specialty. Is this your first time renting out your office?

M: Yes, I've always been my own landlord, so I don't know how to deal with tenants. Also, if something were to need maintenance or replacing, Tokyo is very far away…

W: That won't be an issue—we'll take care of everything. Now, how much do you plan to charge for rent?

M: Actually, I wanted to get your advice on that. What do you suggest?

53-55번은 다음 대화에 관한 문제입니다.

W: Good morning. My name is Michelle Kim. I'm organizing a charity fundraiser at your community center on July 6, and I'm calling to confirm that the Willow Room has been reserved for our company on that date.

M: OK, let me check for you. Yes, we've booked the Willow Room for your organization from 2 P.M. to 7 P.M.

W: That's great. I also wanted to know if it's OK to bring our own snacks and beverages to sell at the event. We thought selling refreshments would be a good idea to raise more money.

M: I'm sorry, but no food from outside can be sold at our facility. However, since your event is for charity purposes, we can probably donate some refreshments from our on-site café. Let me just check with my manager to make sure, though.

신유형 56-58번은 다음 세 화자의 대화에 관한 문제입니다.

W1: The first thing I'd like to discuss at this meeting is our recent decline in beverage sales. How are we going to fix this situation?

M: Well, I think we should go to major sporting events in the city and offer samples of our products. That would get more people familiar with Vita-Juice and promote our image as a sports drink company. Erin, didn't you used to work at Reiner's Stadium?

W2: Yeah, I was in charge of coordinating their events.

M: That's excellent. Erin, for our next department meeting, could you prepare a short presentation on what events have attracted the most people there?

W2: I'd be glad to!

59-61번은 다음 대화에 관한 문제입니다.

W: Now, let's talk about the problem, Raj. In the previous quarter, the number of customers that came to our restaurant was much lower than what we got during the same period last year. Something must be done to bring more people to our place. As you're the head chef, I'd like to hear some ideas from you.

M: Hmm… What if we gave out a special coupon for a free appetizer for certain entrées? I could come up with some recipes for cheaper appetizers to include in the offer.

W: I like that idea! Why don't you prepare those so that I could sample them first?

신유형 62-64번은 다음 대화와 표에 관한 문제입니다.

M: Hey, Fadila, there's a great jazz concert this weekend at Caldwell Hall, and a lot of people from the office are going to attend. Would you like to go with us?

W: Oh, I'd love to! How much do seats cost?

M: Well, let's look at this list. OK, we currently have over 15 people going, so we'll probably qualify for this price here.

W: Oh, that's not bad. And it's this Saturday?

M: Yeah. Will you join us?

W: Sure. How can I get a ticket?

M: Jamie Purvis in Human Resources is handling that. You should stop by her office and ask her to get you one.

Prices	
General	$17
Child	$10
Group (15+)	$13
Caldwell Members	$12

65-67번은 다음 대화와 메뉴에 관한 문제입니다.

M: How was your shrimp pasta? If you'd like, I can bring out your dessert now—it is part of the chef's special you ordered.

W: It was amazing! But I'm too full to eat dessert. By the way, I was wondering… Do you provide rooms for private events?

M: Yes. Let me get you a brochure with information on that. But before I do, do you need anything else?

W: I just need the check, thanks. Oh, and I also have this voucher for 15 percent off my dinner. I can use it, right?

M: Ah, sorry, but this voucher can only be applied to regular items on our menu; special deals are excluded.

Bellanore Bistro
Chef's Special

Monday - Crab cakes
Tuesday - Pulled pork burgers
Wednesday - Shrimp pasta
Thursday - Eggplant parmesan
Friday - Roast chicken

68-70번은 다음 대화와 도표에 관한 문제입니다.

M: I'm looking forward to our trip next Monday, but I hate departing from McGruder Terminal. It's always full of people and has long lines.

W: Yeah, but it offers online booking. I'm looking at their Web site on my phone right now. Where do you want to sit? How about the first standard car?

M: Hmm… Actually, I have to do some work on my presentation, and I need to plug in my laptop to do that. But there aren't any outlets at the seats in the regular cars.

W: OK. There's one business car with seats left, so let's get that one.

M: How are you going to pay for this?

W: I'm going to put it on the corporate card, so I don't have to worry about getting reimbursed.

---

http://www.arrowlines.com

Choose Your Car

Select	Type	Availability	Car
■	Regular	Seats open	A
■	Regular	Seats open	B
■	Regular	Seats open	C
■	Business	Seats open	D
■	Business	Full	E

PART 4

71-73번은 다음 전화 메시지에 관한 문제입니다.

M: Good afternoon, Ms. Rossi. I just got your message about the fish delivery that you received from us yesterday. We are very sorry that you received the wrong fish. I have just shipped the correct items to you by express delivery. They should reach you by the end of the day today. Again, please accept our apologies for any inconvenience this may have caused you. We will investigate what went wrong and will ensure this doesn't happen again. Thank you for your business as always.

74-76번은 다음 안내방송에 관한 문제입니다.

W: Attention all passengers. Europa Airlines regrets to announce the cancellation of its 7 P.M. flight to London. We apologize for any inconvenience this may cause. We request that all passengers scheduled to take this flight proceed to the customer service desk, next to Gate 24, where representatives are waiting to book you onto another flight. Complimentary sandwiches will be provided while you wait. We thank you in advance for your patience in this matter.

77-79번은 다음 뉴스 보도에 관한 문제입니다.

M: Good afternoon, this is Andy Halaby with Channel 9's evening business report. In tonight's segment, we'll tell you about some new developments in the home appliance industry. Kimstar, a local refrigerator maker, has created a new type of compartment for food storage. This compartment constantly controls the amount of water in the air, which means that fruits and vegetables will stay fresh much longer than they would in an ordinary refrigerator. Kimstar, which began production just last year, will present the new model at the annual Inventors' Trade Exhibition in December, and then begin selling it in stores next January.

신유형 80-82번은 다음 전화 메시지에 관한 문제입니다.

M: Hello, Jennifer, it's Raymond. The CEO wants our firm to participate in next month's fashion convention in Hollywood, and she'd like for us to get started on creating a display. Now, I realize that we were supposed to invest most of our time working on our product catalog this month, but this request is also important. It isn't up to me. Anyway, I'll let the other team members know so that we can set up a meeting this week to come up with plans for the display. Meanwhile, can you get in touch with the convention coordinators to see how much a booth costs? Thanks in advance.

83-85번은 다음 공지에 관한 문제입니다.

W: Today, I'd like to inform you about a change that's going to be made to our company's vacation policy. Until now, new staff members have been allowed only one vacation day per month for the first six months of employment. This caused problems for some employees, who sometimes needed to take more time off than was permitted. In some cases, it even led to staff leaving the company, meaning that we had to spend time and money again on hiring and training new workers. In order to prevent newly hired employees from quitting over this issue, they will be entitled to their full 15 days of time-off from their first day of work. Please let your team members know about this change, and make sure that they always follow the correct procedures.

신유형 86-88번은 다음 회의 발췌록에 관한 문제입니다.

M: There is one last matter I need to cover before we conclude today's new employee orientation. It's regarding our security policies and procedures. Here at PX Software, we take strict measures to keep our product development confidential and secure in order to prevent our competitors from making similar programs. Certain documents that you need to use for your work are stored electronically in our company's restricted files, which require a password to open. These passwords are changed regularly for added protection. You'll be emailed a new password when they change.

신유형 89-91번은 다음 회의 발췌록에 관한 문제입니다.

W: Before we begin this morning's meeting, I'd like to make an announcement. I just found out that the company's president, Anne McDonald, will be coming here next Friday. Ms. McDonald has been visiting all the remodeled stores, and our branch is next on her list. This won't be a formal inspection, so we don't need to make any special preparations. We'll be organizing a special luncheon for Ms. McDonald on that day, and I'd like to ask you all to attend to welcome her. Please confirm your availability as soon as you can.

신유형 92-94번은 다음 광고에 관한 문제입니다.

M: Is your exercise tracker too difficult to use? Well, you don't have to worry about that with Fitness Friend, which can be worn like a wristband. With most exercise electronics, you have to navigate through a lot of menus to check how far you've run or to track your heart rate. Why bother with all that? Fitness Friend shows this information at the simple push of a button, so you don't have to spend so much time finding it. As an added bonus, for this week only, the price of Fitness Friend is 15 percent off to celebrate its market debut. So get one today!

신유형 95-97번은 다음 공지와 지도에 관한 문제입니다. 미국

M: Attention all Energy Sonic, Inc. staff members. This is a reminder that, due to the town's yearly marathon, the road that the East Entrance faces will be closed between 8:00 A.M. and 4:00 P.M. tomorrow. Please plan your commute to work accordingly. All other roads around our building will stay open. Even if you normally don't use the affected road to work, you are advised to allow more time for your commute tomorrow morning since traffic is expected to be heavier than usual on all routes in the area.

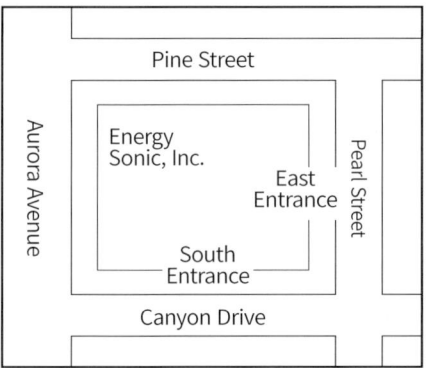

신유형 98-100번은 다음 담화와 점검표에 관한 문제입니다. 영국

W: I've asked everyone to arrive earlier than usual for work this morning to go over the process for receiving furniture deliveries. I'm worried that we're wasting valuable time when we don't follow procedures properly. Recently, several deliveries of merchandise from the regional hub were sent to the wrong retail store. Inspecting merchandise that should have been sent elsewhere is not an efficient way of using our time. That's why I'm asking that everyone carefully look at the warehouse code that's printed on the delivery packaging. It has to match up with the code on the delivery report. If it doesn't, just send the package back. This is of extra importance now that we are receiving a large amount of merchandise for the sale that begins on Saturday.

Procedure Checklist:
1. ___ Check code on packaging
2. ___ See that the items match the order
3. ___ Look for damaged merchandise
4. ___ Transfer items to storage

TEST 02

PART 1
P. 32

1 한 사람

(A) A vehicle is stopped at a traffic light.
(B) Pedestrians are crossing the street.
(C) Boxes have been loaded onto a van.
(D) A driver is opening a car window.

2 두 사람 이상

(A) People are approaching an archway.
(B) People are descending some steps.
(C) People are shopping outdoors.
(D) People are leaning against a wall.

3 두 사람 이상

(A) The men are cleaning a kitchen appliance.
(B) The men are stacking logs in a corner.
(C) The men are seated side by side.
(D) The men are pouring some coffee into mugs.

4 한 사람

(A) There is a shelf above a desk.
(B) The man is closing a drawer.
(C) The man is adjusting his chair.
(D) There is a lamp hanging from the ceiling.

5 두 사람 이상

(A) The woman is sampling some dessert.
(B) A customer is putting items in her bag.
(C) Some people are setting up a tent in a market.
(D) A vendor is selling some merchandise.

6 사물/풍경

(A) A fence is being installed.
(B) A bridge crosses over a road.
(C) A traffic light is being repaired.
(D) Some trees have been cut down.

PART 2   P. 36

7 What 의문문

What time will you be arriving at the venue?
(A) That's on the first floor.
(B) Around noon.
(C) Yes, but I usually don't.

8 제안/청유문

Would you mind if I closed the door?
(A) Sure. You can borrow it.
(B) Just put it in my drawer.
(C) Isn't it a little hot in here?

9 부가 의문문

The meeting room is available, isn't it?
(A) No, with a new client.
(B) The mailroom is downstairs.
(C) Someone's using it.

10 When 의문문

When is the new theater going to be open?
(A) The seats are in the front row.
(B) I just saw a play there.
(C) Yes, it's a great movie.

11 How 의문문

How do I change my password?
(A) It's written in the manual.
(B) Sorry. We can't let them in.
(C) No, it hasn't changed.

12 선택 의문문

Have customers been buying more chocolate or vanilla ice cream?
(A) I'll have some after lunch.
(B) In the frozen goods section.
(C) About the same of both.

13 Where 의문문

Where was your previous place of employment?
(A) An accounting agency in Montreal.
(B) No, the next one.
(C) For about five years.

14 부정 의문문

Isn't there a concert at the community center this weekend?
(A) Let me find out for you.
(B) Where was it held?
(C) I'm sure she is.

15 선택 의문문

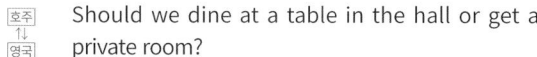
Should we dine at a table in the hall or get a private room?
(A) I'll have a pasta dish.
(B) Yes. Arrange the chairs, please.
(C) They have rooms here?

16 제안/청유문

Why don't we continue reviewing this after dinner?
(A) OK, let's get back in an hour.
(B) No, I prefer a vegetarian dish.
(C) They moved to the second floor.

17 Where 의문문

Where do you suggest we have our company picnic?
(A) Some sandwiches.
(B) I've been to the park.
(C) It's been canceled.

18 제안/청유문

Could you cover my shift on Thursday evening?
(A) From 5 to 9 P.M.
(B) Have you checked with the supervisor?
(C) It's on the back cover.

19 부가 의문문

The guest speaker was excellent, wasn't she?
(A) An information booklet.
(B) I just arrived.
(C) No, it's at 10 o'clock.

20 Where 의문문

Where did the CEO choose to hold the annual event?
(A) On December 23rd.
(B) An awards ceremony.
(C) We won't know until Friday.

21 평서문

We're seeking new employees for various positions.
(A) How many are you looking for?
(B) We've seen it.
(C) The facilities are new.

22 Why 의문문

Why hasn't the licensing agreement been signed yet?
(A) Yes, I agree with you.
(B) It's still being reviewed.
(C) We signed up for a class.

23 Which 의문문

Which vehicle would you like to rent today?
(A) I bought it yesterday.
(B) Any midsize car will be fine.
(C) 300 dollars a month.

24 Who 의문문

Who's preparing the employee training session?
(A) I'm assigning that task to you.
(B) My train leaves in an hour.
(C) New accounting software.

25 Have 의문문

Have you found a caterer for our office party?
(A) Where did you lose it?
(B) Most people are planning on coming.
(C) I'm still looking into it.

26 When 의문문

When are the yearly health check-ups scheduled for our workers?
(A) I'll lead the training session.
(B) Everyone needs to make an appointment by February.
(C) Approximately 300 workers.

27 부가 의문문

The presentation won't be longer than 15 minutes, will it?
(A) Actually, it's a pretty close to the office.
(B) That depends on how many questions are asked.
(C) I thought it was an interesting session.

28 평서문

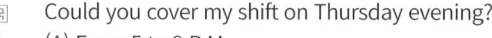
I couldn't read the subtitles during the movie.
(A) It's one of my favorite books.
(B) A newly remodeled theater.
(C) Were you sitting far from the screen?

29 How 의문문

How do you turn on the heater in this room?
(A) Let me close all the windows first.
(B) Between 22 and 25 degrees.
(C) No, I doubt it.

30 부정 의문문

Hasn't our company's logo been redesigned yet?
(A) We just finished it.
(B) She hasn't been here before.
(C) A graphic design company.

31 평서문

We received many excellent submissions for the photography competition.
(A) The deadline can't be extended.
(B) It won't be easy to choose the winner.
(C) There's no photography in the museum.

PART 3

P. 37

32-34번은 다음 대화에 관한 문제입니다.

W: Hello, my name is Dianne Richter. I moved from Arnada to Koryville last month. I got a utility bill in my mail today, but I had already paid this bill before moving. It was forwarded from my previous home. I don't understand what happened.

M: We apologize for that. Our company recently switched to a different software program, and our records have not been completely updated yet. Give me your previous address so that I can look up your account.

W: It's 36 Rotham Road in Arnada. Can you make sure to correct the information so that this doesn't happen again?

M: Of course, Ms. Richter. I just updated your address in our system. But it'll take about 5 business days for the error to be corrected. I suggest you call back after to check that everything is fine.

35-37번은 다음 대화에 관한 문제입니다.

M: Hello, Ms. Hurst. This is Roger calling from Northern Auto Mechanics. You scheduled a routine maintenance check with us for 5 P.M. on April 3rd. But would it be OK if I moved it to 4 P.M. instead?

W: Hmm… I have a long lunch meeting with a client that day, but I should be able to make it by 4 o'clock.

M: Great. Thank you for understanding. We're planning to close early that day to make some minor repairs to our shop.

W: Sure. I'll make a note of this change in my planner right now.

38-40번은 다음 대화에 관한 문제입니다.

M: Good morning, Sarah. It's James Owens calling from Rowlett Law Firm. Would you be able to come in for a second interview this Thursday?

W: Hello, Mr. Owens. It's great to hear back from you. I'm afraid I have to be in the office all day on Thursday. But I can take a day off this Friday, so I can come by then.

M: That'll work. When you arrive, you'll take a short test so that we can get a better understanding of your analytical and problem-solving skills. Shall we say 10 o'clock on Friday morning? We should be done before lunch.

41-43번은 다음 대화에 관한 문제입니다.

W: Hello. I'd like to get a camcorder. I've never bought one before, so I was hoping you could give me some recommendations.

M: I'd be happy to help. If you could be more specific about your needs and what your price range is, I can assist you better.

W: Well, I'm mainly going to use it while traveling. I'm going to Europe this month, and I want to record all the memories. I'm not that great using electronics, so I need something that isn't too complicated.

M: Oh, then the Tonika G56 is perfect for you. I have one myself, and I like it because it has easy-to-use functions. As this is your first time using a camcorder, I would go with this one.

44-46번은 세 화자의 대화에 관한 문제입니다.

W1: We appreciate you coming in for the interview today, Mr. O'Connor. I'm Joanna Perez, the director of personnel here at Channel 9.

W2: And my name's Elizabeth Shultz. I'm one of the producers here.

M: Pleased to meet both of you.

W2: We've reviewed your résumé, and we're very impressed with your qualifications. We'd like to ask you about your availability. If you were to become a member of our film crew, you'd often need to go out on assignment on very short notice.

M: Yes, I'm aware of that aspect of the job, and it's not a problem for me.

W1: Great. Let's take a look at some of your work then. Did you bring your video with you?

M: Yes. I'll show it to you on my laptop right now.

47-49번은 다음 대화에 관한 문제입니다.

M: Sally. Why are you still in the office? I thought you were volunteering at the fundraising event this afternoon.

W: Actually, I went last year. Besides, some of our deliveries unexpectedly became behind schedule.

M: Sorry to hear that. What went wrong?

W: Well, our suppliers were late in sending some items. I'm sure we're going to get complaints from our customers. I'm a little worried because I don't know how I should handle them.

M: I guess you'll have to figure out a way to take care of this. I have to go to the fundraiser now, but let's discuss this matter at the staff meeting tomorrow.

50-52번은 다음 대화에 관한 문제입니다.

M: Hi, Isabella. Welcome back to the office. How was the publisher's conference?

W: It was good. But I didn't go to the final presentation because it was on the same topic as the one I had already heard at another conference earlier this year.

M: I see. What about your own session? You worked so hard to prepare for it.

W: Fortunately, it went smoothly. Speaking of which, there is going to be a similar opportunity at the upcoming conference in June. They need someone who can lead a panel discussion on global marketing. You should definitely consider doing it since that's your area of expertise.

53-55번은 다음 대화에 관한 문제입니다.

W: Hi, my name is Alice Mendia, and I'm calling in regard to my subscription to The Middleton Daily. After I moved last month, I provided you with my new address. But since last week, I haven't received a single issue. Can you tell me what happened?

M: Alright, I'll check the system. OK, it looks like your subscription expired last week. Have you considered trying our newspaper's digital version? For a limited time, customers who purchase our electronic version will receive the first month free.

W: Umm… Do you have any similar offers for the print version? If so, I'd rather get the print version.

56-58번은 다음 대화에 관한 문제입니다.

M: Hi, Chrissie. I have a couple of tickets to the Elvira Symphony Orchestra's concert this Friday night, but I can't go. You said your friend is visiting from abroad, so I thought it might be a good idea for you to take her there.

W: That's very thoughtful of you Robert. I would love to go, but we've already made plans to watch a football match at the Penn Stadium that night. Why don't you post a notice in the company chat room? I'm sure one of the employees will be interested.

M: You're right. I'll do that right now. Thanks for the suggestion.

신유형 59-61번은 다음 대화에 관한 문제입니다.

W: Alex, I heard that you're leading the orientation for the incoming interns.

M: That's right. There's a lot to do, and it's this Friday. I have been spending so much time preparing my presentation for the orientation that I haven't been able to do much else.

W: Really? Well, I completed my assignments early today. Anything I can do for you?

M: Oh, that would be great! Then can you contact the security desk and see if they made access cards for the interns? I submitted a request for them on Monday, but I haven't received an update yet.

W: Of course. I'll call them now.

신유형 62-64번은 다음 대화와 안내 책자에 관한 문제입니다.

W: So I just found out at today's meeting that our branch manager, Ms. Coretta, is transferring to the head office next month. And it looks like the company is looking for an internal replacement.

M: Yeah, I heard. I've been wanting to become the next manager for a while now, but I'm pretty nervous about applying. The executive board might think that I don't possess strong business management skills.

W: Hmm… You know, the public library is currently offering a series of business courses. You should register for one.

M: That's a good idea. I wonder if there's one available for me. I'm at the store from 9 A.M. to 6 P.M., so hopefully, they have a class at night.

Neherville Public Library Business Course Series	
Session A	Tuesdays, 10 A.M.
Session B	Wednesdays, 4 P.M.
Session C	Thursdays, 11 A.M.
Session D	Fridays, 7 P.M.

신유형 65-67번은 다음 대화와 메뉴에 관한 문제입니다.

M: Welcome to Orga's Global Bistro. Are you ready to order?

W: Not quite yet. My sister suggested that I come here because you have an excellent vegetarian menu. She said the pumpkin soup was great, but I can't find it on your menu.

M: Ah… Unfortunately, we only offer that during the fall. We change our menu choices based on what ingredients are the freshest during that season.

W: Oh, I see. OK then… what else is good here?

M: The mushroom sandwich is always popular with customers. And it's actually a personal favorite of mine. The price is quite reasonable, too.

W: That sounds good. I'll go with that then. Thank you.

Orga's Global Bistro Brunch Menu	
Greek salad	$5.00
Potato pizza	$4.50
Shepherd's pie	$7.50
Mushroom sandwich	$6.00

신유형 68-70번은 다음 대화와 원형 도표에 관한 문제입니다.

M: Alright, now let's talk about recruitment. We've always been able to hire plenty of new employees by participating in college career expos, but this year, I want to try something different.

W: Oh? What's the reason?

M: Well, some of our staff members invest too much time visiting various colleges, and sometimes that causes them to miss other project deadlines.

W: That's true. How about directing more resources to our second-most effective recruiting tactic? As you know, at least one third of our staff were hired in that manner.

M: Great idea! Can you meet with Charles from Human Resources and discuss how we can go about this?

PART 4

P. 41

71-73번은 다음 회의 발췌문에 관한 문제입니다. 미국

W: First of all, I'd like to share some exciting news. We have just signed a deal with Wiztech to design earphones for their new smartphone, the WZ800. Wiztech wants us to create earphones that can connect to the device without a cord. Wiztech has also provided a more detailed list of the features they want included, based on a recent consumer survey. I'll hand this list out to everyone right now. Please review it and decide which tasks should go to which person.

74-76번은 다음 전화 메시지에 관한 문제입니다. 호주

M: Kevin, this is Derek from the IT Department. I received your request to find out why your video wasn't working during the web conference this morning. I've checked it out, and it turns out the cause of the problem was that the video system setup was incorrect. Some of the cables were inserted into the wrong connectors. Anyway, it should be okay now, but just to be safe, test out the equipment before the next web conference in the afternoon. If you have the same problem again, let me know and I'll come down to the boardroom and help you.

77-79번은 다음 전화 메시지에 관한 문제입니다. 미국

M: Hi, I wanted to let you know about an issue with one of your bus lines. I take Bus 510 every morning to my office. Today, I waited over 40 minutes for the bus before deciding to just take a cab to work. I visited your home page to find information about any delays, but nothing was posted, so I called this number. Have you made changes to your bus schedule? I'd like to know by today so that I can plan tomorrow morning's commute. You can reach me at 555-3925. Thank you.

신유형 80-82번은 다음 공지에 관한 문제입니다. 호주

M: OK, I'll start today's HR meeting with some information about the East Asia Regional Manager position we've been trying to fill. As you're aware, our goal is to hire someone before the end of the year. But as of now, we haven't found any suitable external candidates, and… well, it's already mid-December. So we have accepted some applications from our own staff, and I want our department to look over them tomorrow. I'll send you their files after this meeting, so check your e-mails later today.

83-85번은 다음 공지에 관한 문제입니다. 영국

W: Attention shoppers, we would like to let you know about an event on the first floor here at our department store this afternoon. At 2 o'clock, we'd like you to join us for a special cooking demonstration. During the event, we'll be displaying a number of kitchen appliances from well-known manufacturers. After the demonstration, you'll have a chance to ask top chefs questions about the equipment and techniques they use to prepare their delicious dishes. And one of the participating manufacturers, Chickbee Appliances, has just begun selling its products on the 6th floor. This is their first month in business, and they have a lot of special offers to share with you.

86-88번은 다음 뉴스 보도에 관한 문제입니다. 〔미국〕

W: You're listening to WCY Radio, Bayville's number one station for news, weather, and traffic. The top story today is the announcement by Mayor Heidi Mackenzie to initiate the revitalization of the city's tourism industry. Bayville's beautiful mountains have always drawn many visitors from all over the country. However, the national high-speed rail system that was completed last year doesn't extend as far as Bayville, and the number of tourists has declined. The main reason is that most tourists prefer to visit destinations where they can arrive by train. The city will attempt to increase tourism by providing a free shuttle service from the closest train station to the city center and back. The buses will start operating in April and will run all year round.

신유형 89-91번은 다음 담화에 관한 문제입니다. 〔영국〕

W: As all of you know, during the safety inspection on Monday, one of our facilities was cited for violations. This is not OK. We at Teris Medical are dedicated to safety, which is why I gathered everyone here today. We'll start off by going over some safety procedures. There are folders on each of your desks for you to keep. Inside, you'll find information on all of our safety policies, which has been divided into different categories. But the thing is… We didn't have a lot of time to prepare the materials. You'll notice that not all of the sections are in the right order.

신유형 92-94번은 다음 설명에 관한 문제입니다. 〔미국〕

M: Thank you for joining our first vegetarian cooking class here at the recreation center. I'm Ehren, your instructor. I'll start by calling your attention to the lockers near the entrance. Each of you can use one locker to store your cooking tools for the class. Now, I know this class officially runs from 9 A.M. to 1 P.M., but we'll always stop at around 12:40 so that we can clean our work areas. There's another class that uses this room. Oh, and also, before you leave today, please remember to visit the registration office to submit your payment for this class, if you have not already done so.

신유형 95-97번은 다음 담화와 지도에 관한 문제입니다. 〔미국〕

W: I have some good news for our investors. The construction of the Slatington Arts Center is almost finished. It's true that the project cost more than we had initially planned, but the additional performance areas should make it possible to host a variety of events and sell tickets to a lot more patrons. I'm really looking forward to this. Now, the final step will be to add the center's logo. The original plan was to put it over Exit 1, but there's been a change of plans. It's now going to be placed over Exit 3 instead, so it faces Main Street. I want it to be visible to all those potential center visitors who drive by every day to see Slatington's logo.

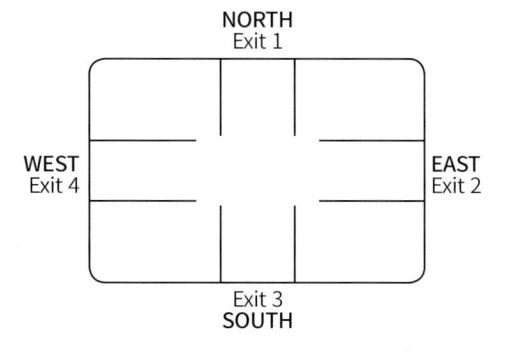

신유형 98-100번은 다음 전화 메시지와 일정에 관한 문제입니다. 〔호주〕

M: Hello, Mandy, this is Joe. I'm glad that we'll be recruiting four new accountants for our company. It's been clear for some time that we need more people to deal with all of our clients. It's been a while since we hired someone, so I wanted to go over the application process with you again. I'd like to do this sometime during the afternoon as I'm busy in the morning. According to Friday's schedule, we're going to be in the same meeting after lunch, so how about we get together as soon as that finishes? I'll be free from then until the workshop begins in the afternoon. Let me know if this works for you. See you later!

Friday Schedule	
09:00	
10:00	Monthly department meeting
11:00	
12:00	LUNCH
13:00	Senior managers' meeting
14:00	
15:00	Safety training session
16:00	
17:00	
18:00	

TEST 03

PART 1
P. 46

1 한 사람

(A) She is looking at some paintings.
(B) She has her arms crossed.
(C) A drawing is being framed.
(D) Some artwork is being mounted on the wall.

2 두 사람 이상

(A) One of the people is holding a paddle.
(B) A sailor is waving from a boat.
(C) Passengers are lined up on the pier.
(D) People are fishing on the dock.

3 사물/풍경

(A) Display racks have been cleared of items.
(B) Potted plants are being removed from a shelf.
(C) Some produce has been placed in baskets.
(D) Some vegetables are being delivered to a store.

4 두 사람 이상

(A) They are setting up some lounge chairs.
(B) They are walking on the beach.
(C) They are putting on their sandals.
(D) They are relaxing under an umbrella.

5 두 사람 이상

(A) Some people are leaving a lobby.
(B) One of the women is combing her hair.
(C) A woman is taking off her sunglasses.
(D) A man is writing on paper.

6 사물/풍경

(A) A vase of flowers has been placed on the floor.
(B) There's a door beneath the staircase.
(C) Ceiling lights are being repaired.
(D) Some decorative items are propped against a railing.

PART 2

P. 50

7 Where 의문문

Where do you keep your extra business cards?
(A) I didn't order any.
(B) She's at a conference.
(C) They're in the drawer.

8 제안/청유문

Can you help me carry this shelf down to the basement?
(A) Give me one minute.
(B) Shelve them, please.
(C) Yes, we carry this product.

9 Who 의문문

Who contacted the manufacturing plant?
(A) Diego called them.
(B) That's a great plan.
(C) They make office furniture.

10 How 의문문

How did your exit interview go?
(A) The exit is that way.
(B) Yes, the view is great.
(C) I haven't had it yet.

11 부가 의문문

I can park my car in front of the store, can't I?
(A) Sorry, we don't have that item.
(B) These trees are beautiful.
(C) It's for customers only.

12 When 의문문

When will the driver arrive at the airport to pick me up?
(A) He's stuck in traffic.
(B) At the Rabada Hotel.
(C) A 6 o'clock flight to London.

13 How 의문문

How do I order tickets in advance for the upcoming music festival?
(A) Yes, I'll order a drink.
(B) To advance my career.
(C) You can do it on our Web site.

14 선택 의문문

Should I prepare printouts of the presentation for everyone or email it to them afterwards?
(A) Just send them the file.
(B) It was very informative.
(C) A sales presentation.

15 Why 의문문

Why did you want to see the McNeil file?
(A) I meant the O'Neil file.
(B) To Daniel's e-mail address.
(C) In the filing cabinet.

16 Where 의문문

Where can I get an extra key made for my office?
(A) I found it here.
(B) It's a nice office.
(C) Try the hardware store.

17 How 의문문

How long is the train ride to Chicago?
(A) I prefer a window seat.
(B) You should have enough time to take a nap.
(C) In front of the Central Station.

18 Should 의문문

Should we request a deadline extension for the research project?
(A) We have a projector.
(B) Yes, he's a researcher.
(C) No, it's nearly completed.

19 제안/청유문

Could you drop Ms. Thompson off at the airport?
(A) The new corporate trainer.
(B) What time is her flight?
(C) I received it. Thank you.

20 부정 의문문

Didn't they talk about the merger at yesterday's staff meeting?
(A) I was visiting a client.
(B) No, in the large meeting room.
(C) Sure, if you'd like.

21 평서문

It's much colder today than I thought it would be.
(A) A new winter coat.
(B) Do you want to take a taxi?
(C) Next week's weather forecast.

22 Who 의문문

Who's responsible for cleaning the break room?
(A) I did it last week.
(B) It fell on the floor.
(C) Please reserve a room.

23 부가 의문문

Mr. Daubert usually leaves the office right at 6, doesn't he?
(A) I usually take a bus.
(B) He has a report due tomorrow morning.
(C) No, it's on the left side.

24 When 의문문

When does the flower shop open on Sundays?
(A) For a wedding this weekend.
(B) It just opened last month.
(C) Same time as the weekdays.

25 Have 의문문

Has your manager approved your product design?
(A) Display the new product line.
(B) I haven't submitted it yet.
(C) The graphics team.

26 선택 의문문

Are the visitors from different companies or the same one?
(A) To tour our facilities.
(B) We picked them up at the airport.
(C) They're all from AKS Corporation.

27 평서문

This hotel has the most amazing view of the city.
(A) Many locations throughout the city.
(B) 24-hour room service.
(C) I guess you haven't stayed at Canlane Hotel.

28 What 의문문

What companies were at the international trade fair this year?
(A) A company lunch with clients.
(B) I have the list on my phone.
(C) To expand our business overseas.

29 부정 의문문

Won't Gallapo Tech be hired to redesign our Web site?
(A) It's up to the CEO.
(B) That's a new sign.
(C) They're available online.

30 제안/청유문

Please have the videoconferencing equipment set up before the meeting.
(A) It was very useful.
(B) He's in the recording studio.
(C) Jason just finished his break.

31 When 의문문

When are the representatives from Nomar Incorporated scheduled to arrive?
(A) A direct flight from Spain.
(B) Didn't Roger make those arrangements?
(C) Gate 3 at the airport.

PART 3   P. 51

32-34번은 다음 대화에 관한 문제입니다.

M: Pardon me, but I believe that's my seat. That's 20C, right?

W: Oh? Let me check my ticket. Umm… I think this is where I'm supposed to be. Look here on my ticket. It says 20C.

M: Hmm, but this is the east section of the auditorium. I think you're in the wrong area.

W: Ah, you're right. Sorry! I should be on the other side. My laptop's plugged into this outlet, so give me a minute to put it into my bag.

신유형 35-37번은 다음 세 화자의 대화에 관한 문제입니다.

M1: Thank you for visiting Conway Convention Center. How can I be of assistance?

W: Hello, I'm Bridgette Taylor from Lead Trainers, Inc. I booked your main event hall for this evening. My associate and I wanted to make sure everything would be ready by 6 P.M.

M1: OK, let me check my list. Ah, here you are. I will need to see a photo ID first, please.

W: Not a problem. Here's my driver's license. Is there anything else?

M2: Wait, Bridgette. We originally arranged for 15 tables, but we'll need more.

W: Thanks for reminding me. Is it possible to bring six more tables into the event hall?

M1: Definitely. I'll let the staff know and have them set up the tables now.

38-40번은 다음 대화에 관한 문제입니다.

W: Marcus, I was told you're organizing the orientation for the new employees. Can I ask you a question regarding the new associate attorneys? Am I still in charge of explaining the company policies to them?

M: Yes, you are. We'll be training them on how to use the client database on Tuesday afternoon. So I was thinking of having you speak sometime in the morning.

W: Umm… That's not going to work. I have back-to-back meetings all morning on that day. Can't I just do it in the late afternoon?

M: Well, the schedule is pretty much set for that day. I'll see if Kim can cover for you. She should be available.

W: OK, thank you.

41-43번은 다음 대화에 관한 문제입니다.

M: Marta, this is David. I'm on my way to pick you up for the company luncheon, but it looks like I'm going to be about 20 minutes late. There is heavy traffic on Hills Avenue. One of the lanes is closed for repaving. I have to take a detour to your place.

W: OK, thanks for calling me. But we also have to pick up the pies on our way to the luncheon. Maybe I should call the bakery and ask if they could deliver the pies to the venue for us.

M: I have a better idea. Christina from the Marketing Department lives just across the street from the bakery. I'll give her a call and see if she would be able to pick it up.

44-46번은 다음 대화에 관한 문제입니다. 　호주 ⇄ 영국

M: Hello, Suzy. Have the flyers for our upcoming sale been printed?

W: Well, I received some samples from the printing company this morning, but they forgot to include the directions to our store. So I gave the company's manager a call right away, and she said they would fix the problem and send them by Thursday.

M: Unfortunately, that won't work. We're planning to pass out the flyers at the mall on Wednesday afternoon, so we need them before then. Do you mind calling the printing company again and request that our order be delivered by no later than Wednesday morning?

47-49번은 다음 대화에 관한 문제입니다. 미국 ⇄ 영국

M: Olivia, how are you doing with the flower arrangements for Willington Hospital? The hospital has to receive them this morning.

W: I know. I'm running a bit behind. When I came in this morning, I noticed we were out of wires and tape. I had to go out and buy some before getting started.

M: Hmm, I'm pretty sure we had some in the back room. I'll reimburse you for those expenses.

W: Thank you. I'll give you the receipt later. Anyway, I'll make sure the flowers are prepared in time for the 11 A.M. delivery.

신유형 50-52번은 다음 대화에 관한 문제입니다. 　호주 ⇄ 영국

M: I'm really looking forward to hearing Bill Castello's presentation at this marketing training seminar. I've read all his books on sales techniques.

W: I agree. And look at all these people! We're not going to find any seats here. Let's try up in the balcony.

M: The balcony? Is that the best we can do? I was hoping to get a closer view.

W: It'll be fine. If you look up there, there are two large screens on the stage, so we can get a good view from wherever we are. Why don't we go up now?

53-55번은 다음 대화에 관한 문제입니다. 　미국 ⇄ 호주

W: Hi, my name is Maria Herrera. I was a former student at your college. I recently applied for a job at Techmo Software, so I requested that my transcript be mailed to their office, but the HR team hasn't received it yet.

M: Ah, yes, Ms. Herrera. We do have your request form here, but since it's missing your signature, we weren't able to send your transcript.

W: Hmm… I thought I'd signed it. Do I have to go back there to do that?

M: That won't be necessary. I'll send you the form by e-mail. Please sign it this time and either fax it or mail it back to us.

신유형 56-58번은 다음 대화에 관한 문제입니다. 미국 ⇄ 미국

W: Hey, John! It's Denise calling from Sales. I think you should know that the projector here in meeting room 9 isn't working.

M: Really? I'll go there now and check it out.

W: Actually… I have a meeting here in ten minutes. But I don't need to use the projector during the meeting, so it's not urgent…

M: Ah, OK. Then I'll deal with it later this afternoon when you're finished using the room. I see the room isn't booked for any other meetings today. Do you have everything you need in the room?

W: Yes, everything's here, thanks. We're finally bringing together all the regional sales people for a face-to-face meeting. It's going to be a nice change from the usual video conference meetings.

59-61번은 다음 대화에 관한 문제입니다. 　영국 ⇄ 미국

W: Hello, I parked my van here, but I forgot to bring cash with me. Do you take credit cards for payment?

M: Yes, but you can't use your credit card here. If you go over to parking lot C, you'll find a payment machine near the elevators that will accept it. You also have the option of paying on our Web site with your smartphone or tablet.

W: Mmm… I'll pay online then. Can you give me the Web site's address?

M: Actually, it's listed right there on your parking permit.

W: Ah, OK.

M: After you've made your payment, you'll be sent a confirmation message to your phone. Just show that to the attendant on your way out.

신유형 62-64번은 다음 대화와 목록에 관한 문제입니다.

W: Hello, I bought a Woodwick cabinet at your store today, and I'm trying to set it up right now. However, I just noticed that not all of the necessary parts were included in the box.

M: I apologize for that. What are you missing?

W: Some of the nails are missing. It says in the manual that there should be ten of them. But I only see seven here.

M: OK, if you come back to our store and go to the guest services center, we can give you a new set of ten of them. We'll also need to see your receipt to verify your purchase.

Woodwick Cabinet (List of Parts)	
Contents	Quantity
Casing nails (C392)	6
Box nails (B787)	4
Sinker nails (S109)	10
Finish nails (F453)	14

신유형 65-67번은 다음 대화와 평가서에 관한 문제입니다.

W: Hi, Cameron. Our restaurant received several negative reviews on the Local Bites site. Look at one here.

M: Hmm… I see we have some areas that need some serious improvement. With these kinds of reviews, I'm concerned that customers will stop coming to our place.

W: Well, we're expanding our dining area this month, so we should have more space soon.

M: Right, but we still have to discuss what we're going to do about this other low rating at our employee meeting next week.

W: How about bringing in an outside consultant to help us address this situation? We can't afford any more negative reviews.

```
www.localbites.ca/review_section
     Review of La Sorrento Bistro
```

Rating Area	Rating (out of 10)
Dining space	3
Menu choices	3
Pricing	8
Customer service	8

신유형 68-70번은 다음 대화와 도표에 관한 문제입니다.

W: Hi, Mr. Alvarez. We need to talk. You've seen the report on this week's fabric production, haven't you?

M: Yes. Which part did you want to discuss?

W: Well, if you look at the last page of this report, you can see that one of our large knitting units was running at less than 25 percent of its normal efficiency yesterday. That's a lot slower than any of the other units.

M: Hmm… OK, let's stop using this machine immediately, and I'll call a mechanic now to check it out. We have a large order of sweaters to fill by next week, so we need to make sure this machine is up and running at its maximum capacity.

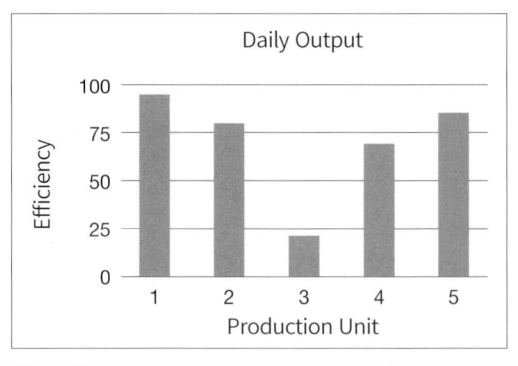

PART 4

P. 55

71-73번은 다음 공지에 관한 문제입니다. 호주

M: Before we open our doors for business today, I'd like to inform everyone about a new recycling policy that will come into effect starting next month. After opening the boxes of shipment that arrive at our store and unpacking the merchandise, take all of the boxes and packing material to our recycling area as usual. However, from now on, you have to separate the cardboard boxes and the plastic wrap, and put them into different containers. This is a new regulation that all businesses in the city must comply with. Collection day will still be Friday, so make sure to sort all recyclable items by then.

신유형 74-76번은 다음 방송에 관한 문제입니다. 미국

W: Good afternoon, and thank you for tuning into WMEE's weather news. It is going to be extremely hot today as temperatures will rise to over 36 degrees Celsius in the early afternoon. As most of you know, Fort Wayne is hosting the annual bicycle race today, with more than 5,000 people expected to watch the competition. If you are planning on attending this event, we highly recommend bringing plenty of juice or water so that you don't get dehydrated.

77-79번은 다음 회의 발췌문에 관한 문제입니다. 영국

W: Now, let's discuss Sana, a jewelry brand we will begin offering at our retail locations this year. As you're aware, our main clientele is young office workers. Our Marketing Department conducted a survey on style preferences, and most respondents said that "a wide variety of fashionable designs" was very important to them. And that's why we have decided to carry Sana's products at our stores. Just check out all the different designs in their catalog. Next, Marcella will give a presentation on the advertising campaign to promote Sana's line of products.

80-82번은 다음 담화에 관한 문제입니다. 미국

M: Good afternoon. It's been great having you all here as interns. You've done some valuable work for our museum, and I hope you have benefited from the experience you've gained with us. For your final task, I'd like you to help us out today with promoting our upcoming local history exhibit. Each of you will be given 350 brochures to hand out all around the city. You'll not only be giving them to people you pass by on the street but also to businesses. We've prepared a map and marked the areas you need to go to. Please work together to decide who goes where, and try to be back by 4 o'clock. Good luck!

83-85번은 다음 소개에 관한 문제입니다. 미국

W: Welcome to this month's County Business Forum. Tonight, we have a very special guest speaker, Mr. Sanjiv Singh. He's the owner of Singh Financial Planning. His firm offers customized investment management services to more than 100 small businesses. Today, he'll talk about some of the growth strategies that worked best for him when he first started to build his business 20 years ago, with a small office and just one employee. You can text your questions to the number you see on the screen on the stage. Seminar coordinators will review the questions and share them with Mr. Singh after he has finished his main presentation. OK, let's welcome Mr. Singh to the stage with a big round of applause!

신유형 86-88번은 다음 공지에 관한 문제입니다. 영국

W: Good afternoon, all shoppers. Thank you for shopping at Danny's Supermarket. Today, we are asking all customers to fill out a short survey. It will take just a few minutes of your time. You'll find two booths in the store—one next to the main entrance and one near the frozen foods aisle—where our employees are distributing the questionnaires. Our aim is to better understand our customers' needs so that we can provide even better service. All customers completing the survey will be given a 10 percent off coupon valid on all purchases in the store today.

89-91번은 다음 회의 발췌록에 관한 문제입니다.

M: Hello, everyone. Before we begin today's meeting, I'd like to remind everyone that we'll be updating our company's e-mail system tonight. Once the new version has been installed, you will see a huge improvement in our system. The update will be done overnight, so all of you must log off from your computer before you leave today. You may access the system again tomorrow morning. Ms. Kelley, a member of the technical support team, is here to explain the new features of the system. Now, let's give our attention to Ms. Kelley.

92-94번은 다음 광고에 관한 문제입니다.

W: Do you rely on secure payments via the Internet for your business? If so, Master 2000 is the system for you. With most Web-based payment applications, you need to manage credit card numbers, passwords, and special security software just to get paid for your services or products. Don't you have better things to do? With Master 2000, all you have to do is add our link to your Web site, and it will redirect your customers to our payment page. Go to our Web site to view a short clip of how to use the system. Master 2000: a smarter way to get paid.

95-97번은 다음 지시문과 좌석 배치도에 관한 문제입니다.

M: Good evening. It's great to see so many talented comedians here today! I hope you're all ready for tonight's comedy contest here at the Maywood Theater. Before your final rehearsals, I'd like to give you a brief overview of how things will proceed tonight. While you wait to go on stage, each of you should be seated in the theater. We've reserved the first three rows in the seating area nearest to the exit for you so that you can easily access the stage when it's your turn. Finally, after the winner is announced and the event ends, please wait a while in the theater. We've organized a professional photo shoot, which will begin as soon as the audience has left. The photos will be used by the press covering the event.

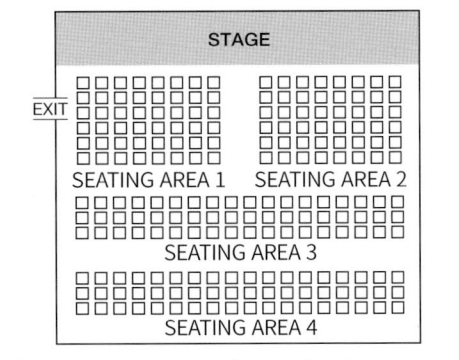

98-100번은 다음 전화 메시지와 경비 내역서에 관한 문제입니다.

M: Good morning, Ms. Matsumoto. This is Alan Rucker calling from the Finance Department. I have a question about the travel expenditure sheet you provided for your trip to the expo last week. I compared your information with the receipts, and it looks like there's a mistake. The restaurant receipts add up to 50 dollars less than what you listed on your sheet. Please check this so that I can process it. Oh, and by the way, the reimbursement form has been revised, and every employee should have been emailed the new one. Please use it for future expenditures. Thanks!

| Request for Reimbursement ||
Expenditure	Amount
Rental car	$835.00
Accommodation	$345.00
Meals	$380.00
Flight	$530.00

TEST 04

PART 1
P. 60

1 한 사람

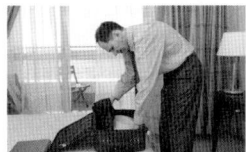

(A) The man is turning off a lamp.
(B) The man is closing a drawer.
(C) The man is drawing the curtains.
(D) The man is looking in his suitcase.

2 두 사람 이상

(A) A man is setting up a projector.
(B) A woman is raising her hand.
(C) Some people are facing the presenter.
(D) Some people are entering a meeting room.

3 한 사람

(A) Customers are paying at the counter.
(B) Racks have been stocked with merchandise.
(C) Workers are organizing items on the shelves.
(D) Some fruits are being taken out of a shopping cart.

4 두 사람 이상

(A) Some trees are being planted along the river.
(B) Some people are walking toward the water.
(C) A gardener is mowing the grass.
(D) A ship is passing under the bridge.

5 한 사람

(A) A man is pouring water into a bucket.
(B) Some tools are laid out on the floor.
(C) Some dishes are being washed in a sink.
(D) A man is installing handles on a cabinet.

6 사물/풍경

(A) A rug has been rolled up in a corner.
(B) The room is unoccupied.
(C) A computer is positioned next to the window.
(D) The curtains have been left open.

PART 2
P. 64

7 Who 의문문

Who signed for the parcel?
(A) I sent it already.
(B) The assistant manager did.
(C) At the post office.

8 How 의문문

How's the conference you attended at the Yokovich Center?
(A) Across from the hotel.
(B) I enjoyed it a lot.
(C) By Russell Kim.

9 When 의문문

When will the construction of the company cafeteria be finished?
(A) On the tenth floor.
(B) Not until next month.
(C) Yes, try the new menu.

10 Have 의문문

Has Mr. Crowe visited the dentist's this week yet?
(A) I brush my teeth twice daily.
(B) It's important to go regularly.
(C) Yes, his appointment was on Monday.

11 평서문

I found yesterday's seminar to be quite informative.
(A) It's tomorrow. Not today.
(B) A training workshop.
(C) Yes, I learned a lot.

12 Why 의문문

Why is David going to another company?
(A) I'm going to a staff meeting.
(B) They offered him a higher salary.
(C) At a job fair.

13 How 의문문

How do you usually get to work?
(A) I drive my car.
(B) Communication skills.
(C) We finish at six.

14 What 의문문

What was discussed at today's board meeting?
(A) The board of directors was present.
(B) I've been out of the office all day.
(C) In the conference room next to reception.

15 When 의문문

When is your performance review meeting?
(A) No, that's not what he said.
(B) Not for another month.
(C) Approximately six months.

16 제안/청유문

Would you mind switching work shifts with me this Friday?
(A) No, you can't exchange this item.
(B) I'm taking that day off.
(C) Today has been busy.

17 Where 의문문

Where do you want me to put the new items that arrived today?
(A) In the display case by the entrance.
(B) In different sizes and colors.
(C) They should be here tomorrow.

18 선택 의문문

Should I discuss the proposed merger at today's meeting or next week's?
(A) Competition has increased.
(B) With an accounting firm.
(C) Today's has been canceled.

19 What 의문문

What does Ms. Patel think about our company's new logo?
(A) I didn't think so.
(B) I'm meeting with her tomorrow.
(C) I'll accompany you.

20 Which 의문문

Which catering company did we hire for the president's birthday party?
(A) The one we used for the anniversary event.
(B) I think she's 50 years old.
(C) To work in the Maintenance Department.

21 Do 의문문

Did it seem like there were more attendees this year than before?
(A) This was my first time participating in the conference.
(B) It's going to be held this Friday.
(C) I put them on your desk.

22 평서문

The marketing director will be leaving the company next month.
(A) Do you know who's replacing him?
(B) They'll be arriving here soon.
(C) A new advertising campaign.

23 선택 의문문

Do you want to go directly to the head office or visit the factory first?
(A) I'm fine with either.
(B) There's room in my car.
(C) Yes, that's correct.

24 부가 의문문

You're coming to the company sports day on Saturday, aren't you?
(A) Over a hundred people came.
(B) I'm working all weekend.
(C) A gym membership discount.

25 Why 의문문

Why didn't you take any photos at the museum?
(A) Anytime in the afternoon.
(B) A famous art gallery.
(C) It wasn't allowed.

26 Have 의문문

Have they rearranged the furniture in here?
(A) It does look more spacious than before.
(B) They are made of wood.
(C) Next to the fridge.

27 제안/청유문

Please put my purchase in a box and gift wrap it.
(A) I wrapped it myself.
(B) Sure. Give me one minute.
(C) This is a discounted item.

28 How 의문문

How long will it take you to complete the financial report?
(A) I just received the data.
(B) Next year's budget.
(C) Sure. I'll bring it.

29 부정 의문문

Wasn't the photocopier on the 10th floor just recently fixed?
(A) Colored photocopies, please.
(B) No, the meeting is on the 11th floor.
(C) Is it not working again?

30 When 의문문

When do I get reimbursed for my business expenses?
(A) A trip to Hong Kong last week.
(B) Have you submitted a report?
(C) About 500 dollars.

31 부가 의문문

The Internet connection is quite slow this morning, isn't it?
(A) Business was unexpectedly slow.
(B) I haven't noticed.
(C) That's the Web site.

PART 3

32-34번은 다음 대화에 관한 문제입니다.

W: Hello, this is Paula Jones in Accounting. There seems to be a problem with my computer. The fan inside is making a loud noise and distracting me from my work.

M: Hmm. I see. Why don't you try shutting off your computer and turning it on again?

W: That was the first thing I did. Unfortunately, it didn't fix the problem.

M: OK. I'm free for about 30 minutes right now. I'll come to your desk and have a look at it.

35-37번은 다음 대화에 관한 문제입니다.

W: Good morning. I'm here to pick up my medicine. My doctor sent the prescription to this pharmacy yesterday. Could you check if the order is ready? My name is Beatrice Fallon.

M: I'll take a look for you. Yes - we did receive the prescription, but unfortunately the order isn't ready yet. We've been extremely busy, so we're behind schedule. Would you mind waiting five minutes? I'll get it for you now.

W: Sure. Actually, I have some things to buy at the store across the street, so I'll do that now and then come back here in 20 minutes.

38-40번은 다음 대화에 관한 문제입니다.

M: Good afternoon. My name's Josh Brennan, and I'm calling from Downtown Appliances. As you're a valued customer, we wanted you to be the first to know about our special promotion this month. We're offering a 30 percent discount on all dishwashers.

W: Well, my dishwasher is getting old, but it's still in good condition. I'll probably need to replace it sometime, but not right now.

M: OK. If you'd like me to, I could add your name to our e-mail list. That way we can let you know about all our promotions as soon as they're announced.

신유형 41-43번은 다음 대화에 관한 문제입니다.

W: Hey, Stan. Do you remember the questionnaire our gym distributed two weeks ago?

M: Yeah. It was to have members comment on their experience with us, right? How was the response?

W: Well, most of them said they'd like to spend a little more time with their personal trainers. Currently, each training session is one hour long. Would it be possible to lengthen them by 10 minutes?

M: That might cause conflicts with our schedules. We'll have to leave the decision up to senior management.

신유형 44-46번은 다음 세 화자의 대화에 관한 문제입니다.

M1: Good morning, Carl. Jennifer and I just wanted to make sure you are settling into your position here at JCF Energy. We're so pleased that our first choice for the new engineering position was selected.

W: That's right, and as long as we're here, I can teach you how to log your work hours, which you will have to report to Accounting every two weeks. Can you spare some time to do it right now?

M2: Actually, I have a meeting in the lab in about five minutes to learn more about the first project I've been assigned to.

M1: Oh, it sounds like no one told you. Unfortunately, the lab is undergoing some urgent repairs, so it's closed for the day. Your meeting has been moved to tomorrow morning.

신유형 47-49번은 다음 대화에 관한 문제입니다.

W: Tim, we're going to leave soon to cater Salafran Dental Association's dinner banquet, but we're short on plates. Are there some in our storage room?

M: No. I put in an order with our local vendor on Monday, but it still hasn't arrived. This isn't their first time, you know.

W: Well, we have to deliver everything to Salafran's office by 5 P.M., so what should we do? I don't have enough time to drop by a store.

M: I'll take care of it. I can purchase some on my way to their office.

W: OK, that sounds good. Give me a call when you arrive, so I can help you bring them inside.

50-52번은 다음 대화에 관한 문제입니다.

M: Hey, Dalia. The news just said that a big storm is headed here. The buses might not be running tomorrow, and I'm supposed to work in the morning.

W: Yeah, I heard. If it's bad outside, it'll be hard for our workers to come in. I'll decide tomorrow morning whether to open the restaurant or not.

M: All right. If you want me to help you contact everyone working tomorrow, let me know.
W: I'd really appreciate that. Thank you.

53-55번은 다음 대화에 관한 문제입니다.

W: Hi, I have a subscription to your weekend newspaper, but I didn't get Saturday's and Sunday's this past weekend. My address is 241 Creighton Meadows in Branton.
M: I'll check your account. Oh, it seems your subscription expired last Friday, which explains why you had no weekend deliveries. Would you like me to renew your subscription for you?
W: Yes, please. I used my credit card when I subscribed online last time. I'm sure you still have the information.
M: Okay. Let me just go over the payment details with you to check that they're correct.

56-58번은 다음 대화에 관한 문제입니다.

W: Hello. Last week, I ordered a laptop from your online store, but I haven't received it yet. My name is Wanda Jones. Can you tell me what happened?
M: Please give me a minute while I check our system. OK, it says here that the driver tried to make the delivery, but he didn't have the correct address.
W: I don't understand why no one tried to contact me then. Someone should have called me right away to check my address. Frankly, I'm quite disappointed.
M: I'm really sorry about that. If I can confirm your address now, I'll arrange your delivery for tomorrow. Also, to make up for our mistake, I'll reimburse the shipping fee to your bank account.

59-61번은 다음 대화에 관한 문제입니다.

W: Mr. Harper. I'm really sorry, but I don't think I can finish the Web site design I've been working on for Nonia Pharmaceuticals by the deadline.
M: Oh, I was planning on showing the new Web site to the Nonia Pharmaceuticals representatives this Thursday. When do you think you can get it done by?
W: Well, I'm still in the process of creating the color schemes and font styles. I know the deadline is 5 P.M. tomorrow, but I'm going to need at least three more days to get everything just right.
M: Okay then. I'm going to call Nonia and reschedule the meeting to next week.

62-64번은 다음 대화와 정보에 관한 문제입니다.

W: Thanks for coming by, Mr. Moore. I've been reviewing your travel expenses incurred while away on business. But I've found some issues with your report.
M: Um… do I need to submit more documents to get paid back for the costs incurred during my business trip?
W: No. It's just that the company no longer covers hotel room service costs.
M: So I won't be reimbursed for that?
W: I'm afraid not. But you will get money back for the rest of the items.
M: Okay. It seems like I was not fully aware of the newly revised regulations. I'll make sure it doesn't happen again.

ITEM	AMOUNT
Hotel X 6 Nights	$480
Room Service	$90
Business Lunch	$120
Airfare	$620

65-67번은 다음 대화와 지도에 관한 문제입니다.

W: Hey, John. I'm so happy to see you. I'm completely confused by this station. I'm trying to get to the airport, but I don't know which subway line to take. I was planning to take one of the express lines, but they're both temporarily closed for repairs.

M: Let's look at the subway map over here. Hmm… I think you should take this route. The train stops at Airport Approach—but it's actually quicker than the other non-express service.

W: Thanks so much. I can't be late for my flight to Miami.

M: Are you going for business or pleasure?

W: For business. There is a convention there that I have to go to. I'll be giving a report about it at next month's staff meeting.

M: I see. Hope the trip goes well.

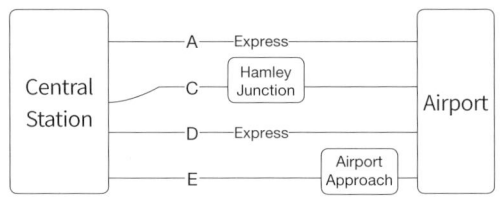

68-70번은 다음 대화와 연극 안내서에 관한 문제입니다.

W: Hi, Tom. What are you doing after work tonight?

M: Well, I was thinking of watching a play. I've been browsing this theater guide to decide what I should watch. I don't think I'll make it in time for The Village Riot, which I heard got great reviews.

W: Do you mind if I look, too? Ah… actually I watched Children of One recently. The actors did a great a job, but the plot was a little dull.

M: Thanks for letting me know. I suppose I'll check out The Roof Peddler then. How about you? What will you do tonight?

W: I'll just stay home. I'll be at a convention both Saturday and Sunday, so I need to relax tonight.

Play	Starting Time
The Village Riot	6:30 P.M.
Harkin's Past	7:00 P.M.
The Roof Peddler	8:00 P.M.
Children of One	9:30 P.M.

PART 4

71-73번은 다음 담화에 관한 문제입니다.

W: Welcome to today's opening of our latest exhibit here at the Ingram Museum. This new exhibit brings together some very rare landscape drawings by some of the finest 17th-century Dutch artists. Before you enter, I will hand out an audio player to everyone. The device will provide information about the artists and their drawings. When you're done looking around the exhibit, please stop by the video room at 2 o'clock. We'll be showing a 30-minute film about some of the artwork featured.

74-76번은 다음 라디오 방송에 관한 문제입니다.

M: This is Campton Radio 22 with your community's weekly news bulletin. This weekend, the Orleans Blues Quartet will be presenting several new jazz pieces. Anna Rethom, the leader of the group, recently won the Armstrong Award for the Best Jazz Composer of the Year. Tickets are available on the Campton Theater's Web site for both the Saturday and Sunday performances. We'll be back in a moment with the local traffic report right after a quick commercial break.

77-79번은 다음 회의 발췌록에 관한 문제입니다.　[영국]

W: As we discussed in our last team meeting, we will be making more use of video conferencing this year. All our meeting rooms have now been equipped with computers and Web cameras. The IT Department will be providing training on how to operate the equipment over the coming weeks. Our team's training is scheduled for next Thursday at 3 o'clock in Meeting Room 9. Please make a note of this on your calendars. I'm aware that some of you won't be able to make it since you'll be at the advertising conference in Shanghai. But no need to worry—other sessions will be scheduled at a later date.

신유형 80-82번은 다음 회의 발췌록에 관한 문제입니다.　[미국]

W: Thank you all for attending our monthly staff meeting. First of all, make sure to check out the latest issue of City Life Magazine. You'll be happy to see that the magazine selected us as the best fitness center in the area. But let's not forget that another new gym just opened up down the street. To stay ahead of the competition, we plan on ordering additional workout machines and also recruiting more personal trainers. The new machines should be available to our members at the beginning of next month.

신유형 83-85번은 다음 전화 메시지에 관한 문제입니다.　[미국]

M: Hello, Julia, it's Mark. Unfortunately, I still haven't heard back from the airline about my missing luggage with the prototype of our new potato peeler inside. Based on the conversations I've had with the airline employees, I don't think I'll get my luggage back before Wednesday's presentation. Without the prototype, there is really no point in making the presentation. So, the best solution would be for you to fly out here with another prototype. I realize it's a long trip, but I can't think of any other solution.

86-88번은 다음 광고에 관한 문제입니다.　[호주]

M: Do you find that you spend too much time managing your business's accounts? Then why not use AC Genie to manage your company's finances? AC Genie is the best-selling accounting software on the market. Specifically designed for the needs of small and medium-sized businesses, its automatic invoicing feature allows you to effortlessly monitor income and expenditure. Customized reports can be easily generated and real-time financial data is always available at the click of a mouse. Call 555-8261 and speak with one of our representatives to try out AC Genie today! Training and support are provided free to all customers.

신유형 89-91번은 다음 전화 메시지에 관한 문제입니다.　[영국]

W: Hi, Tiffany. It's Gwyneth Kane calling about my scheduled talk at the workshop for your biologists. I have several subjects in mind for my lecture. But if you'd like me to discuss my latest study on muscle regeneration, which has attracted a lot of attention, the data will not be published for a while. Please call me back so that we can finalize the topic. By the way, in regard to the fee list on my Web site, since I've worked with your firm on many occasions, I won't charge you my standard speaking fee.

92-94번은 다음 공지에 관한 문제입니다.　[미국]

M: Before I close this meeting, I'd like to remind all floor managers that students from Dillard Technical School will be coming to our manufacturing plant tomorrow afternoon. The school wants their students to see the process of how goods are manufactured in a factory such as ours. Remember that the students and teachers may ask our workers to demonstrate how a machine works. So when you go back to your production floor, be sure to inform the members of your team about this and address any concerns they might have about the visit.

신유형 95-97번은 다음 전화 메시지와 목록에 관한 문제입니다. [호주]

M: Good morning. I'm calling for Noel Wright. I just wanted to confirm the order you placed with us here at Red Office Supplies yesterday. It looks like you ordered an unusually large quantity of toner cartridges this time, and I wanted to make sure it wasn't an error. If it was a mistake, please let me know right away so that I can correct the order for you. Also, I'm going to be out of town on business for a week starting tomorrow. If you call tomorrow, please ask for Danica. She'll be taking care of my customers while I'm away.

Order List	
Item	Quantity
Highlighter	20
Poster paper	35
Toner cartridge	170
Envelope	200

신유형 98-100번은 다음 공지와 도표에 관한 문제입니다. [미국]

M: The first item on today's agenda is the recent survey that we conducted regarding our plant's dining area. So let's briefly go over the results. According to the graph, the most popular request was for the seating area to be expanded. Although we'd like to do this, we just don't have the budget for it right now. But we can definitely address the next most popular request. So we're going to begin work on that right away. And remember: all employees who participate in the survey will receive a complimentary bottle of juice every day for a week.

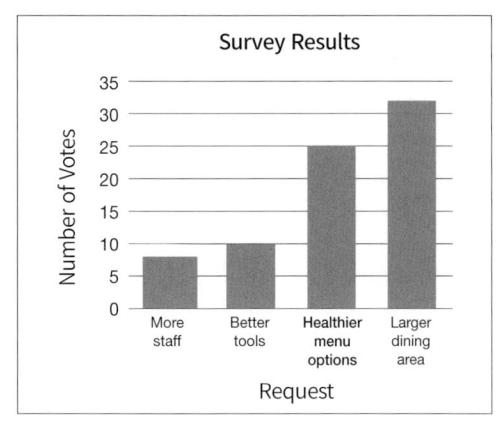

TEST 05

PART 1   P. 74

1   한 사람

[영국]

(A) She's chopping vegetables.
(B) She's turning on a faucet.
(C) She's putting on an apron.
(D) She's wiping a countertop.

2   사물/풍경

[호주]

(A) Windows are being washed.
(B) A row of bicycles is facing a wall.
(C) Cars are parked in a garage.
(D) A fence is being painted.

3   두 사람 이상

[미국]

(A) They're planting some flowers in a pot.
(B) They're arranging merchandise on a shelf.
(C) They're looking into a shop window.
(D) They're attaching tags on some items.

4 두 사람 이상

(A) Fans are waiting in line to purchase tickets.
(B) Musicians are packing up their instruments.
(C) Some of the performers are wearing hats.
(D) Musicians are rehearsing in a studio.

5 한 사람

(A) A wheelbarrow is being pushed at a worksite.
(B) A vehicle is being filled with sand.
(C) Some men are leaving a construction site.
(D) Some people are putting up a fence.

6 사물/풍경

(A) Some curtains are being opened.
(B) Some cushions have been placed on the floor.
(C) A lamp has been put on a table.
(D) A light fixture is hanging from the ceiling.

PART 2

P. 78

7 Who 의문문

Who's in charge of the renovation project?
(A) Two to three weeks.
(B) Kumar, the construction manager.
(C) Charge it to my account.

8 Where 의문문

Where is our summer sportswear being manufactured?
(A) It was made in Vietnam last year.
(B) Water-resistant fabric.
(C) Ms. Murphy is good at sports.

9 Do 의문문

Did you get the key to the storage room from Lisa?
(A) I haven't seen her today.
(B) She works at the store.
(C) A meeting room is available.

10 Have 의문문

Has the new marketing director been named yet?
(A) It was a promotional event.
(B) About the new advertising campaign.
(C) I think it's going to be Mr. Cho.

11 부정 의문문

Isn't our monthly sales report due today?
(A) It's a monthly magazine.
(B) Oh, I almost forgot about that.
(C) He's an outstanding salesperson.

12 Why 의문문

Why was Amelia late for the seminar?
(A) Around 10:45.
(B) She had a client meeting.
(C) The current employment rate.

13 제안/청유문

Could you take this customer's call?
(A) The customer service center.
(B) I'll take it to her office.
(C) Sure. Put the call through.

14 When 의문문

When can I expect to receive payment?
(A) On the last day of this month.
(B) In the Accounting Department.
(C) Approximately 600 dollars a week.

15 Do 의문문

Does the fitness center you go to have a parking lot?
(A) Many people jog in the park.
(B) Brand-new exercise equipment.
(C) There's an underground garage.

16 평서문

If you're not in a hurry, I suggest you take a bus rather than a taxi.
(A) No, three more stops.
(B) Here's your change.
(C) Yes, that would be cheaper.

17 선택 의문문

Would you like me to reserve a restaurant for the office party or is it going to be catered?
(A) Everyone is going to attend.
(B) The food was delicious.
(C) We found a caterer.

18 Why 의문문

Why is your membership application form so long?
(A) You don't have to fill out everything.
(B) She applied for the job.
(C) How much is the membership fee?

19 How 의문문

How many desktop computers did we sell this month?
(A) We have office furniture.
(B) I'll need to look it up.
(C) It's easy to use.

20 평서문

The room should be set up before the board members arrive.
(A) Who attended the meeting?
(B) It's already been done.
(C) From 10 to 11.

21 평서문

Management has recently hired several new employees.
(A) I didn't think we had the budget for that.
(B) A seminar on business management.
(C) He wasn't able to start last Monday.

22 Which 의문문

Which bus do you take?
(A) He's rather busy right now.
(B) I usually drive.
(C) Why don't you take some?

23 부정 의문문

Didn't Janet postpone her vacation to September?
(A) A travel agency.
(B) From Spain to France.
(C) Yes, she rescheduled it.

24 Where 의문문

Where is the closest print shop?
(A) Printouts for the presentation.
(B) Yes, we close at eight.
(C) There's one on the next block.

25 평서문

I thought we were replacing the desks in the office this week.
(A) Yes, we sell office supplies.
(B) Didn't you read the notice on the board?
(C) Place the chairs on the desks.

26 Do 의문문

Do the security staff know that guests will be visiting our facilities today?
(A) I'll visit you later.
(B) They've been informed.
(C) The ladder is secure.

27 부가 의문문

You haven't received a package for me today, have you?
(A) What's it look like?
(B) Pack it in a box.
(C) A courier company.

28 평서문

Excuse me. You need a membership card to enter here.
(A) Let me get the door for you.
(B) Oh, how do I get one?
(C) I'll pay in cash.

29 Have 의문문

Have you considered joining a gym near the office?
(A) They're working on a project.
(B) Yes, but it's too expensive around here.
(C) He's really considerate.

30 When 의문문

When will the offices on the third floor be vacant?
(A) Around 900 dollars a month.
(B) Ms. Sato might know.
(C) A long-term lease.

31 선택 의문문

Is today's meeting going to be held in conference room A or B?
(A) Some teleconferencing equipment.
(B) I think it's been canceled.
(C) It will end before noon.

PART 3

32-34번은 다음 대화에 관한 문제입니다.

W: It's good to see you back, Paul. How was your break?

M: It was wonderful! I spent most days climbing the mountain outside the city.

W: Did you do any shopping?

M: No. There were so many people in the area, so getting around was really difficult to do.

W: That's too bad. At least you were able to relax.

M: Yeah. Anyway, what did I miss at work?

W: Well, there is some big news. Last week, we finally began work on the marketing campaign for Risha Tech's new product. We need to bring you up-to-date on what's going on.

35-37번은 다음 대화에 관한 문제입니다.

M: Hello, this is Ralph from the Logistics Department. I don't think I'm going to be able to submit my expense claim by tomorrow. Would it be possible to get an extension?

W: That's only permitted under special circumstances. What's the reason?

M: Well, I seem to have misplaced a few receipts. I have to find them before I can complete the form.

W: Hmm… Let me speak to my manager about that. But for now, why don't you turn in what you have filled out so far? That way, I can begin processing the claim.

38-40번은 다음 대화에 관한 문제입니다.

W: Hey Karl, I was planning to check out the new museum exhibit with the tour group tomorrow. But I just called guest services and found out that all of the tickets are sold out.

M: I see. Well, I read about a modern art show that's open at a different location. It's right on Main Street. Why don't you also suggest it to the tourists?

W: That's a good idea. I've got to attend a meeting now, but I'll come by your desk after. Let's talk more then.

신유형 41-43번은 다음 세 화자의 대화에 관한 문제입니다.

W1: Mr. Lentz, we appreciate you looking over the ad campaign we've created for Conway Apparel.

W2: Yes, thank you so much, Mr. Lentz. So… What do you think? We're going to discuss it with Conway's representatives next Tuesday, and we'd like some feedback before we do.

M: Well, I'd place more emphasis on how this ad campaign will attract people in their 20s.

W1: That's a good point. We can use popular social media networks to reach out to them. Should we include this in the plan?

M: Definitely. I'm sure Conway's representatives would like it.

W2: Alright, we'll make the necessary revisions. If you have some time tomorrow, we'd like to have another meeting with you to discuss this further.

신유형 44-46번은 다음 대화에 관한 문제입니다. 호주 ⇄ 영국

M: Catherine, I just completed the additions you requested to the company's Web site. Would you like to take a look before I upload the new pages?

W: Sure. Hmm, yes, everything looks good. Oh, hold on, I spotted an error. The Chief Financial Officer's surname should be all one word, not two separate words.

M: Ah, yes. I forgot that it's one word. I'll fix that right away.

W: I get confused sometimes, too. Anyway, all that matters is that the information in the final version of the Web site is correct.

47-49번은 다음 대화에 관한 문제입니다. 호주 ⇄ 미국

M: Hi, Ms. Engleton, I'm a reporter for *Haymont Daily*. I'd like to talk to you about the new fitness program you introduced at your office. I hear the response has been very positive.

W: Yes, that's right! We want to encourage our staff to be more physically active. So we hired a trainer to lead exercise classes before and after work. Now, employees can take this opportunity to work out.

M: That seems like a great idea, but the program must cost your company a lot of money.

W: Yeah, it does. But we believe it's worth it when it comes to the well-being of our staff.

신유형 50-52번은 다음 세 화자의 대화에 관한 문제입니다.

M1: Hello, Mary and Joe. Thanks for coming back to look at the house again. As I told you on the telephone, the seller has decided to reduce the asking price.

W: The new price works better for our budget, but we do still have some concerns about the property.

M2: Yes, we think some major renovations may be needed. For example, the roof looks like it might need some work, and we noticed a lot of mold in the bathroom. We'd also want to install a new kitchen. We're concerned about the potential costs of doing all this.

M1: Well, I know the roof was replaced three years ago so that should be in pretty good shape.

M2: Oh, I see. We also wondered why the owner reduced the price. Why is she so keen to move?

M1: She needs to move for work reasons. She's being transferred to another city, so she wants to sell it as quickly as possible.

53-55번은 다음 대화에 관한 문제입니다.

W: I just got off the phone with Jemima Kelly. She's supposed to give the opening speech at the awards ceremony next week, but she needs to travel overseas urgently, so she won't be able to attend.

M: Oh, what a shame! The program for the event has to be printed soon, so we're going to need to find a replacement quickly.

W: Yes, you're right. Can you think of anyone suitable who might be available at such short notice?

M: Well, one person who would be great is Danni Lee. She is well-respected in the company and is also a great speaker. I'll ask her right now to see if she'd be interested.

신유형 56-58번은 다음 대화에 관한 문제입니다.

W: Hello, and thank you for calling Cooper Medical Center. How may I help you?

M: Hi. My name's Peter Davidson. I'm going to be working overseas starting next week, and I'd like to receive some vaccinations. Could I make an appointment?

W: I'll check our appointment schedule, Mr. Davidson. OK, I see that we have a few openings this Wednesday afternoon. Is 1:00 P.M. okay?

M: Well, I work until 2 o'clock on Wednesdays.

W: OK, then how about 3 o'clock? Would that give you enough time to get here?

M: Yes, that'll work for me. Thanks.

59-61번은 다음 대화에 관한 문제입니다.

M: Vera. I remember you telling me that your office used Dacon Staffing Solutions to find temporary workers. Were you satisfied with them?

W: Yes, we've used Dacon's services quite a few times over the years.

M: I see. Well, now that the busy tourist season is coming, my diner will need some extra help. I'm hoping to hire some experienced servers.

W: Hmm. Dacon specializes in filling clerical positions, so they're probably not your best option. However, if you search the Web, I'm sure you'll find an agency that can suit your needs.

62-64번은 다음 대화와 내비게이션 화면에 관한 문제입니다.

W: Larry, we're nearing the port, so let's stop and refuel the car. The rental agency will charge an additional fee if we don't refill the gas tank.

M: Right. We would end up paying more than we need to.

W: Should I take this street then?

M: No, that's the rest stop. Just go a little further and turn right on the next street.

W: Ah, OK. Let's hope we can find some snacks there. Then we can eat them on our ferry ride to the island.

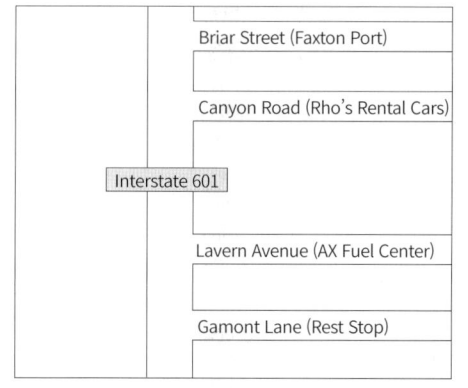

65-67번은 다음 대화와 차트에 관한 문제입니다.

W: Good morning. This is Jane calling from Premier Engineering. I was recently at a demonstration event for your supply chain management software. I'm considering using it for my company. Could you tell me about the different options you have available?

M: Certainly. As you probably know, we have various license levels. Which license level will suit your company best really depends on the size of your staff. How many employees will be using the software?

W: Our Supply Chain Management Department is quite small, though we'd probably want some of our sales team to also be able to access the software. So… maybe around 50 users?

M: The Professional license allows up to 60 users so that would be your best option.

W: That sounds perfect. I'll purchase it now.

License Level	Annual Cost
Basic	$1,600
Professional	$2,800
Team	$4,000
Enterprise	$6,500

68-70번은 다음의 대화와 승객 목록에 관한 문제입니다.

W: Hello, I'm Nicole Brunski from San Marco Industries. I'm one of the people on that sign who is going to the management conference. Are you the one driving us to the hotel?

M: Yes, I am. Welcome to Chicago, Ms. Brunski. You're actually the first person to arrive at the airport. I just heard that some of your coworkers' flight from Sydney has been delayed for two hours.

W: Really? We won't be able to make it to the orientation if we have to wait that long.

M: It'll be fine. We'll leave as soon as your coworker from Houston arrives in 30 minutes. I'll take you both to your hotel. Then I'll come back for the other two. Let's head over to the lounge and wait there.

Name	Arriving from
Reeya Singh	Houston
Chris Walker	Sydney
Bill Keen	Sydney
Nicole Brunski	San Diego

PART 4

P. 83

71-73번은 다음 안내방송에 관한 문제입니다.

> M: Attention Upshaw Railway passengers. We are pleased to inform you that a new automated ticketing system has just been installed on the main floor. These machines are situated near the entrances. They have easy-to-use touchscreens that make purchasing train tickets quick and convenient. In addition, instructions for using the system are available in several languages, including: Italian, Japanese, Spanish, and English. If you require help with these machines, an Upshaw Railway representative will assist you.

74-76번은 다음 전화 메시지에 관한 문제입니다. 미국

> W: Hi, Mr. Saunders, I'm calling from Vivre Energy Solutions. I would like to inform you of the services we offer to help small businesses such as yours save on the use of energy. We conduct a thorough study of your company's operations to identify areas where savings can be made. For example, we've worked with many companies and helped them decide whether switching to solar power is right for them. If you'd like to find out more about our services, I can provide references from our past customers. You can reach me at 555-1290.

신유형 77-79번은 다음 뉴스 보도에 관한 문제입니다. 영국

> W: Good afternoon. This is Antonia Giordano from TBN News with today's business report. Several years ago, local factories were struggling to fill positions at their manufacturing plants. They just couldn't find many skilled candidates, and this resulted in slower production. To help out with the situation, technical schools in the city have added more classes. Lowerton Technical School, for example, has nearly doubled the number of welding and machine operating classes it offers. Nowadays, local factories all say they're getting applications on a daily basis.

80-82번은 다음 회의 발췌록에 관한 문제입니다. 미국

> M: Good morning. I know many of us use the snack vending machines in the company cafeteria. But we're debating whether to switch to a different vending machine company. So tomorrow afternoon, a potential new supplier will be stopping by to let us sample their products. In addition, they'll give everyone a complimentary bag of cookies and chips, which are their most popular items. All we ask is that you provide some feedback on the products you sample so we can make a better decision. It'll only take a couple of minutes to complete the feedback form, and you can leave it on Andrew's desk when you're done.

신유형 83-85번은 다음 전화 메시지에 관한 문제입니다. 미국

> W: Hi, Sven. I'm glad to see that preparations are going well for our German investors' visit. I reviewed the plans you sent me, and I have some comments. First, I was just informed that one more person will be joining the group. Can you contact the inn and book an additional suite? Also, it looks like you were going to take our guests to watch the new performance at the Galplex Theater. That performance got poor reviews. What do you think about the Reuger Museum?

86-88번은 다음 방송에 관한 문제입니다.

M: Thank you for tuning into Inland Update on Radio 909 here in Redlands City. Town officials stated that last Saturday's music festival fundraiser at Caroline Park was a big success. More than $100,000 was raised from ticket and food sales to pay for the development of a new music education program in Redlands schools. Although organizers had to reschedule the event because of an unexpected storm, turnout was very high. However, another $50,000 will be needed before the schools can purchase all the needed instruments and supplies. To learn more about how you can help, check out the Redlands City Web site.

89-91은 다음 전화 메시지에 관한 문제입니다.

W: Hi, Mark. It was nice meeting you, and I hope you found this morning's consultation for your business helpful. I'm just calling to give you some additional comments. As a management consultant, I'm very impressed with how you run your stores. You oversee five different locations all by yourself. Not many people can do that. So don't worry if you're having a little trouble with record keeping. There is an Executive Education Seminar coming up in May, and I highly suggest you attend it. They have speakers covering some very useful material on client files and bookkeeping.

92-94번은 다음 회의 발췌록에 관한 문제입니다.

M: We'll start off today's meeting by briefly going over our new shipment tracking system. This new software is quite different from the one we've used in the past. The program will enable us to see the exact location of any shipment, even while it's in transit. This will be helpful for our clients, since we will be able to offer them more accurate information regarding the status of their orders. We'll start offering training on the system this month. Robert Benfer, an expert in the use of the new system, will be visiting all of our branches to conduct training and answer questions.

95-97번은 다음 담화와 기능 목록에 관한 문제입니다.

W: Welcome, everyone. Today, we are launching our clinic's My Wellness smartphone program. This new software will help us keep a close eye on our patients and provide them with quick health assistance via their smartphones. So, now, I'd like all of you to test the app on your own smartphones. The My Wellness app displays a list of available features when you open it. As you can see, the Calorie Tracker can help our doctors to monitor nutrition. However, the feature patients will find most useful is at the top of the screen. This allows them access to our medical professionals 24 hours a day, wherever they may be.

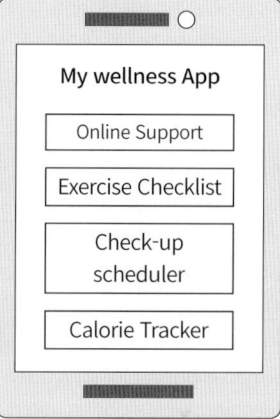

98-100번은 다음 전화 메시지와 설문에 관한 문제입니다.

W: Hi, it's Katie Merrell, the membership coordinator at Skylane Fitness Club. I'm just calling to thank you for completing our member satisfaction survey. We're giving each of our survey participants a special coupon for 10 percent off at any restaurant in this building. I mailed it out this morning. Also, while looking through your form, I noticed you mostly gave high ratings to our club. I appreciate that. But I'd like to talk to you about the one category you gave a 3 to. Whenever you have a moment to talk, please call me at 555-2293.

Satisfaction Survey	
Category	Rating (Out of 5)
Equipment	4
Pricing	3
Cleanliness	4
Customer service	5

TEST 06

PART 1
P. 88

1 한 사람

(A) She's putting on her glasses.
(B) She's writing on a notepad.
(C) She's picking up the phone.
(D) She's reading a book.

2 두 사람 이상

(A) The man is leaning over a railing.
(B) The man is posing for a picture.
(C) People are using a photocopier.
(D) People are adjusting some light fixtures.

3 두 사람 이상

(A) A park area is unoccupied.
(B) People are lined up to buy tickets.
(C) An outdoor stage is being set up.
(D) A crowd has gathered to watch a performance.

4 사물/풍경

(A) A rug has been rolled up against the window.
(B) Some cushions have been stacked on the floor.
(C) A picture frame has been mounted on a wall.
(D) Some potted plants have been placed on a shelf.

5 한 사람

(A) A woman is wiping a counter with a towel.
(B) Lab equipment is laid out on a work area.
(C) A woman is putting some tools in a drawer.
(D) The windows in the room are open.

6 두 사람 이상

(A) People are stocking some merchandise.
(B) People are putting labels on cartons.
(C) People are stacking boxes in a corner.
(D) People are standing in an aisle.

PART 2
P. 92

7 제안/청유문

Why don't you turn up the volume?
(A) The microphone is new.
(B) It's over there.
(C) Sure, I'll do that.

8 When 의문문

When is the best time to visit Ms. Yamamoto?
(A) Any day except Thursday.
(B) I'm in a hurry.
(C) At her office.

9 평서문

Let's reorganize the cabinet so we can locate our files more easily.
(A) 50 dollars only.
(B) I emailed them to you.
(C) Should we do it now?

10 Have 의문문

Has the data from the customer survey been analyzed yet?
(A) They aren't what we anticipated.
(B) To complete the questionnaires.
(C) A password for the database.

11 How 의문문

How are we supposed to meet the assignment's deadline?
(A) It was a short meeting.
(B) What team is he assigned to?
(C) We're going to have to work overtime.

12 When 의문문

When did the store close down?
(A) At another branch.
(B) After the owner moved.
(C) It's close to the highway.

13 제안/청유문

Shall we discuss some ideas for the food festival?
(A) Everything was very delicious.
(B) I'm not that hungry.
(C) Sure. Let's brainstorm.

14 Have 의문문

Has Gordon finished reviewing the safety manual?
(A) This is our latest machine.
(B) No, he's been out all day.
(C) The factory inspector.

15 What 의문문

What kind of books does your company publish?
(A) An online booking service.
(B) No, I didn't read them.
(C) Mystery and adventure.

16 제안/청유문

Please shut down your computer when you leave the office.
(A) We recently purchased more computers.
(B) In the company manual.
(C) Ernie already told me.

17 부가 의문문

You wanted help with that video, didn't you?
(A) A 30-minute clip.
(B) No, he's the director.
(C) Yes, but I resolved the issue.

18 Where 의문문

Where should I put Ms. Kensington's file?
(A) Around 3 o'clock, if possible.
(B) She arrived just this morning.
(C) On the shelf next to the printer.

19 Why 의문문

Why hasn't the invoice been sent?
(A) Before July 8th.
(B) I haven't processed it yet.
(C) An original receipt.

20 평서문

There must be an easier way to get to the factory.
(A) On the assembly line.
(B) He lives far away.
(C) I'm not sure there is a better route.

21 부정 의문문

Didn't Shana say she put the dishes on the table?
(A) No, they're in the sink.
(B) A vegetarian menu.
(C) The restaurant purchased new chairs.

22 평서문

The login page on our Web site isn't working.
(A) You should call tech support.
(B) In order to save electricity.
(C) That's your new password.

23 Have 의문문

Have you reviewed the sales presentation?
(A) Yes, I read it three times.
(B) When is he speaking?
(C) The transfer request form

24 부가 의문문

The product launch is planned for this Friday, right?
(A) No, We require another week.
(B) Yes, I just ate lunch.
(C) My plane got delayed this afternoon.

25 Which 의문문

Which of these wallpapers should I use for the living room?
(A) I didn't know it was used.
(B) I like the striped one.
(C) Yes, in the other room.

26 How 의문문

How long is the flight to Los Angeles?
(A) He's on vacation.
(B) Around three hours.
(C) At 2 o'clock.

27 Where 의문문

Where are the responses to the questionnaire?
(A) At 11 A.M. on Wednesday.
(B) I believe Dave has them.
(C) Almost 500 replies.

28 부정 의문문

Didn't Ms. Lee book a room for tomorrow's staff meeting?
(A) No, none were available.
(B) It's on the third shelf.
(C) Yes, everyone attended.

29 선택 의문문

Do you want me to send a photocopy of the contract or the original document?
(A) For the marketing presentation.
(B) Let me check with Benjamin.
(C) No, I thought you did.

30 부정 의문문

Shouldn't we inform the client about the updated budget?
(A) Please fill out this form.
(B) Kenny said he will do it.
(C) I was reimbursed for the expenses.

31 평서문

I'm afraid the weekly staff meeting has been postponed.
(A) That's the second time this month.
(B) In the large meeting room.
(C) Did you attend it?

PART 3

32-34번은 다음 대화에 관한 문제입니다.

W: Hello, can I get one ticket to the 3:30 P.M. showing of *Marine Underground*? I have read great things about it.

M: Sorry. That play is quite popular, and we don't have any more seats for the afternoon. But there are some left for the 7 P.M. show.

W: Ah, I have plans for the evening. I'll just return another day. Can I book a ticket for next Friday right now?

M: We do sell tickets in advance, but that's only offered to theater members. If you aren't a member, you can register here to become one.

W: All right. I'd like to do that now.

신유형 35-37번은 세 화자의 대화에 관한 문제입니다.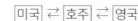

M1: Thank you both for coming. We have to create a presentation for next week's investors' meeting. How do you think we should begin?

M2: Well, we need to grab their attention right away. So our introduction has to be very appealing.

W: I think we should make a video that shows people giving testimonials about how much they enjoy our products. Can the media team help with that, Allan?

M2: That shouldn't be a problem, but I'm a little concerned about the schedule. We'll have to shoot all the scenes in the next day or two in order for the file to be edited in time for the meeting.

신유형 38-40번은 다음 대화에 관한 문제입니다.

W: Oh, Kevin, I'm glad you're here. I'm meeting with the accounting director at 4 o'clock and… I need the marketing team's budget proposal.

M: I'm just about done. There's just one small concern I have about the estimated cost of advertising next year. Based on the conversations I've had with most of the city's papers, we're going to need to spend quite a bit more this time.

W: Hmm… That's definitely an issue. Our budget doesn't have a lot of flexibility. I'll mention it at this afternoon's meeting. Maybe we can negotiate a deal with the local newspapers where we offer them promotional products in exchange for better rates.

41-43번 문제는 다음 대화에 관한 문제입니다.

M: I'm looking for an office chair. I saw in your online ad that you're offering 25 percent off on all office furniture.

W: Ah, unfortunately, the last day of that deal was yesterday. However, we do have another fantastic promotion that might interest you: Buy any type of chair and get another one at half-price.

M: Hmm, I don't really need two of them. Is there any way you could give me a price cut on just one chair?

W: I don't have that kind of authority. But I can ask my supervisor and see if he is able to do anything for you.

신유형 44-46번은 다음 대화에 관한 문제입니다.

M: Lucy, you know that presentation I sent you for the pharmacology symposium…

W: Oh, I forgot about that. I was supposed to give you feedback. I'm sorry.

M: It's OK. I know you've been really busy with the trial for the new cold medication.

W: Yeah, that's finally coming to an end now. It'll be ready for launch before the end of the year.

M: Fantastic! So do you have a moment to check some of my slides now?

W: Yeah, sure.

M: Great. I want to make sure that all of the researchers' names are included in these slides.

W: OK, let's take a look. Mmm… Oh! Didn't Dr. Chen take part in the project?

M: That's right. It's a good thing you caught that.

47-49번은 다음 대화에 관한 문제입니다.

M: Hey, Monica. How's your day going?

W: Not bad. Actually, I was hoping to run into you. I heard you just bought a new apartment. I'm planning to save to buy one, too.

M: Yeah, I just moved in last week. It's the first time I managed to save up for such a big purchase. I used a budgeting software online, which really helped me.

W: Oh, really?

M: Yes. It's called SimpleBudget.com. You should use it to help you save for your new place.

W: Hmm… But how much does it cost? I'm trying to save money, not spend it!

M: Well, you can use it for free for a month. After that, it costs 20 dollars a year.

W: That seems reasonable. I'll check it out. Thanks for the advice.

50-52번은 다음 대화에 관한 문제입니다.

M: Hello, Ms. Simms? This is Vincent Rossi. Did you get a chance to look at the initial design that I drafted for your store's newspaper ad?

W: Yes, I did, Vincent. I'm quite impressed with the design. I think using a photo of my gift shop instead of just the logo makes it look much more appealing.

M: It's good to hear that you like it. What do you think about the layout of the text? Would you prefer it to be in the center rather than on the left side?

W: Oh, yes, that's a good idea. I think doing that would make the whole ad more eye-catching.

53-55번은 다음 대화에 관한 문제입니다.

W: Good morning. My name's Gemma Peterson. I'm a customer service agent at Inter Bank. I'm calling about the message you left regarding your credit card.

M: Oh, yes. Thanks for returning my call. I recently got a credit card with your bank, but I didn't receive any instructions on how to view my account online. I'd like to be able to see the transactions that I make with my card.

W: All our credit card accounts can be viewed online, but you'll need to go to an Inter Bank branch to sign up for the service in person.

M: I see. There is a branch right across the street from my office, so I'll drop by at lunchtime. Thanks for your help.

56-58번은 세 화자의 대화에 관한 문제입니다.

W1: Hello, my coworker and I are here about the announcement you just made. You need passengers willing to take the evening train to London, right?

M: That's correct. The next departing train has been overbooked. If you are OK with leaving at 8 P.M. tonight, I can offer both of you a half-price voucher.

W1: Hmm… Our presentation is tomorrow afternoon, so I guess it doesn't really matter. How about it, Sue?

W2: I have no problem with that. Why don't we grab some food in the mean time?

W1: That sounds good. Let's try that diner near the waiting area. I've heard great things about the dishes there.

59-61번은 다음 대화에 관한 문제입니다.

W: Laszlo, I've been searching for a suitable venue for our department's annual summer celebration, and I've found an affordable option: the Waterview Loft. I just need to find a caterer. Do you have any ideas?

M: Well, since we're looking to reduce costs, maybe we should hold the event without a catering service this year. Couldn't we just set up a barbecue ourselves and ask everyone to bring their favorite meats and side dishes?

W: That would certainly lower the cost. We should probably check first that people are willing to bring their own food.

M: Yes, I agree. Let's mention it at the weekly meeting tomorrow morning and see what kind of reaction we get.

62-64번은 다음 대화와 건물 안내도에 관한 문제입니다.

M: Hi, I'm here for my dental check-up at 11 A.M. I parked in the lot right in front of the building, but this ticket doesn't indicate how much parking is.

W: Guests can park there for free for two hours, but we start charging $1.00 for every 30 minutes after that.

M: OK. Oh, and this is the first time I'm seeing Dr. Hurley in this building. Can you direct me to his office?

W: Sure. Dr. Hurley moved here several days ago, so we didn't get a chance to revise the directory. He's located in Suite 205.

Stumerick Building Directory	
Business	Suite #
Haxwell Eyewear	105
Stuvesant Associates	107
Maycare Health Clinic	202
Ranz Publishing	205

신유형 65-67번은 다음 대화와 사업 계획서에 관한 문제입니다. 미국 ⇄ 호주

W: Hello, Joe. How's the landscaping project coming along?

M: It's going well. It's a big job, but we're making good progress. I think you're going to be very pleased with the results.

W: That's good to hear. When do you think the work will be completed? I'd like to have the property on the market before autumn.

M: Let me take a look at the project plan. We've just finished the soil preparation, and we'll be moving on to planting next week. So we're on schedule to have everything done by the end of August.

W: Great! When you can, could you send me an estimate of how much will be spent on the project in total? I'll take the cost into account when deciding on the asking price for my home.

Project Plan	
Stage 1	Construct porch, decks, and patio
Stage 2	Prepare soil
Stage 3	Plant trees and flowers
Stage 4	Repave driveway

신유형 68-70번은 다음 대화와 청구서에 관한 문제입니다. 영국 ⇄ 호주

W: OK, so you're getting a new phone and upgrading your service plan. Is there anything else I can help you with today?

M: Actually, I have a question before I pay. Will I be able to check my phone bills online? I work overseas a lot, so I'm often not at home when the bill arrives.

W: Of course. You just need to go to our Web site and set up an account. There's also a mobile application that you can download to check your account status whenever you like.

M: I'll definitely use that. Hmm… I know I agreed to the extended warranty, but on second thought, I won't need it. Could you take that off my bill please?

W: No problem.

PRODUCT	COST
Mobile phone	$280
Extended warranty	$68
Monthly global roaming plan	$30
Leather case	$25
Total	$403

PART 4 P. 97

71-73번은 다음 담화에 관한 문제입니다. 미국

W: Welcome to *Financial Matters* here on KGW Radio. With us in the studio today is Professor Martin Murray, an expert in microeconomics from Southshore University. His recent book, *The Cost of Everything*, has quickly become a bestseller. This morning, Professor Murray will be giving us some important tips on how to handle your personal finances. We'll be taking calls throughout the show, so we invite you to call in with questions for the professor. The number is 555-7812.

74-76번은 다음 회의 발췌문에 관한 문제입니다. 영국

W: During this month, we are going to change the way employees access the office building. You won't have to type in a number code on the keypad in front of the main door anymore. Instead, all employees will be given a photo ID card that you can swipe through an electronic card reader to enter the building. Before this transition occurs, all of our staff members must stop by the security office to get their pictures taken. To speed up the process, I have sent all of you an e-mail with the assigned time slot for each person. If you can't make it to your appointment due to your work schedule, please let me know right away.

77-79번은 다음 공지에 관한 문제입니다.

M: Good morning. Thank you for joining us here at Manheim Employment Solutions. We recruit staff for companies, ranging from publishing firms to clothing retailers. Today, we have representatives from various industries to meet with you one-on-one and provide you with professional advice. But as there are so many of you here today, you might have to wait a bit. While you're waiting, you should consider taking advantage of our résumé review service, available at the desk in the lobby.

80-82번은 다음 전화 메시지에 관한 문제입니다.

W: Hi, this is a message for Daniel Henderson. My name is Patricia, and I'm calling from the Radcliffe Charity Group. Thank you for your interest in volunteering to help with our fundraising event next month. We actually already have enough volunteers signed up, but we'll keep your information on file so that we can get in touch with you when we need volunteers in the future. Also, I suggest going to our Web site and completing an online application form to volunteer with us. By doing so, you'll receive e-mails notifying you about all of our upcoming events. Thank you again, and we hope to work with you soon.

83-85번은 다음 녹음 메시지에 관한 문제입니다.

M: Hello, you've reached Carlos' Diner. We are currently closed for renovations and will reopen on May 20 with a new menu and a bigger dining area. In addition to our popular selection of burritos, tacos, and nachos that our customers have always enjoyed, we will now be offering a deluxe choice of coffees. If you'd like to reserve a table for our grand reopening day on May 20, visit our Web site at www.carlosdiner.com. And don't forget to print out a complimentary dessert coupon while you're there!

86-88번은 다음 담화에 관한 문제입니다.

W: OK, before we get started today, I've got some news to share. Demand for our custom-built motorcycles has increased, but some buyers have expressed dissatisfaction. Six weeks is quite a while to receive an order. That's why I've decided to hire more mechanics, all with plenty of experience. They'll be joining us later this week, and this should really cut down the time we need to fill customer orders. Another thing slowing us down has been old equipment, so I'm going to begin upgrading our tools. Today, I picked up a welding machine. Can I get someone to help move it from my truck to our factory floor?

89-91번은 다음 담화에 관한 문제입니다.

W: Thank you for attending today's meeting of the Wollaston City Community Group. We're in the planning process of building a playground in the city center, but we are still in need of additional funding. As you know, the land for the playground was donated by the local government, and the blueprints were drawn up free of charge by local architects. But we haven't yet raised enough money to buy all of the necessary equipment. I'd like to ask you all to spend some time this week calling owners of local stores to see if they would be willing to assist us.

92-94번은 다음 전화 메시지에 관한 문제입니다.

M: Hello, it's Leo Goodwin. I just got word on a studio apartment vacancy that we haven't listed in our ads yet. I think this one really matches your needs. It's right by the subway station, as you had hoped. The one issue I should mention is that it's not as spacious as you wanted, but that also means the rent is well below the amount you were willing to pay. If you're OK with downsizing a little, this could be ideal. Anyway, please contact me immediately if you want to check it out. I can hold off on listing it until this afternoon, but I can't wait any longer than that, and this one will go quickly.

신유형 95-97번은 다음 공지와 시간표에 관한 문제입니다. 호주

M: Attention all passengers. We are sorry to announce that due to strong winds, the 4:00 P.M. ferry to Georgetown Port has been canceled. Since the wind is forecast to decrease later today, we do expect to be able to run the last scheduled departure to Georgetown Port. As demand for this last service will be higher than usual, we will use a larger ferry to accommodate the greater number of passengers. Please note that the larger ferry is an older boat that has outdoor seating on its upper deck, so passengers are advised to wear a thick sweater or a heavy coat. Thank you.

Georgetown Port Ferry	
Departure	Arrival
7:45 A.M.	8:30 A.M.
11:30 A.M.	12:15 P.M.
4:00 P.M.	4:45 P.M.
8:00 P.M.	8:45 P.M.

신유형 98-100번은 다음 담화와 도표에 관한 문제입니다. 영국

W: Welcome to this week's class on marketing your own business. We're going to talk about designing a letterhead that looks appealing. This is the first thing clients see, so you need to grab their attention straight away. Let's look at the first slide. We'll review every part in detail, but first, let's look at the part that says, "Happily Clean in Moments." This will give customers a better understanding of your business. OK, now, it's your turn to come up with some creative messages that suit your company. There are some paper and pencils in the folder on your desk.

TEST 07

PART 1
P. 102

1 한 사람

(A) A plant is being watered.
(B) A lamp is being turned on.
(C) The woman is typing on a computer.
(D) The woman's arms are resting on a desk.

2 두 사람 이상

(A) The woman is holding a map.
(B) They're climbing some rocks.
(C) The man is taking items out of a backpack.
(D) They're cycling along a trail.

3 한 사람

(A) Some plates have been placed on a table.
(B) The man is hanging some frames on the wall.
(C) A rug has been laid on the floor.
(D) The man is arranging cushions on a couch.

4 사물/풍경

(A) Some stools are lined up on the floor.
(B) A potted plant is hanging from the ceiling.
(C) The shelves are being stocked with books.
(D) The drawers behind the desk are closed.

5 두 사람 이상

(A) A woman is talking in front of an audience.
(B) A man is closing a laptop.
(C) Some handouts are being distributed.
(D) People are arranging some chairs in a row.

6 한 사람

(A) A sink is being repaired.
(B) Some tools are stacked on a counter.
(C) Some equipment is being taken out of a bag.
(D) Water is flowing from a faucet.

PART 2   P. 106

7 Where 의문문

Where's the workshop taking place?
(A) Training for new employees.
(B) I didn't know you were interested in coming.
(C) Friday afternoon.

8 Who 의문문

Who's leading the Paterson project?
(A) By February 15th, at the latest.
(B) I'm in charge of that.
(C) Yes, I agree.

9 부가 의문문

You do know how to use this equipment, right?
(A) Between 3 and 5 o'clock.
(B) I should, after all the training.
(C) An electrical engineer.

10 When 의문문

When did the company decide to hire a new lawyer?
(A) In the Legal Department.
(B) After the merger was announced.
(C) Yes, he might do that.

11 제안/청유문

Can you take me to the new dining lounge?
(A) It's a new menu.
(B) Robert knows where it is.
(C) The daily dinner special.

12 부정 의문문

Won't you need a camera?
(A) Some old photos.
(B) Yes, can I borrow one?
(C) The media room on the 5th floor.

13 When 의문문

When do you want this book back?
(A) I'll order some more tomorrow.
(B) Sometime before Thursday.
(C) There's a library across the street.

14 부정 의문문

Don't we need a security card to enter the office?
(A) Yes, but I forgot to bring mine.
(B) Just outside the main entrance.
(C) She's at the post office.

15 Be 의문문

Are there any deliveries for me today?
(A) I don't think it was deliberate.
(B) Hold on, I'll check for you.
(C) The river is near here.

16 How 의문문

How do I join your fitness center?
(A) All the information is in this brochure.
(B) Seventy dollars per exercise program.
(C) No, I don't have a credit card.

17 부정 의문문

Wasn't Bill going to join us for dinner?
(A) They really enjoyed it.
(B) Yes, let me check if he's ready.
(C) To sign up for a membership.

18 Do 의문문

Do you think the revised manual provides clearer instructions?
(A) OK, I'll clear the table now.
(B) For health and safety reasons.
(C) I would have included more graphs.

19 How 의문문

How did the workshop coordinator decide on the topic for the session?
(A) She received feedback from the managers.
(B) Please pick up your badge.
(C) After the discussion.

20 부가 의문문

You can't fax me the budget proposal before 1, can you?
(A) The new fax machine has been ordered.
(B) It should be prepared by then.
(C) She proposed the idea.

21 Why 의문문

Why was the speaker from Toronto late to the conference?
(A) I attended it last month.
(B) No, it was a sales conference.
(C) Probably because of traffic.

22 Be 의문문

Are you flying out to Osaka early next week?
(A) A free upgrade to business class.
(B) Actually, I'm leaving at the end of the month.
(C) I prefer a direct flight.

23 평서문

I'll be away on business next Monday.
(A) Yes, leave the door open.
(B) Then I'll attend the sales meeting in your place.
(C) One block away from our office.

24 Who 의문문

Who's seen the latest copy of the budget report?
(A) Around 80 pages.
(B) Have you checked the group folder?
(C) Sometime this week.

25 What 의문문

What is the warranty period on this laptop?
(A) Six months, but it can be extended.
(B) To repair the screen.
(C) With an extra battery.

26 Be 의문문

Is the rental car out of gasoline?
(A) The contract was received on Tuesday.
(B) A new customer.
(C) No, John just filled it.

27 평서문

We'll be extending the store's hours today for the holiday promotion.
(A) They're not on sale.
(B) She works for an advertising agency.
(C) Alright, I'll place a sign near the entrance.

28 Why 의문문

Why aren't we allowed to use the staff kitchen?
(A) Do you think it's too loud?
(B) They're replacing the floor tiles.
(C) In the sink, please.

29 What 의문문

What's the enrollment fee at the design school on Staad Avenue?
(A) The store's located on Parkview Road.
(B) Two thousand dollars per quarter.
(C) They were recently renovated.

30 Be 의문문

Is the road still blocked?
(A) It's about five kilometers away.
(B) Yes, the item also comes in black.
(C) No, the parade is now over.

31 평서문

I'm no longer interested in subscribing to your magazine.
(A) Probably on the front cover.
(B) On the 25th of every month.
(C) We'll remove you from our list.

PART 3

P. 107

32-34번은 다음 대화에 관한 문제입니다.

M: Hi, I saw your summer sale ad online this morning, so I thought I'd drop by during my lunch break. Is every item in the store included in the sale?

W: Yes, the sale applies to everything you see in the store. The discounts range from 20 to 60 percent. Did you download the voucher from the advertisement? You'll need to have it printed out to receive the discounts.

M: Oh, I didn't know that. I'll have to do that at my office and stop by here again after work.

35-37번은 다음 대화에 관한 문제입니다.

M: Good morning, Ms. Peterson. I have some more items that need to be dry cleaned. I spilled some food on this tie last night, and I was hoping you'd be able to remove the stain.

W: That's no problem. I'm sure we'll be able to get the stain out. I'll add the tie to your order, and it'll be ready this Friday afternoon with the rest of your items.

M: Actually, I was planning to wear the tie for a conference speech I'm giving this Wednesday morning. Could I possibly get it back before then?

W: In that case, I'll do your tie first, and it'll be ready to collect tomorrow afternoon.

38-40번은 다음 대화에 관한 문제입니다.

M: Hello, I'm calling regarding the annual Technology Convention next month. I'm trying to submit an online form for a booth, but I keep getting an error message. Is there another way to reserve one?

W: So sorry about that. Our Web site hasn't been working quite right recently. Why don't I book it for you over the phone now? Will this be your first time at the convention?

M: Actually, my company had a display space last year. If possible, I'd like to be placed in the same area again.

W: All right, I can help with that. If you give me your company name, I can pull up your file and check if we have an available space.

신유형 41-43번은 다음 대화에 관한 문제입니다.

M: Hello, Janet. I see here on the schedule that you've got me working at the front desk all weekend. But the thing is… I came out last Saturday and Sunday as well. So… I was wondering if I could get this weekend off.

W: Hmm… I don't know. As you're aware, we're short on staff right now. And I was hoping that you could train some new workers this week because they don't have any experience taking calls and handling room reservations. After their training is done, I can give you some time off.

M: OK. Let's hope they learn quickly!

44-46번은 다음 대화에 관한 문제입니다.

M: Hello, Jeanine. The technician who normally does repair work for Pacific Associates just called in sick. Is there any way you could cover her 3 o'clock appointment for her today?

W: Not a problem. But I've never been to their office before, so you'll have to give me directions. What's the quickest way of getting there from here?

M: It's best to take Highway 56 to the coast, and then go south on Highway 5. When you get there, remember to get the client to sign a copy of the invoice.

47-49번은 다음 대화에 관한 문제입니다.

W: Good morning. This is Monica Galdon. I'd like to book a physical therapy session for tomorrow morning. Carmelo is my therapist.

M: OK, let's see… Mmm, unfortunately, according to the schedule, Carmelo is fully booked tomorrow. If you want, you can see him on Thursday. Or we could fit you in with Jessica at 3:00 P.M. tomorrow.

W: Well, my foot really needs attention, so I'll just go with Jessica this time. Is she as experienced as Carmelo? I'm going to be walking quite a bit during a nature tour on Thursday, so I really need the best treatment.

M: Actually, Jessica is our most experienced therapist. She's been with us for over 15 years now. If you want, I can ask her to give you a call so that you can tell her about any concerns you may have.

신유형 50-52번은 다음 세 화자의 대화에 관한 문제입니다.

M: Hello, I'm Michael Rogers. I spoke to you earlier today on the phone. I asked for a copy of my optical prescription because I'm moving overseas in a few weeks. I'm here to pick it up.

W1: Ah, yes, I remember. Could you tell me who your optician is?

M: It's Dr. Spinelli.

W1: OK, let me check to see if my colleague, Paula, already dealt with this. Just a moment, please. Paula?

W2: Yes?

W1: Did you print out Mr. Rogers' prescription?

W2: Yes, it's right here. Mr. Rogers. Could I just get you to sign this request form? It's for our record purposes.

M: Sure.

신유형 53-55번은 다음 대화에 관한 문제입니다.

M: Angela, check out this handbag! It's exactly your style.

W: Actually, I bought one last month. It's made by hand in Italy from high-quality leather. When I first saw it, I couldn't resist getting it!

M: Hmm… I bet my personal assistant at work would love one. It'll be her birthday soon, and I've been looking for a gift for her. But the only thing is… payday is still weeks away.

W: Would you like to borrow some money? You can pay me back later.

M: Oh, that'd be great, thanks! Which color did you get? I don't remember ever seeing you with the bag.

W: It's blue. My mom really liked it, so I just let her have it.

56-58번은 다음 대화에 관한 문제입니다.

M: I appreciate you coming over so promptly, Ms. Andrews. As you can see, the new brick walkway between our office buildings is perfectly flat and looks great. But, behind the building… right here; your employees still haven't finished. The path is marked, but the bricks are just here in a pile.

W: Ah… You're right. The crew was supposed to finish this on Sunday, but the unexpected snowfall set their schedule back.

M: I understand. When is the earliest that you can come back and resolve this?

W: Well, now that I'm aware of the issue, I'll move you to the top of tomorrow's schedule now. Everything should be completed by late afternoon tomorrow.

59-61번은 다음 대화에 관한 문제입니다.

W: Hi, I'm organizing a community meeting for Allenheimer Construction. Does your library have any vacant large rooms on December 2?

M: Before I check our system, can you tell me approximately how many guests will be coming? I want to make sure I find the most suitable room.

W: Of course. We're expecting around 80 people. Also, we will need a projector and a podium set up on the day of the event.

M: Alright, then I would recommend either the Reynold Room or the Stanley Room. Both are quite spacious and have all the features you want. You can find complete details about them on our home page. Let me give you the link, so you can look through them.

62-64번은 다음 대화와 회의실 일정표에 관한 문제입니다.

M: Ms. Perez, I just got off the phone with the vice president of Lamar Productions. They're looking for a new financial company to manage their expenses, so he wants to come see us on Monday morning at 10 to learn about our accounting services.

W: That's great! Lamar Productions has a lot of offices, and they would be our largest client. Please reserve the large conference room on the 20th floor for that meeting. It has the best facilities.

M: Hmm… It looks like that room has already been reserved at 10.

W: Mmm… Let me see… Oh, I see that Alexandra's the one who booked it. I think she'll be OK with using the small room instead since only three people are attending her meeting.

M: Probably. I'll send her a text now and see if she would be fine with the switch.

20F Large Conference Room [Monday]	
9:00 A.M.	Quarterly financial review
10:00 A.M.	Sales planning
11:00 A.M.	New product education
12:00 P.M.	Employee safety training

65-67번은 다음의 대화와 평가에 대한 문제입니다.

M: Hi, Francesca, did you see the latest issue of *Asian and Fusion Magazine* with its ratings of the top Chinese restaurants in town? They gave us 5 out of 5 for the quality of our food. You have done a great job as head chef!

W: Thanks, Huang! I'm so glad we decided to send the cooks for training in Beijing last year. We were really able to impress the customers with more authentic dishes.

M: I agree, but I wish we had done a lot better in some of the other categories. I mean, we can't do much about our location at the moment, but there's really no excuse for getting just a two on this one. We've got to find a way to fix this.

W: Why don't we hand out questionnaires to our diners? They may have some ideas our own staff never thought of.

Review of Haochi Chinese Grill

Food quality: 5
Table service: 3
Restaurant location: 1
Interior layout: 2

68-70번은 다음 대화와 전광판에 관한 문제입니다.

W: Franco. I'm surprised you don't have more luggage. The conference lasts for a week, but you only have that small suitcase.

M: That's because I won't be staying for the whole conference. I have an important meeting back at the office on Thursday, so I'll be flying back on Wednesday afternoon.

W: Oh, I didn't know that. Anyway, we'd better head over to the departure gate. Do you know which gate our flight leaves from?

M: Hmm… Let's see. My boarding pass says Gate C19. Oh, it's up on the departure board now. It looks like the flight's on time. Let's grab a coffee on our way over to the gate.

Destination	Gate	Time	Status
Detroit	A21	13:25	Canceled
Seattle	C19	13:45	On time
Pittsburgh	B16	13:55	On time
Los Angeles	C23	14:00	Delayed

PART 4

P. 111

71-73번은 다음 광고에 관한 문제입니다.

W: Having trouble getting rid of an old laptop, cell phone, or other electronic devices? Then your solution is Techno Depot. We collect and recycle your used electronics. Also, when you drop off your device, we will give you a discount voucher that can be used at our store. To find out how to get to Techno Depot, please check our Web site at www.technodepot.com.

74-76번은 다음 공지에 관한 문제입니다.

M: Attention all assembly line personnel. Several of our machines have broken down. Until the issue is resolved, the assembly line will be closed. All assembly line workers should report to their supervisor for temporary reassignment. Should any schedule changes be required for tomorrow's shift, you will be informed by your supervisor by text message this evening.

77-79번은 다음 회의 발췌문에 관한 문제입니다.

W: Lastly today, I have some great news for you. As you know, we began this year aiming for a 15 percent increase in sales of our Do It Yourself home improvement products. Well, today I am thrilled to tell you that we have met that goal this year, thanks to our targeting of customers on the East Coast. Now, as a result of our company's newfound success on the East Coast, we'll be looking to expand our business there even further. As a result, we'll be opening a new regional branch office in New Jersey in the next quarter. That means that we'll have a new job available: Managing Director of the East Coast Region. Ideally, we would like to hire for this position from within our existing pool of supervisors. So if you're interested in relocating east, and if you'd like the challenge of establishing our brand in a new region, why not give it a try? The closing date for applications will be June 28.

80-82번은 다음 담화에 관한 문제입니다.

M: It is my pleasure to announce this year's winner of the Best Global Advertisement Award, Mazak Advertising. The firm was selected for its creative ad campaign for Probert Motor's new hybrid automobile. Their ads effectively show how the hybrid cars emit only half as many pollutants as regular cars, and therefore, cause less damage to the environment. Mazak Advertising plans on donating a portion of the profits from the advertisements to a local organization dedicated to preserving clean air. I want to congratulate all of the employees of Mazak Advertising for their dedication and innovation.

83-85번은 다음 전화 메시지에 관한 문제입니다.

W: Hi, my name is Wanda Lakes. I own a beauty salon on Ferris Avenue, and I would like to have the salon redecorated. I got your contact information from a business acquaintance of mine, and he also showed me the work your designers did on his boutique last month. I was hoping you could do the same for my place. My main concern is that my salon is quite small, so I want to make the inside look more spacious. I was thinking of using a lighter paint color. Anyway, if you decide to accept this project, please contact me at 555-4923 so that I can set up a convenient time for you to visit the salon.

신유형 86-88번은 다음 회의 발췌록에 관한 문제입니다. 영국

W: Welcome to today's meeting. I'd like to go over some customer feedback on our new audio player, the N22. Among the product's many features, customers named the removable battery as the most important because it can easily be replaced when its power runs out. Anyway, since we've added so many additional features, the online demo video is now 30 minutes long. But our production team is going to shorten it.

89-91번은 다음 라디오 광고에 관련된 문제입니다. 호주

M: Are you looking to work part-time during the winter? Bondra Limited, the country's number one packaging company, is recruiting delivery workers for several branches in the southern Langway area. This is an ideal position for local students and those looking for temporary work. No prior delivery experience is required. You will be trained by us in all shipping and delivery procedures required for the position. Please come to the Bondra Limited office at 397 Middleton Road to apply.

신유형 92-94번은 다음 전화 메시지에 관한 문제입니다. 미국

M: Hello, Mr. Miyashita. This is Eric Gruber. I was a temporary programmer at your firm for the recent winter season. The reason for my call is I still haven't received the check for my last month of work. After my contract with your company ended, I terminated my apartment lease there and moved back to my hometown, Little Rock. So I'm guessing you might have sent the payment to my previous address. I'm searching for a job now, and I need to pay my bills. Please call me at 555-4788. Thanks.

신유형 95-97번은 다음 공지와 평면도에 관한 문제입니다. 미국

W: So that brings us to the end of our tour of the statues exhibit. We have a book about the exhibit in the bookstore on the first floor. It's an excellent purchase if you'd like to learn more about the statues we've seen during the tour. I'll leave you now to explore the rest of the museum on your own. You'll find a map of the museum on the wall over there. I highly recommend visiting the Chinese jewelry exhibit in our special exhibits gallery. That's the one right next to the coffee shop. This is actually the last day you can see this exhibit.

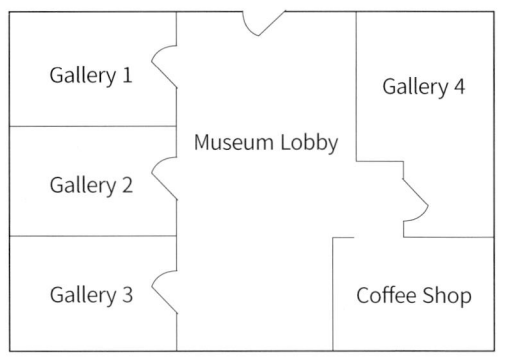

신유형 98-100번은 다음 회의 발췌록과 설문조사에 관한 문제입니다. 호주

M: Now we've reached the final item on today's agenda: the results of our customer survey. The survey was carried out at all our stores during the last three months. Since satisfying our shoppers is our company's primary goal, the survey results provide us with some very important insights. Let's take a look at the top four responses to the survey question, "What can we do to make our store better?" As you can see, most would like us to give them larger discounts. Unfortunately, we are already doing the best we can in this area. We can, however, do something about the second-most-requested change. We can either take on a couple of new employees or give extra hours to existing staff members. Please let me know if any of you would be interested.

Survey Responses

Bigger discounts – 38%
Fresher fruits and vegetables – 18%
More foreign foods – 17%
Longer Sunday hours – 27%

TEST 08

PART 1

P. 116

1 한 사람

(A) She's walking along a rocky path.
(B) She's wearing a backpack.
(C) She's tying her shoelaces.
(D) She's taking out a water bottle.

2 한 사람

(A) The man is washing some windows.
(B) Poles are being installed inside a building.
(C) Potted plants are being placed on the floor.
(D) The man is sitting on a vehicle.

3 사물/풍경

(A) A boat is sailing on a lake.
(B) The walls of a home are being painted.
(C) Some buildings overlook the water.
(D) Lampposts line both sides of a staircase.

4 두 사람 이상

(A) The men are shaking hands.
(B) The men are assembling a desk.
(C) One of the men is writing on a document.
(D) One of the men is handing a folder to his coworker.

5 두 사람 이상

(A) Some furniture is being rearranged.
(B) The walls have been covered with curtains.
(C) Workstations have been set up in an office.
(D) Some windows are being cleaned.

6 두 사람 이상

(A) A woman is paying for some jewelry.
(B) A vendor is stacking some items on a table.
(C) Hats are being hung on a line.
(D) Some merchandise is being displayed.

PART 2

P. 120

7 제안/청유문

Could you locate the McPherson file for me?
(A) It's important to save your documents regularly.
(B) I like the blue filing cabinet.
(C) Who was the last person to use it?

8 Who 의문문

Who can I contact for a cost estimate on garden renovations?
(A) It was very costly.
(B) Samwell Landscaping is recommended.
(C) About a year ago.

9 When 의문문

When will the Stanson Hotel on Arrow Street be built?
(A) In room 310.
(B) Yes, the amenities were nice.
(C) The project will start next week.

10 Do 의문문

Did the Audit Committee accept the recommendation we made?
(A) In the meeting agenda.
(B) A letter of recommendation.
(C) They should let us know by Friday.

11 What 의문문

What does the manager think about the new project?
(A) I need it for my presentation.
(B) From September to November.
(C) He's quite interested in it.

12 Who 의문문

Who needs to know about the new shipment arriving on Tuesday?
(A) Mark, the warehouse manager.
(B) Yes, I started the job today.
(C) It's from China.

13 Where 의문문

Where do I hand in my application?
(A) That's indicated on the second page.
(B) A potential candidate.
(C) On March 10th.

14 How 의문문

How long will this promotion last?
(A) About five miles.
(B) No, the first one.
(C) Throughout this entire week.

15 Do 의문문

Did you speak with the new publishing director?
(A) The directions are clear.
(B) Yes, the other day.
(C) Our online magazine.

16 Why 의문문

Why are so many rooms booked?
(A) On the top floor of the hotel.
(B) If there's enough room for our group.
(C) There's a big conference this week.

17 평서문

The main door to the office is locked.
(A) I'll call the building manager.
(B) Room 101, on the first floor.
(C) Close it when you leave.

18 선택 의문문

Do you want to discuss your proposal here or in the meeting room?
(A) No, I didn't see them.
(B) He proposed it yesterday.
(C) Why don't we do it here?

19 부정 의문문

Don't you usually get off work by six?
(A) I get off at the next stop.
(B) I don't have any more time now.
(C) Yes, but I have to finish something today.

20 Be 의문문

Is this fruit juice fresh?
(A) At the new grocery store.
(B) I need some fresh air.
(C) Check the date on the container.

21 How 의문문

How often does your supermarket offer specials on meats?
(A) Usually twice a week.
(B) Let's meet on Friday.
(C) The shuttle bus runs every 15 minutes.

22 제안/청유문

Could I get your e-mail address?
(A) Yes, it's been sent.
(B) Sure, no problem.
(C) I'd rather drive.

23 부정 의문문

Doesn't Brian normally start at 9?
(A) A list of office supplies.
(B) Yes, but he's taking the morning off.
(C) I'm afraid he's got none.

24 간접 의문문

Can you tell me where the copy room is?
(A) Yes, you can copy mine.
(B) No, I don't have any.
(C) There's one next to the lounge.

25 평서문

I think you might be in my seat.
(A) Oh, you're right. Sorry about that.
(B) An online reservation.
(C) Tickets for the balcony area.

26 What 의문문

What did Mr. Hayes think about the survey results?
(A) During the discussion.
(B) He said they were informative.
(C) At least 300 questionnaires.

27 How 의문문

How many employees attended the sales workshop at the head office?
(A) There's a sale this week.
(B) Around 50.
(C) He's an experienced trainer.

28 부가 의문문

I was impressed by the presentation given by Professor Jones yesterday, weren't you?
(A) Yes, let's have him speak again next time.
(B) I printed out all the slides.
(C) I'm planning to finish it by tonight.

29 평서문

I wonder if the new appliance store is open yet.
(A) I just bought a heater there.
(B) Next to the shopping center.
(C) It was very interesting.

30 선택 의문문

Would it be cheaper to use a mobile phone or a landline?
(A) Use this cord here.
(B) Where will you be calling?
(C) You need to recharge it.

31 부가 의문문

You said you'd finish the marketing proposal by this Thursday, didn't you?
(A) The stationery is in the storage room.
(B) I did, but I'll need one more day.
(C) No, it wasn't advertised.

PART 3

32-34번은 다음 대화에 관한 문제입니다.

W: I'm happy to see that your shop has Pro-Maker's new food steamer. I've been looking everywhere for it.
M: Yes, a lot of professional cooks say it's the best!
W: What sizes does it come in?
M: Small, medium, and large. But as so many people have been looking for this item, we don't have all three in stock at the moment.
W: Hmm, which sizes are available then?
M: Well, we're out of the large ones at the moment, but our next shipment will come in next week.
W: Actually, I just need a small one.
M: Great! If you come with me to the cash register, I'll ring you up. I'm sure you'll enjoy using this product!

35-37번은 다음 대화에 관한 문제입니다.

W: Good afternoon. I'd like some information on transporting equipment from Chicago to Philadelphia. My company needs to transport 4 photocopiers, 10 printers, and 20 computers to our new branch in Philadelphia.

M: Of course. Our business specializes in moving office property. When do these items need to arrive?

W: Well, several clients are coming to tour our new facility in two weeks, so we need everything before the 15th. Can you give me a rough estimate of how much it will cost?

M: Well, before I can do that, I would need to know the exact length and width of every item. If you could, please send an e-mail with that information to lmont@mztransporters.com.

38-40번은 다음 대화에 관한 문제입니다.

M: Hello, Ms. Terrence, this is Jake Harwood calling from Lee Valley Tires. We were pleased to meet you at the interview, and we'd like to offer you the junior accountant position.

W: That's wonderful! I'm so glad to hear that. But I'm a little concerned about getting to work. There are no public transportation options that I know of, and I don't have a car.

M: Actually, you don't have to worry about that. We provide a shuttle service for our employees from Kipling Train Station, which is nearby our office. I'll send you the details about the shuttle with the offer letter.

41-43번은 다음 대화에 관한 문제입니다.

W: Harry, I've got some great news. Jim Hawthorne, the tax consultant, just told me that he can hold a workshop for our firm's employees on the third week of this month.

M: That's good to hear. I understand that many companies want him as a consultant, so I'm happy that we were able to book him. Now, we must verify the number of individuals planning on attending so that we can make sure our room is large enough to accommodate everyone.

W: I'll handle that. I'll email all of the department managers and ask them to let me know how many people will be going to the workshop.

44-46번은 다음 대화에 관한 문제입니다.

M: Excuse me. Could you help me? There is a pair of pants in the display window, and I'd like to know how much it is.

W: Of course. Which pair are you talking about?

M: The jeans right over here. I really like them. But I don't know what the price is.

W: Let me take a look to see if there is a tag on it.

M: Umm… I don't think there is one.

W: OK. Then, I'll need to look it up in our database. Please wait a moment.

신유형 47-49번은 다음 세 화자의 대화에 관한 문제입니다.

M: Sherry, Jane, I'd like to know if you two are almost finished transferring our students' records to the new database.

W1: We're nearly done. Most of the files for the students have been created, and Jane is finalizing the course registration system.

W2: That's correct. I'm updating it so that this system is connected to our students' records.

M: Perfect. Hopefully, everything will be completed by next week. By the way, what do you think about holding a staff training session regarding the new system?

W1: I think that's a great idea.

50-52번은 다음 대화에 관한 문제입니다.

M: Viviana, since our company has been getting a lot more clients lately, I think we should consider having our own accountant.

W: I agree. We just don't have any time for bookkeeping tasks. But do we have the budget to recruit a full-time bookkeeper?

M: Well, one of my friends also runs his own business, and he uses an outside firm whenever they need someone to take care of their accounting. A consultant comes to his company to do the bookkeeping, and he only pays for the services received. Why don't we give this a try?

W: That sounds like a great idea. Can you get the consulting firm's name and phone number from your friend? I'd like to call them and get more details about their services.

53-55번은 다음 대화에 관련된 문제입니다.

M: Hey, Candice. I've tried to log in to the company system several times, but I keep getting the same error message. Are you having similar issues?

W: No, I signed in with no problems. The tech team made some modifications to our server yesterday evening, so maybe the update is why you're having trouble.

M: Then I'll have to talk to one of the tech people. Do you know who I'm supposed to contact?

W: I'm not sure, but all you have to do is submit an online work request form. Why don't I do that for you from here?

56-58번은 다음 세 화자의 대화에 관한 문제입니다.

M: Alright. So we're going to include a section about historic sites in the next month's issue of our magazine. Would either of you like to take on this project?

W1: I'd be interested. I actually wanted to do a piece on the Rogan Gallery ever since it was remodeled in April.

M: Thank you, Jill. Please arrange a meeting with the curator there.

W1: OK. Maya, would you be able to accompany me and take some pictures?

W2: Yes. I was already planning on visiting the gallery, so this works out perfectly.

W1: Great. I'll reserve a meeting room tomorrow, so we can go over the details.

59-61번은 다음 대화에 관한 문제입니다.

M: I'm confident that the executives at Liou, Inc. will be satisfied with the new headquarters we're designing for them. I admit it took a while to finalize the plans for the building, but the design turned out really well.

W: Yeah, and the whole place will be energy-efficient, which is exactly what the executives want.

M: Right. I'm glad that we were able to get this done on time.

W: Same here. By the way, you know I'm in the city orchestra group, right? Well, our final concert is this Friday. Do you think I could leave an hour early that day?

M: Hmm… There will still be more work to finish, but I think Ryan should be able to assist us on Friday.

62-64번은 다음의 대화와 평면도에 대한 문제입니다.

W: Good morning. Welcome to Harrington Bookstore. Can I help you with anything today?

M: Yes, I'd like to get a copy of *The Tiger Biologist's Diary*. I'm in charge of the book club at my school. People say this one is great for generating a lot of questions and discussion.

W: That's a good choice. It made me look at things in a new way. You can find it in the corner next to the lounge. Everything is arranged in alphabetical order. Please let me know if you need further assistance.

M: Thank you for your help.

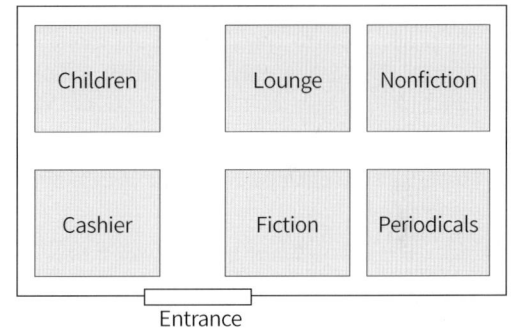

65-67번은 다음 대화와 차트에 관한 문제입니다.

M: Hi, I'd like to find out more about the oriental lily flowers your garden carries. I want to plant them out in front of my company's building. They would really make our property a lot more beautiful. I'm browsing your home page right now.

W: Alright. If you scroll all the way down, you'll see a flower size chart.

M: Hmm… I'm not sure which of the smaller types to choose.

W: Well, Type 1 flowers are planted in pots and usually placed in balconies. Type 2 flowers, on the other hand, are larger and must be planted in the ground.

M: Oh, I don't want any pots. We have plenty of space for flowers around our building. Do you have a delivery service?

W: Yes. And for a small extra fee, we'd also be glad to plant them for you.

Oriental Lily Flowers Size Chart			
Type 1	Type 2	Type 3	Type 4
3 feet tall	4 feet tall	5 feet tall	6 feet tall

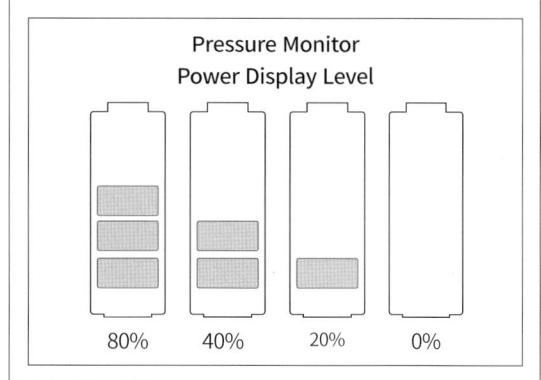

신유형 68-70번은 다음의 대화와 그림에 관한 문제입니다.

M: For your plant technician training today, I'd like to explain how to check a pressure monitor's battery. The device may not properly indicate the tank's pressure level if the battery is too low.

W: Does the pressure monitor come with extra batteries or another power source in case of an emergency?

M: No, we don't have any backups. You'll have to check the battery often; be sure to look at the display.

W: When should I replace the batteries?

M: As you can see in the factory's operating manual, the battery power levels are shown on the display screen. Change the batteries when they reach 20 percent. We must make sure that the pressure monitor always has enough power to work properly.

PART 4

P. 125

71-73번은 다음 날씨 보도에 관한 문제입니다.

W: Now for the weather forecast. All areas of the city will begin to clear today, but a severe weather warning has been issued for late tonight as a major snowstorm will arrive. As a result, heavy delays are expected on all main roads tomorrow morning. Local travelers are advised to take the subway as all lines will be operating on increased schedules for the next few days. According to the Meteorological Department, this weather is expected to end in about a week.

신유형 74-76번은 다음 전화 메시지에 관한 문제입니다.

M: Hello, Jeremy. I wanted to briefly go over the plans for the employee transition as Krista's last day of work is today. At our last meeting, we decided that Lester would take over her job duties. Krista was supposed to teach him how to prepare the monthly financial reports, but there will be a department meeting in the afternoon today. So instead, I will meet with him tomorrow morning and show him how to make the reports myself. Feel free to contact me with any questions you have. See you later.

77-79번은 다음 방송에 관한 문제입니다.

W: Hello, and welcome to today's edition of *Money Matters*. With us in the studio today is a well-known financial advisor, Justin Mills. You have probably heard of his hugely popular monthly newsletter, *Mills on Money*. Justin is here today to talk about something new that he'll be embarking on. Starting next month, he's going to be giving a series of seminars around the country, advising people on how to best manage their personal finances. Attendees will also receive a free one-year subscription to Justin's newsletter. Later in the show, Justin will be taking your questions, so please post yours on our program's Web site, www.moneymatters.tv.

80-82번 문제는 다음 안내에 관한 문제입니다.

W: Hello. My name is Janet, and I'm your instructor for the Introduction to Boxing class. It is possible to hurt your hands during training, so please be sure to wear gloves every time. If you don't have your own, there are some in the cabinet by the entrance. As you know, this is a two-month course. After this introductory course, you should consider joining the intermediate-level class. Space is limited, so tell me if you plan to do so. OK, the first thing you'll do in every class is jump rope. Let's check out this video where some of my advanced students demonstrate the correct technique.

83-85번은 다음 회의 발췌록에 관한 문제입니다.

M: I'm delighted to announce that our company has been nominated for the Global Marketer of the Year Award. This is all due to the effort made by everyone here today. I'd like to bring special attention to the outstanding work done by Raj Singh and his team members. The team's international campaign for Dewson Electronics received high praise from many customers and organizations. As you know, the campaign was the main reason Dewson's sales rose by almost 30 percent. Raj, I'd like to ask you to talk about what made the campaign so successful.

86-88번은 다음 방송에 관한 문제입니다.

W: Hello and welcome to today's health news bulletin on Channel 4. According to a study published in *Wellbeing Magazine*, home cooking is an important factor in living a healthy life. Participants in the study were asked about their dietary habits, and the results showed that those who cooked their own meals at home consumed more fiber and vitamin-rich foods than those who ate pre-prepared meals. The study's lead researcher, John Umunna, urges people to prepare their own meals as much as possible. A complete list of the questions asked in the study can be found on the *Wellbeing Magazine* Web site.

89-91번은 다음 투어 정보에 관한 문제입니다.

M: Alright, everyone, I've stopped the bus because I want to show you something special. The view from this particular spot is absolutely stunning. If you'll look to the left, you can see the beautiful town of Slatington. These days, it's mainly an agricultural town, but it was once an important mining town where coal and a variety of other minerals were bought and sold. Merchants would trade materials here, then use the Lehigh Canal to move them to other parts of the state. Next, we'll stop at the Old Post Inn in Slatington for lunch before continuing our tour.

92-94번은 다음 회의 발췌록에 관한 문제입니다.

M: I appreciate you having me over at your office. We're delighted that you're thinking about hiring us to help recycle your old computers and other office equipment. My firm, Camcomp, Inc., is dedicated to offering electronics recycling services to various businesses. By allowing us to dispose of your electronics in a clean manner, you'll help reduce pollution and conserve natural resources. Many companies are signing up. Now, before I answer any questions, I want to play a video clip of our CEO's speech from when our firm received the Top Environmental Business Award at a convention last fall.

신유형 95-97번은 다음 공지와 일정에 관한 문제입니다. [호주]

M: Ladies and gentlemen, I hope that you have all been enjoying the presentations at this year's conference on jewelry design. Our jewelry organization has gathered several well-known speakers who we believe will interest professional jewelry designers like you. Now, I do need to tell you about one change to today's agenda. Ms. Nadia Wong missed her flight from Osaka, so she won't be able to make it today. That's why Angelito Paraiso from Manila will be taking her place. He'll give a lesson on designing accessories that can be worn both at work and casually. Also, remember to turn in your conference feedback card before you leave. Participants who submit a card will be entered in a raffle to win a free trip to Paris.

Time	Presenter
First presentation	Nadia Wong
Second presentation	Gary Almont
Third presentation	Lewis Walton
Fourth presentation	Mayumi Kosaka

신유형 98-100번은 다음 회의 발췌문과 표에 관한 문제입니다. [미국]

W: Good morning. I'd like to briefly go over something with all of you today before we open for business. From the chart here, you can see which cake flavor was the most popular this week. As we promised our customers, we will take 30 percent off the flavor with the most votes for one week. I want to give a special thanks to Michelle for giving us the idea of holding this contest. Many customers enjoyed the promotion, and it has nearly doubled our sales. I'm sure everyone here has good ideas as well, so I encourage you to bring them up to me whenever you can.

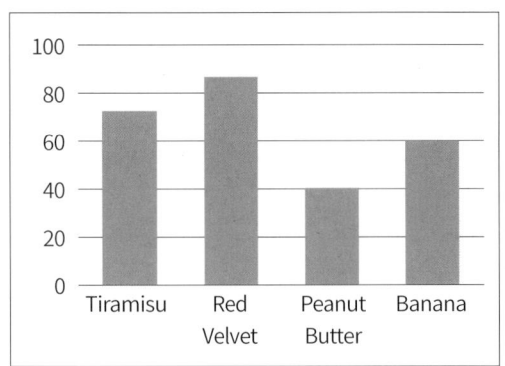

TEST 09

PART 1
P. 130

1 한 사람

(A) A man's adjusting some lamps.
(B) A man's reaching for an item on a shelf.
(C) A man's stacking some books on a desk.
(D) A man's working in front of a computer screen.

2 두 사람 이상

(A) A woman is mopping the stairs.
(B) A woman is putting on a jacket.
(C) A man is opening a laptop.
(D) A man is grasping a railing.

3 두 사람 이상

(A) They're placing food on a mat.
(B) They're trimming some bushes.
(C) They're sitting outdoors.
(D) They're hiking through the trail.

4 두 사람 이상

(A) Some people are sitting across from each other.
(B) Some people are attending a presentation.
(C) Some people are entering a room.
(D) Some people are handing out some paper.

5 사물/풍경

(A) There are baskets above a cabinet.
(B) A wooden floor is being polished.
(C) Some drawers have been left open.
(D) Garments are being hung on clothing racks.

6 한 사람

(A) Some furniture is being assembled in a lounge.
(B) A man is wheeling a machine on a ramp.
(C) The ladder is being placed against the truck.
(D) Workers are resurfacing the road.

PART 2   P. 134

7   What 의문문

What time can you pick me up tonight?
(A) A monthly pass.
(B) The clients from New York.
(C) My car is in the repair shop.

8   Where 의문문

Where will the architecture expo take place this time?
(A) Yes, she could make it.
(B) In Madrid, Spain.
(C) October and November.

9   Why 의문문

Why am I unable to access my online account?
(A) Did you enter the correct password?
(B) At the customer service center.
(C) No, it's only available online.

10 제안/청유문

Can we talk about this report today?
(A) I'll be at a client meeting in Auckland.
(B) No, every few hours.
(C) I'd like to stay for two days.

11 When 의문문

When's the supervisor scheduled to inspect the new facility?
(A) Sometime before Thursday.
(B) Behind the parking facility.
(C) That was a big surprise.

12 Where 의문문

Where can I find Mr. Farzad?
(A) I'm afraid he's out of the office all week.
(B) Every Tuesday, from 10 to 6.
(C) The lost and found is over there.

13 What 의문문

What did you do on the weekend?
(A) I actually worked both days.
(B) Sorry, I'm busy then.
(C) OK, we should go see a movie.

14 부정 의문문

Weren't you supposed to submit the marketing proposal by today?
(A) I suppose that'll solve the problem.
(B) No, at the advertising agency.
(C) Yes, but some figures had to be updated.

15 부가 의문문

The conference is scheduled to be held on March 7, isn't it?
(A) You should've been there.
(B) I think it's in April.
(C) About the company's new product.

16 평서문

I don't mind organizing the catering for the annual awards banquet.
(A) The event coordinator
(B) That'd help a lot, thanks.
(C) Yes, snacks will be provided.

17 Do 의문문

Do we have enough handouts for all the seminar participants?
(A) Well, some people can share.
(B) She conducted the training.
(C) The event has been confirmed.

18 부가 의문문

You'll be here when the shop opens tomorrow, won't you?
(A) It never closes that late.
(B) They prefer to shop on weekends.
(C) I always am on Fridays.

19 Which 의문문

Which warehouse stores the new leather boots?
(A) This winter, I believe.
(B) The one in Adamstown.
(C) Yes, they're really comfortable.

20 Will 의문문

Will the annual mechanical engineering conference be held in Mumbai?
(A) Actually, it's in New Delhi this time.
(B) She's a well-known engineer.
(C) I'd like to stay longer.

21 선택 의문문

Do you prefer to fill out an electronic form, or are you more comfortable with a paper application?
(A) Either is fine.
(B) It looks comfortable.
(C) I feel pretty good, thanks.

22 평서문

Let's find a cheaper venue.
(A) A large concert hall.
(B) The Regent Theater is an option.
(C) They found it in my office.

23 부가 의문문

The turnout at the company party was low, wasn't it?
(A) Sure, it can be lowered.
(B) It's part of the admission fee.
(C) Yes, a lot of people are on vacation.

24 Who 의문문

Who can help me assemble this bookcase?
(A) I'll be available in a minute.
(B) An advance booking.
(C) They're in the display case.

25 간접 의문문

Do you know why the training session has been rescheduled?
(A) The instructor is on a business trip.
(B) About a new safety policy.
(C) In your department.

26 부가 의문문

You only produce clothes for adults, right?
(A) No, we also have a children's line.
(B) I'll be working today.
(C) That was very productive.

27 선택 의문문

Should we send the package to Ms. Kang, or will she pick it up?
(A) Some computer parts.
(B) No, I don't need it.
(C) She's dropping by later.

28 평서문

Let's get Maria to look over the expense report.
(A) Travel and accommodation costs.
(B) She said she's very busy.
(C) Around three to four hours.

29 선택 의문문

Do you think we can drive, or should we take the subway?
(A) How bad is the traffic now?
(B) Sure, you can take some.
(C) I've been driving for a few years.

30 부정 의문문

Isn't the company banquet going to be on June 20th?
(A) For the finance director's retirement party.
(B) No, it's been rescheduled.
(C) A lot of people attended.

31 부가 의문문

You've checked the charts and graphs in the presentation slides, right?
(A) A monthly paycheck.
(B) She's an excellent speaker.
(C) Yes, all the errors have been corrected.

PART 3

P. 135

32-34번은 다음 대화에 관한 문제입니다.

M: Good morning. I purchased this food blender here recently. It's only been a week, but the blades aren't spinning that fast.
W: Hmm… Have you tried checking the speed setting? The blades for this model don't turn as quickly on the low and medium settings.
M: Yes, I made sure that it was set to the highest speed. Anyway, I'd like to get a refund for this blender. Here is the original receipt.

35-37번은 다음 대화에 관한 문제입니다.

M: Good morning, Sonya. You remember how we were going to review the questionnaires our hotel guests completed? Well, I'm almost done reading them.
W: That's right! Sorry, the remodeling project has been taking up all my time. What were you able to find?
M: Mmm… Quite a few people said that we should extend the hours of our fitness center.
W: That's probably a good idea. We should try to accommodate our guests' schedules as best as we can.
M: I agree. I'll make sure to bring it up during the weekly meeting next Tuesday.

38-40번은 다음 대화에 관한 문제입니다.

M: Hello, my name's Paul. I'm with Ferndale Heating and Cooling. I'm scheduled to visit your office to repair your air conditioner at 5:30 today, but I'm running a little late. I'm afraid I won't be able to get there until around 6:30.
W: Thanks for calling. Most people in the office go home around 6 o'clock. I'll let the security guard know you're coming. He's here all evening, so he can let you in.
M: Thank you. By the way, what should I do with the invoice when I'm done? Should I leave it with the security guard?
W: Could you email it to me instead? I wouldn't want it to get lost.

41-43번은 다음 세 화자의 대화에 관한 문제입니다.

M1: Good afternoon. Can I help you with anything?
W: Yes, please. I'm looking for a gift for my nephew. I was thinking of getting some children's storybooks. Do you carry them here?
M1: Hmm… I'll have to check with my coworker. Rodrigo, do you know if we have children's storybooks?

M2: Sure. They're on the second floor though. If you follow me, I'll take you there.

W: Thanks! Also, would it be possible to have them sent straight to my nephew's home?

M2: Of course. Any item from our store can be delivered within the city at no additional cost.

W: Oh, that's great.

신유형 44-46번은 다음 대화에 관련된 문제입니다.

M: This morning, we are pleased to have time management specialist Joanne Friedman on our show. Ms. Friedman, would you share an important tip on managing time efficiently in the office?

W: Certainly. One of the easiest things to do is to prioritize your daily assignments so that you complete the important ones first.

M: That's good advice. Now, I know that you're going to write a book covering this subject. When do you think it will be released?

W: Hmm... That's tough to say. Right now, I'm still in the process of interviewing executives of different companies and getting their input.

47-49번은 다음 대화에 관한 문제입니다.

M: Hello, my name is Sam Clemens, and I am with a delivery person from your store. He has brought a single-sized bed to my house, but I ordered a queen size, not a single. The order number is 1368.

W: OK, I just checked your account on the computer, and I think I know what happened. It looks like the code for the bed was entered incorrectly. I'll correct it right now.

M: When can I expect to receive it? I just moved in to a new home, and I have no bed to sleep in.

W: Well, the queen-sized bed you want should be in the warehouse. I'll mark 'Rush' on the order so that it can be delivered tomorrow. I apologize for the error.

50-52번은 다음 대화에 관한 문제입니다.

W: Good morning, Vincent. Are you done compiling the regional sales figures? I need to present them to the board members at the headquarters tomorrow.

M: I was planning on entering the rest of the data yesterday, but the system went down yesterday afternoon. How soon do you need the final figures?

W: Well, I'm supposed to be at the headquarters at 3 P.M. tomorrow, but I have to leave the office earlier to have lunch with a client. So it would be great if you could get them to me by tomorrow morning.

53-55번 문제는 다음 세 화자의 대화에 관한 문제입니다.

M1: Welcome to Vidia Business Solutions. My name is Larry, and this is Kenneth. We'll address any inquiries you have regarding our firm's client management services. You can leave it to us to help you keep track of your clients.

W: Thank you. We really need experts to assist us with handling our clients and our relationships with them. We just can't do it alone anymore.

M2: Oh, did something recently change at your company?

W: Well, Kenneth, three months ago, we purchased one of our rivals. Now, we have almost double the number of clients and accounts.

M2: Well, we offer several service packages that I think are especially well-suited for your newly expanded business. If you want, I can discuss these options with you right now.

56-58번은 다음 대화에 관련된 문제입니다.

M: Sarah, I hope you had a great time in Germany. I understand you met with some of our business partners. But I also heard you found another potential distributor for our furniture.

W: Yeah, they are a major firm called Branworth Distribution. They have a reputation for being dependable. But the main problem is that their distribution costs are a lot higher than their competitors'.

222

M: Well, if you think they are that reliable, we should consider using them. How about if we negotiate a three-month contract with them to see how well they do? If we're satisfied with them, we can sign a longer deal with them afterwards.

59-61번은 다음 대화에 관한 문제입니다.

M: Hi. I bought some merchandise here this morning, and when I got home, I noticed on my receipt that I had been charged twice for the same item.

W: We're so sorry about that. It seems that our automated checkout machines had some software issues this morning, and a few customers have reported duplicate transactions.

M: Ah, I see.

W: I'll go ahead and give you a refund right away.

M: Thanks. Here's the receipt.

W: And while you're here, would you like to take part in a quick customer survey?

M: Sure. I've got some time to spare.

62-64번은 다음 대화와 목록에 관한 문제입니다.

W: Hi, David, are you able to access our server?

M: Yes—I haven't had any problems with it.

W: Well, I can't log in to it, so I have no way to view our company's files. Can you check if this week's sales report has been uploaded yet?

M: Umm… Give me a second. OK, yes—I see it.

W: Great, can you go ahead and print it for me? I'll need the report for my meeting later.

File	Created by
The World Economy	Rex Kamata
Investment Portfolio	Brian McCurdie
Weekly Sales Report	Tom Avery
Employee Evaluation Form	Jeong-Seok Ok

65-67번은 다음 대화와 건물 안내도에 관련된 문제입니다.

W: Charlie, I realize that you're driving over to LPS Motors' headquarters soon. But… um… can you spare a few minutes to look over the new layout for our office before you go?

M: No problem. Alright, what do we have here?

W: So, the R&D division will occupy rooms 303 and 304. And as you frequently use the media room, I've put your office right next to it.

M: Looks good to me. I assume you'll be in the corner office?

W: That's right. I work a lot with the R&D team, so it's best that I'm close to them.

M: True. Well, I'm sure the employees will be pleased with the new arrangement at the meeting tomorrow morning.

Lounge		Restrooms ♂ ♀
Room 304		
Room 303		
Room 302	Room 301	Media Room

68-70번은 다음 대화와 파이 차트에 관한 문제입니다.

M: Amy, did you hear the news? According to today's newspaper, our company may purchase JMP Parts. I have the article right here.

W: Oh, I didn't know. Does the article give any details?

M: Well, it points out that the takeover would make us more competitive than we are now. Look— the article breaks down the market share of each of the four major companies in the industry.

W: I see. Acquiring JMP Parts would give us a market share that is equal to that of Fazio Corporation.

M: Yes. It seems like a good move on our company's part.

W: But actually, I'm not so sure about that. It says here in the article that JMP Parts' profits are down for the second quarter in a row—Maybe our company should reconsider.

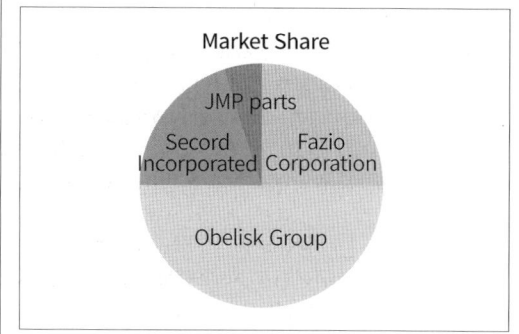

PART 4

P. 139

71-73번은 다음 방송에 관한 문제입니다. [미국]

W: The Guild Performing Arts Association will be holding its tenth annual film festival next weekend. This time, the association has added three new categories: Best Student Director, Best Animation, and Best Youth Film. The event's coordinator, Catalina Murphy, said that she hopes these new additions will attract a younger crowd to the festival. Over 50 submissions from independent film makers have been received. Visit the association's Web site at guildperformingarts.com for more information on screening times and tickets.

74-76번은 다음 공지에 관한 문제입니다. [호주]

M: May I have your attention please? I'll be your driver this evening on the 8:30 trip to Glasgow. We'll be leaving 20 minutes later than scheduled as the mechanic is replacing one of the tires on the bus. Despite the delay, I still anticipate that we'll reach Glasgow on time as traffic is usually light in the evenings. I appreciate your understanding.

77-79번은 다음 전화 메시지에 관한 문제입니다. [영국]

W: Hello, Mr. Oshiro. It's Mary from the Northwest Fitness Center. You cancelled your membership with us last month and stated our locker rooms as the reason. You indicated that there were many occasions on which you couldn't find any empty lockers to use to store your personal belongings. Well, we recently renovated our locker rooms and doubled the space in the area. We'd like to offer you a special deal. If you resume your gym membership by next week, we'll give you four free personal training sessions. These sessions are designed to create and help achieve your fitness goal. All of this will be provided to you at no additional cost. Again, this offer will expire in one week, so please let us know as soon as possible if you're interested.

신유형 80-82번은 다음 전화 메시지에 관한 문제입니다. [미국]

M: Hello, it's Brennan from Hercatz Automotive. I'm looking through the documents you emailed me in preparation for your first day next Monday as a new employee. One thing; it looks like you didn't include an introduction about yourself. We're planning to put it in our newsletter for next week. If you aren't sure how to start, just review the sample in your company packet. Feel free to contact me with any questions or concerns you might have. I look forward to seeing you soon.

83-85번은 다음 회의 발췌문에 관한 문제입니다. [호주]

M: Hello, and welcome to the monthly staff meeting. First, I have some news for everyone. Last week, our library received a generous donation of rare 19th century history books. They will be made available on the first floor, and I'm sure that many patrons will be fascinated by the books. Since the books are very valuable, we need to make sure that people treat them with care. I brought instruction sheets on how to handle these rare books. Please pass these sheets out to patrons before they enter the multimedia room.

신유형 86-88번은 다음 지시문에 관한 문제입니다. [호주]

M: I'd like to welcome you all to your first day here at Gellen Industries. We'll begin by checking out the offices and meeting rooms. Then, we'll head over to the cafeteria for lunch. Everyone has their IDs, right? OK, great. Each office has a security system. After eating, everyone will go to their respective workstations and get their computers set up. We renovated our offices last week, so the building map in your binder is not accurate. We'll provide you with a revised one soon.

89-91번은 다음 워크숍 발췌문에 관한 문제입니다. 미국

M: Welcome to today's workshop on developing effective business plans. Let's begin by defining the term business plan. It is a statement which describes your company's goals and how they will be achieved. A business plan that is well-written will increase the chance of making a good first impression, which is extremely important in receiving financial support from those who are willing to make an investment in your company. Now, before we talk about what effective business plans are, I'd like each of you to share your past work experience with the other group members. Let's begin then.

신유형 92-94번은 다음 전화메시지에 관한 문제입니다. 영국

W: Hello, Charles, this is Veronica. Do you have time to meet tomorrow afternoon? We need to start searching for a head chef for our diner. We have less than three months until the grand opening. I have a lot of applications that we need to review together. I'll send the ones that seem the most qualified over to you now by e-mail. Then we can decide which candidates to call in for interviews when we meet tomorrow. Please get back to me and confirm if this is OK with you.

신유형 95-97번은 다음 전화메시지와 표에 관한 문제입니다. 미국

W: Hello, this is Judy at City Tech Apartments. I'm calling to remind you that your rent was due on Wednesday, October 25. Since your payment is now three days past due, we have charged a late fee to your account. Please send your monthly rent plus the extra fee to us no later than midnight tonight to avoid further charges. To prevent this from happening again, I recommend using the automatic payment system on our Web site. To register for this service, you need to provide your bank account details. If you'd like more information about this service, feel free to contact me at 555-1212. Thanks.

Late Fees	
3 days late	€50
7 days late	€100
14 days late	€150
21 days late	€200

신유형 98-100번은 다음 설명과 평면도에 관한 문제입니다. 호주

M: Hello, everybody. I called this meeting to let you know about some changes in the production area. We have found that it takes an average of 10 minutes to gather all the needed parts for a work order. I think we can reduce the time we spend on that if we organize our materials in a more efficient way. Here's a layout of the factory floor. I've placed some new storage cases between the assembly area and the Quality Control Team. We'll put our most commonly used manufacturing components there. One more thing: I need five people to come in on Saturday and help move everything into the new containers. So if you're interested in working some overtime, just write your name on the sheet at my desk.

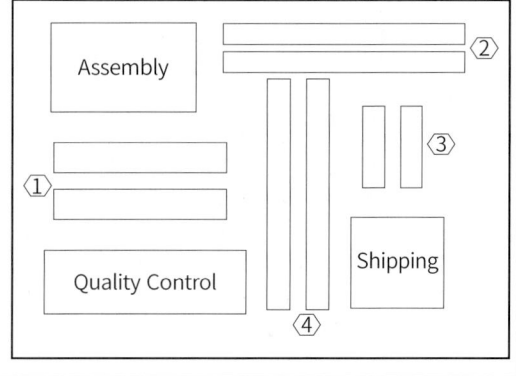

TEST 10

PART 1 P. 144

1 한 사람

(A) A man is washing a plate in the sink.
(B) A man is placing some utensils in a container.
(C) A man is wearing an apron.
(D) A man is picking up a cutting board.

2 두 사람 이상

(A) They're clearing drinking glasses from a table.
(B) They're having some food near a fence.
(C) They're arranging some chairs in a row.
(D) They're strolling in a rooftop yard.

3 사물/풍경

(A) A picture frame is propped against the counter.
(B) A potted plant is being watered.
(C) Some seats are occupied.
(D) Some magazines are spread out on a table.

4 한 사람

(A) She is looking in her bag.
(B) She is putting on her sunglasses.
(C) She is closing a laptop.
(D) She is taking out a notepad.

5 두 사람 이상

(A) The woman is placing a jacket on the sofa.
(B) The man is opening a briefcase.
(C) They are seated in a reception area.
(D) They're putting flowers in a vase.

6 사물/풍경

(A) Some chairs are positioned in a circle.
(B) All of the workstations are taken.
(C) A window is being cleaned.
(D) Computer monitors are set up next to one another.

PART 2 P. 148

7 평서문

 I'd love to watch the new guitarist play.
(A) I'm just here as a tourist.
(B) No, that's not my watch.
(C) That performance is sold out.

8 When 의문문

When are we sending the purchase order?
(A) Once we receive the estimate.
(B) She bought it on sale.
(C) A different buyer.

9 Be 의문문

Are there any available positions on the accounting team?
(A) You are welcome to email your résumé.
(B) The accounting software was upgraded.
(C) He's available until 6 P.M. today.

10 Where 의문문

Where can I hang my coat?
(A) It's not that difficult.
(B) On this rack right here.
(C) It was cold this morning.

11 Who 의문문

Who's picking up the clients at the train station this afternoon?
(A) Go to platform 10.
(B) To our headquarters.
(C) Actually, they're arriving tomorrow.

12 Be 의문문

Is the new accounting program as complicated as it looks?
(A) The office looks great.
(B) I'm not sure how much it cost.
(C) It's not that different from the previous one.

13 Have 의문문

Has the keynote speaker's presentation been canceled?
(A) She conducts research on tropical rainforests.
(B) Did you make a reservation?
(C) I can check the schedule on the Web site.

14 제안/청유문

Could you review the sales report for me?
(A) Sorry, I have an urgent meeting.
(B) I'll make the photocopies.
(C) I really like the view.

15 How 의문문

How did you get a parking space at work?
(A) No, I start next week.
(B) I applied with the HR Department.
(C) 200 dollars a month.

16 평서문

Kevin's going to be assigned to an overseas branch.
(A) I will oversee the manufacturing process.
(B) Yes, that's what he wants.
(C) Please sign here.

17 When 의문문

When can we expect the survey analysis to be available?
(A) Please fill out the questionnaire.
(B) I just received the data.
(C) That's quite surprising.

18 Why 의문문

Why do we have a box of labels in here?
(A) Allie put it there.
(B) On the packages.
(C) After I ship the boxes.

19 How 의문문

How often do you check your bank account?
(A) Here's my bank account number.
(B) A few times a week.
(C) The deposit is 50 dollars.

20 제안/청유문

Would you mind passing me that cup, please?
(A) No, I'll reserve it.
(B) Sure, here you go.
(C) Just some juice.

21 간접 의문문

Can you tell me when our paychecks will be issued?
(A) About three hours.
(B) At the end of the month.
(C) It's 3,000 dollars in total.

22   부가 의문문

Parkview Hospital is admitting patients tomorrow, isn't it?
(A) He needs to have more patience.
(B) No, not on Sundays.
(C) Here are your medical records.

23   Which 의문문

Which of the proposals should be sent to the executive committee?
(A) It was a great proposal.
(B) No, he's not on the committee.
(C) We haven't decided yet.

24   부정 의문문

Wasn't the event coordinating staff supposed to have everything set up by 2?
(A) At least 75 chairs.
(B) Yes, they'll be done in a minute.
(C) The awards ceremony went very well.

25   제안/청유문

Would you be able to visit us on Saturday the 7th?
(A) It would have to be later in the afternoon.
(B) Where does she work again?
(C) My apartment is on Flinders Street.

26   선택 의문문

Should we take the train or drive to the conference?
(A) Go north on West Avenue.
(B) About half an hour.
(C) I prefer public transport.

27   Who 의문문

Who wanted these changes made to the pamphlet?
(A) Great – let's print it.
(B) An advertising campaign.
(C) The director did.

28   부가 의문문

You can cancel the order, can't you?
(A) The item has already been shipped.
(B) They sell it online.
(C) We accept cash or credit card.

29   선택 의문문

Do you want to present your proposal first or should I?
(A) Yes, I got it as a present.
(B) Can I go after you?
(C) You should be fine.

30   Should 의문문

Should I get started on the Stevens Project today?
(A) He's the new project manager.
(B) Sure, if you're finished with other work.
(C) I didn't bring my car today.

31   Do 의문문

Does the security officer know that the clients are arriving shortly?
(A) He's been informed.
(B) A staff identification badge.
(C) Room 406 down the hall.

PART 3

32-34번은 다음 대화에 관한 문제입니다.

W: Hello, my name is Carol Newman. I'm staying in room 505, and I'd like to file a complaint. The people in room 506 have their television volume on too high. I knocked on their door, but nobody answered. Is there anything you can do?

M: Actually, I just saw the guests that are staying next door to you, and it looked like they were heading out to dinner. So I don't think there's anyone in the room right now.

W: Then could you send someone up to turn off the TV in their room? I have to finish a report, and I really need to concentrate.

35-37번은 다음 대화에 관한 문제입니다.

M: Is the advertising campaign for Mendoza Appliances' new refrigerator coming along according to schedule? They're an important client of our agency, so we have to make sure to do a good job. Have you discussed the ad with them yet?

W: Yes, and they're pleased with everything except for the background color. They've asked us to change it from dark blue to dark green. Once we've done that, it'll be ready to be sent to the print shop.

M: OK, but just keep in mind that we won't be able to send it out to them until next week. I heard that the print shop had to send out some printing machines for repairs, so they're backed up a bit.

38-40번은 다음 대화에 관한 문제입니다.

W: Hi, my name is Tiffany Kim. I just received the summer dress that I purchased from your Web site, but there is a small tear in the back.

M: I am very sorry about that, Ms. Kim. If I could just get your order number, I will process a refund or send you a replacement item.

W: OK. The number is 3892, and I would like to get a dress with no defects this time.

M: Absolutely. We'll ship a new dress by express mail, so you will receive it tomorrow. Just place the old dress in the same box to return it to us free of charge. I apologize for the inconvenience.

신유형 41-43번은 다음 세 화자의 대화에 관한 문제입니다.

W1: Hey, Vanessa. Are you still looking for a new apartment?

W2: Yeah. There's a place in Averton's downtown area that I'm really interested in. But I'm worried about my commute to the office.

W1: Oh, David, don't you live in downtown Averton?

M: Yes, it's a great area, and it's not that expensive.

W2: Does it take you long to get to the office?

M: Not really. The best way is to take side streets, since there's usually heavy traffic on the highway in the morning. Here—I'll show you on this navigation app.

44-46번은 다음 대화에 관한 문제입니다.

M: There are two more boxes left in the truck, Ms. Lin. Once we bring those in, my crew will remove the pads that were used to protect your furniture, and then your move will be finished.

W: Wow, that's great! I didn't expect your workers to unload the boxes so quickly from the moving truck. Thank you for your hard work.

M: No problem. But the last two boxes don't have labels that say where they're supposed to go. Should I just put them on the living room table?

W: Actually, I remember what's inside them. They're soap and other toiletries. Do you mind taking them to the restroom?

47-49번은 다음 대화에 관한 문제입니다.

W: Hey, Pablo. I have the schedule for next week's business training seminar right here. And these are the two workshops you'll be leading.

M: OK. But wait. The workshops are one after the other, but one is in Begley Hall and the other is in Pitt Hall.

W: Yeah, and?

M: Well, they're located at opposite ends of the conference center building. But there's only five minutes between the sessions to pack up my equipment, walk to the hall, and get set up again. How could anyone do that?

W: Oh, you're right about that. I'll fix it so that both of your sessions are in the same hall.

신유형 50-52번은 다음 세 화자의 대화에 관한 문제입니다.

W: Hello, I'm thinking of signing up for a membership at your gym. Do you mind telling me a bit about the place?

M1: I'd be glad to. We're open Monday through Saturday, from 6 A.M. to 11 P.M. As a member, you'll have access to all of our facilities including the swimming pool and tennis court.

W: Excellent! Now, I also heard you offer discounts to Radcar Co.'s employees.

M1: Hmm… Let me check with a coworker. Ben, do Radcar workers qualify for the corporate discount?

M2: Yes. If you provide your employee ID card, we'll apply a 25 percent discount.

W: OK. I brought my ID with me, so I'd like to register today. I just need to complete some paperwork, right?

M1: That's right. I'll print them out for you.

53-55번은 다음 대화에 관한 문제입니다. 미국 ⇄ 영국

M: Hi, Sharon. It's Kumar. I apologize for calling on such short notice, but I don't think I can come in to work today at the restaurant. I caught a terrible cold, and I'm afraid I might make others sick as well.

W: Oh, you'd better stay home and get some rest then, Kumar. Have you asked any of the others to cover your shift today?

M: I called Juan earlier, and he said he's available. But he's only been here a week, so I don't think he can explain all of the items on the menu yet.

W: That's fine. I'll ask him to come in an hour early today. This will be a good opportunity for him to get some extra training.

56-58번은 다음 대화에 관한 문제입니다. 미국 ⇄ 미국

M: Hello, my name is Lawrence Carter, and I'm a sales representative from Glisten Dental Products. Would it be okay if I put up this display near the entrance of your store? We're promoting our new children's toothbrushes.

W: Well, most of our customers come here to shop for their children, so they might be interested in them. But can you tell me about the products first?

M: The toothbrushes were made by top pediatric dentists in Europe. What makes these toothbrushes unique is the specially designed handle. Its special shape allows children to securely hold the brush.

신유형 59-61번은 다음 대화에 관한 문제입니다. 미국 ⇄ 호주

W: Frank, this is Christine. I'm having some trouble getting into the building. The scanner won't accept my ID card. It looks like I'm locked out!

M: Don't worry; you're not the first person to have this problem today. Let me have your employee number, and I'll reenter you into the system. That usually gets the scanner working again.

W: Uh… I can't remember my number, and I'm in a hurry to get to a meeting. Could you just come down and open the door for me?

M: That's against company policy. Just hold on a second, and I'll look up your ID number myself. It won't take long.

신유형 62-64번은 다음 대화와 자리 배치표에 관한 문제입니다. 영국 ⇄ 미국

W: Ahm… Excuse me, I think that's my seat. According to my boarding pass, I'm here in seat D.

M: Are you sure? I thought mine was 26D. May I see your boarding pass? Ah… Your seat is right in front of me.

W: Oh, you're right! Sorry. In that case, would you mind switching seats with me? My coworker is going to be in 26E, and during the flight, we need to go over some documents together for a conference.

M: Well, as long as I'm still in an aisle seat, it doesn't matter to me. But we'd better notify one of the crew members about the switch first.

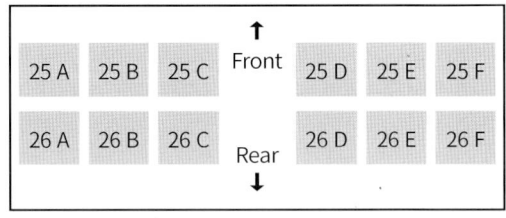

신유형 65-67번은 다음 대화와 목록에 관한 문제입니다. 미국 ⇄ 미국

W: Michael, Mr. Winston called this morning. He said he needs steel frames instead of the wooden ones he initially ordered. But he wants ones that are the same price as the wooden ones.

M: Thanks for telling me. I'll take care of it.

W: Is it going to take long?

M: Not at all. I just need to know the name of the model that the client initially ordered so that I can cancel it first.

W: Hold on. I think I have it written somewhere. Um… Here it is. The model was White Birch Wood.

M: Oh, thanks. I'll call the Production Department now to notify them of the change, and then send a new invoice to the Sales Department.

Model	Price
White Birch Wood	$399
Mahogany Wood	$499
Industrial Steel	$399
Antique Steel	$599

신유형 68-70번은 다음 대화와 목록에 관한 문제입니다.

W: Terrence, I heard that the company will be having a dance competition this year for the annual summer event. I enjoyed the sports festival last year, but I think this year's event will be really fun too.

M: I think so, too. We need to decide on which printing firm we should go with to print the brochures for the event.

W: Let's look at the list right now. OK, I know Satex is highly rated, but we have to choose a firm that's more affordable. We have a much smaller budget this year.

M: Right. How about this one right here in Seattle? They charge reasonable prices, and they received good reviews.

W: OK. Let's go with that one!

Printing Firm	Location
Vercom	Seattle
Satex	Tacoma
Medio	Everett
Gomca	Bellingham

PART 4 P. 153

71-73번은 다음 안내 방송에 관한 문제입니다.

W: All right, I have a special announcement to make. The library recently received a generous contribution from a long-time donor. On Tuesday, the Library Committee held a meeting and decided that the money will be used to repair the broken shelves in the fiction section. This work will begin in the second week of July and probably last for about a month. As this is a huge project, we ask for everyone's help and cooperation. Thanks.

74-76번은 다음 전화 메시지에 관한 문제입니다.

M: Good morning, Ms. Jones. Thank you for taking the time to meet with me yesterday to talk about your store's holiday ad. We will make the design changes you requested to the online ad. During the meeting, you also told me you would like to buy television advertising. I discussed the matter with our production team, and they said that we're currently offering 25 percent off television advertising. If you want to take advantage of the offer, you should tell me as soon as possible because the deal will end next Tuesday.

77-79번은 다음 공지에 관한 문제입니다.

W: Welcome everyone to this evening's financial investment seminar here at First One Bank. Tonight, Mr. Witte is going to talk about how to make your money grow using several proven strategies. Mr. Witte is the current vice president of CLA, Inc. He worked there for more than a decade as a financial advisor before being promoted to his current position last month. In addition, he gives monthly lectures on smart investments at his company's main branch. If you're interested in his lecture and would like more details about it, please speak to Mr. Witte after the seminar. OK, let's now give Mr. Witte a big round of applause.

신유형 80-82번은 다음 회의 발췌문에 관한 문제입니다. 미국

M: Thank you all for attending this meeting. As you know, Bendare Corporation is dedicated to helping the environment, so once again, we'd like our employees to volunteer for clean-up activities. As usual, this year, our company will pick up trash at the local parks on the first Saturday of every month. Now, I know what you may be thinking: we have to give up our weekend to do this, but we don't get anything in return. Well, I'm pleased to announce that this time, there will be some motivation. All staff members who come out and contribute will receive a coupon for a free lunch at Barney's Diner.

신유형 83-85번은 다음 전화 메시지에 관한 문제입니다. 미국

W: Good morning, Mr. Lanson. This is Carla Wong from Hoober Corporation's manufacturing plant. I just received an order this morning from your company for coffee tables. I'm calling because, well… 1,500 is a huge order. I don't think we've ever received an order this big before. Also, I want to mention that our plant does not have enough machines to manufacture that many tables in five days. Please give me a call back to discuss this matter as soon as possible. Thank you.

86-88번은 다음 공지에 관한 문제입니다. 미국

W: Today, I would like to discuss our summer internship program. As we did last year, we were able to find students from the best computer science colleges in the nation, and they will be working under some of you to prepare for a career in software programming. This time, however, the process will be slightly different. Staff members in charge of these students will give weekly evaluations of their progress in addition to the monthly assessments. By doing this, it will allow our Human Resources team to identify the strongest candidates for possible full-time jobs at our company after they graduate.

89-91번은 다음 공지에 관한 문제입니다. 영국

W: OK, before we end today's meeting, I want to make one final announcement. We are going to expand our shipping services. From the first of next month, we're not only going to send our merchandise to our usual local customers but also to customers all across the country. Most of you are aware of this, but more and more people from other cities have shown interest in our products. For that reason, we decided to find a partner to help us better reach our customers. But I will closely monitor our sales over the next quarter to ensure this change is worthwhile for our ongoing success.

신유형 92-94번은 다음 뉴스 보도에 관한 문제입니다. 미국

M: This is Blake Lee for Channel 3 News. I'm on the corner of Adams Boulevard and 10th Street, just outside the entrance to Jenna's Ice Cream Parlor, which just opened for business today. The Chicago-based company is popular nationwide, and this is the first Jenna's Ice Cream Parlor store in our town. As part of its opening celebration, the store is offering a free bottle of juice with every order of ice cream. But only the first 300 customers can take advantage of this offer, and the store has been open for almost two hours now. Even if you miss out, you can still enjoy some delicious ice cream.

신유형 95-97번은 다음 전화 메시지와 경비 보고서에 관한 문제입니다. 미국

W: Good afternoon, Mark. This is Lana in the Finance Department. I was reviewing your expense report for the marketing trip to New York last month, and I noticed that you didn't submit one of your receipts. I see that you requested a reimbursement for $27.50 on August 10, but there is no receipt for that date. In order for me to finalize everything, you'll have to give it to me. If you have lost it, please call me, and I'll go over the necessary process for that case with you.

Business Expense Report		
ITEM	AMOUNT	DATE
Taxi	$23.15	August 7
Hotel	$270	August 8
Sales luncheon	$217.10	August 9
Airport shuttle	$27.50	August 10

98-100번은 다음 담화와 그래프에 관한 문제입니다.

M: Hello, everyone. Let's begin today's fourth quarterly review of our business by talking about how well we're doing with boosting our sales here at Albert's Home Tools. You can see that our store sold the most in September, with the introduction of our new hardware product line. Also, our second most profitable month was when we had the half-off sale to celebrate our anniversary. That event was more successful than we'd anticipated! Looking ahead to the upcoming year, we plan to hire a professional graphic designer to make our product catalog more appealing.

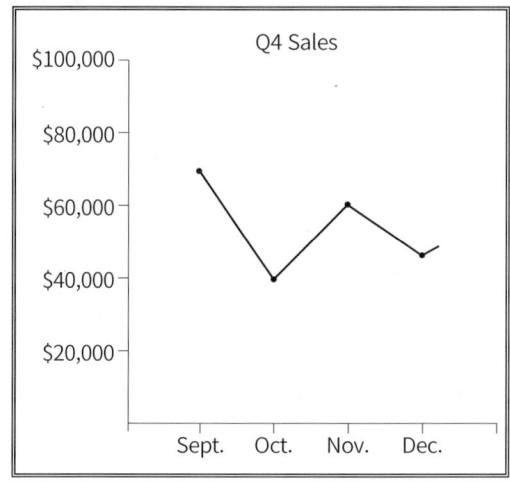

Listening Comprehension

Answers

ANSWERS 빠른 정답 찾기

TEST 01

1 (D)	11 (C)	21 (C)	31 (B)	41 (C)	51 (D)	61 (B)	71 (C)	81 (B)	91 (D)
2 (D)	12 (B)	22 (C)	32 (C)	42 (D)	52 (A)	62 (C)	72 (A)	82 (A)	92 (D)
3 (A)	13 (A)	23 (B)	33 (A)	43 (D)	53 (D)	63 (C)	73 (B)	83 (D)	93 (D)
4 (B)	14 (B)	24 (B)	34 (B)	44 (C)	54 (C)	64 (A)	74 (B)	84 (B)	94 (A)
5 (B)	15 (B)	25 (A)	35 (A)	45 (A)	55 (D)	65 (B)	75 (D)	85 (A)	95 (A)
6 (D)	16 (A)	26 (A)	36 (A)	46 (D)	56 (D)	66 (B)	76 (A)	86 (C)	96 (B)
7 (C)	17 (B)	27 (C)	37 (C)	47 (D)	57 (A)	67 (D)	77 (D)	87 (B)	97 (C)
8 (A)	18 (C)	28 (A)	38 (C)	48 (A)	58 (D)	68 (D)	78 (A)	88 (D)	98 (B)
9 (B)	19 (A)	29 (C)	39 (D)	49 (C)	59 (B)	69 (D)	79 (C)	89 (C)	99 (A)
10 (A)	20 (A)	30 (A)	40 (D)	50 (A)	60 (C)	70 (D)	80 (A)	90 (D)	100 (C)

TEST 02

1 (C)	11 (A)	21 (A)	31 (B)	41 (D)	51 (B)	61 (A)	71 (B)	81 (D)	91 (B)
2 (B)	12 (C)	22 (B)	32 (C)	42 (B)	52 (D)	62 (A)	72 (A)	82 (A)	92 (A)
3 (C)	13 (A)	23 (B)	33 (D)	43 (B)	53 (B)	63 (D)	73 (C)	83 (B)	93 (C)
4 (A)	14 (A)	24 (A)	34 (B)	44 (B)	54 (A)	64 (D)	74 (B)	84 (D)	94 (C)
5 (D)	15 (C)	25 (C)	35 (D)	45 (A)	55 (D)	65 (B)	75 (C)	85 (C)	95 (B)
6 (B)	16 (A)	26 (B)	36 (A)	46 (C)	56 (B)	66 (D)	76 (C)	86 (B)	96 (B)
7 (B)	17 (C)	27 (B)	37 (D)	47 (A)	57 (A)	67 (D)	77 (A)	87 (D)	97 (C)
8 (C)	18 (B)	28 (C)	38 (B)	48 (C)	58 (D)	68 (A)	78 (D)	88 (A)	98 (B)
9 (C)	19 (B)	29 (A)	39 (C)	49 (B)	59 (B)	69 (C)	79 (C)	89 (C)	99 (D)
10 (B)	20 (C)	30 (A)	40 (C)	50 (D)	60 (C)	70 (A)	80 (B)	90 (A)	100 (B)

TEST 03

1 (A)	11 (C)	21 (B)	31 (B)	41 (B)	51 (A)	61 (A)	71 (B)	81 (D)	91 (C)
2 (A)	12 (A)	22 (A)	32 (D)	42 (D)	52 (C)	62 (B)	72 (D)	82 (A)	92 (C)
3 (C)	13 (C)	23 (B)	33 (A)	43 (C)	53 (D)	63 (C)	73 (B)	83 (C)	93 (D)
4 (D)	14 (A)	24 (C)	34 (A)	44 (D)	54 (B)	64 (D)	74 (A)	84 (D)	94 (B)
5 (D)	15 (A)	25 (D)	35 (D)	45 (B)	55 (A)	65 (A)	75 (D)	85 (D)	95 (D)
6 (B)	16 (C)	26 (C)	36 (B)	46 (A)	56 (B)	66 (B)	76 (A)	86 (D)	96 (A)
7 (C)	17 (B)	27 (C)	37 (A)	47 (D)	57 (C)	67 (A)	77 (C)	87 (A)	97 (B)
8 (A)	18 (C)	28 (B)	38 (D)	48 (A)	58 (D)	68 (D)	78 (B)	88 (D)	98 (C)
9 (A)	19 (B)	29 (A)	39 (C)	49 (B)	59 (D)	69 (C)	79 (D)	89 (C)	99 (C)
10 (C)	20 (A)	30 (C)	40 (B)	50 (D)	60 (B)	70 (A)	80 (B)	90 (B)	100 (A)

TEST 04

1 (D)	11 (C)	21 (A)	31 (B)	41 (A)	51 (B)	61 (D)	71 (B)	81 (C)	91 (D)
2 (C)	12 (B)	22 (A)	32 (B)	42 (C)	52 (A)	62 (C)	72 (C)	82 (D)	92 (B)
3 (B)	13 (A)	23 (A)	33 (C)	43 (B)	53 (D)	63 (D)	73 (C)	83 (C)	93 (A)
4 (B)	14 (B)	24 (B)	34 (D)	44 (D)	54 (C)	64 (B)	74 (A)	84 (D)	94 (C)
5 (B)	15 (B)	25 (C)	35 (B)	45 (B)	55 (A)	65 (B)	75 (D)	85 (D)	95 (C)
6 (B)	16 (B)	26 (A)	36 (A)	46 (D)	56 (B)	66 (D)	76 (B)	86 (C)	96 (D)
7 (B)	17 (A)	27 (B)	37 (C)	47 (A)	57 (A)	67 (C)	77 (C)	87 (D)	97 (C)
8 (B)	18 (C)	28 (A)	38 (B)	48 (C)	58 (D)	68 (D)	78 (B)	88 (D)	98 (D)
9 (B)	19 (B)	29 (C)	39 (B)	49 (C)	59 (D)	69 (C)	79 (C)	89 (C)	99 (C)
10 (C)	20 (A)	30 (B)	40 (D)	50 (C)	60 (C)	70 (D)	80 (D)	90 (B)	100 (B)

TEST 05

1 (D)	11 (B)	21 (A)	31 (B)	41 (C)	51 (D)	61 (B)	71 (C)	81 (C)	91 (D)
2 (B)	12 (B)	22 (B)	32 (C)	42 (D)	52 (C)	62 (B)	72 (A)	82 (A)	92 (B)
3 (C)	13 (C)	23 (C)	33 (C)	43 (A)	53 (D)	63 (B)	73 (D)	83 (B)	93 (D)
4 (C)	14 (A)	24 (C)	34 (D)	44 (D)	54 (B)	64 (C)	74 (B)	84 (D)	94 (A)
5 (A)	15 (C)	25 (B)	35 (D)	45 (A)	55 (D)	65 (D)	75 (D)	85 (A)	95 (C)
6 (C)	16 (C)	26 (B)	36 (B)	46 (C)	56 (A)	66 (B)	76 (A)	86 (D)	96 (B)
7 (B)	17 (C)	27 (A)	37 (C)	47 (A)	57 (C)	67 (B)	77 (A)	87 (B)	97 (A)
8 (A)	18 (A)	28 (B)	38 (D)	48 (C)	58 (D)	68 (B)	78 (D)	88 (A)	98 (A)
9 (A)	19 (B)	29 (B)	39 (C)	49 (A)	59 (C)	69 (A)	79 (B)	89 (A)	99 (C)
10 (C)	20 (B)	30 (B)	40 (A)	50 (B)	60 (A)	70 (C)	80 (D)	90 (D)	100 (B)

TEST 06

1 (D)	11 (C)	21 (A)	31 (A)	41 (C)	51 (B)	61 (C)	71 (B)	81 (B)	91 (D)
2 (B)	12 (B)	22 (A)	32 (D)	42 (D)	52 (D)	62 (A)	72 (D)	82 (D)	92 (A)
3 (D)	13 (C)	23 (A)	33 (B)	43 (B)	53 (D)	63 (C)	73 (B)	83 (D)	93 (B)
4 (C)	14 (B)	24 (A)	34 (A)	44 (D)	54 (B)	64 (D)	74 (C)	84 (C)	94 (D)
5 (B)	15 (C)	25 (B)	35 (D)	45 (C)	55 (C)	65 (A)	75 (B)	85 (A)	95 (B)
6 (D)	16 (C)	26 (B)	36 (B)	46 (A)	56 (D)	66 (C)	76 (A)	86 (C)	96 (D)
7 (C)	17 (C)	27 (B)	37 (D)	47 (C)	57 (B)	67 (C)	77 (B)	87 (D)	97 (C)
8 (A)	18 (C)	28 (A)	38 (D)	48 (B)	58 (A)	68 (C)	78 (D)	88 (B)	98 (C)
9 (C)	19 (B)	29 (B)	39 (B)	49 (A)	59 (A)	69 (D)	79 (C)	89 (C)	99 (D)
10 (A)	20 (C)	30 (B)	40 (D)	50 (A)	60 (D)	70 (B)	80 (D)	90 (C)	100 (A)

TEST 07

1 (D)	11 (B)	21 (C)	31 (C)	41 (A)	51 (A)	61 (D)	71 (A)	81 (C)	91 (B)
2 (A)	12 (B)	22 (B)	32 (A)	42 (C)	52 (C)	62 (C)	72 (D)	82 (D)	92 (B)
3 (C)	13 (B)	23 (B)	33 (D)	43 (A)	53 (D)	63 (B)	73 (C)	83 (D)	93 (C)
4 (D)	14 (A)	24 (B)	34 (B)	44 (A)	54 (A)	64 (B)	74 (C)	84 (B)	94 (A)
5 (A)	15 (B)	25 (A)	35 (C)	45 (C)	55 (D)	65 (C)	75 (C)	85 (C)	95 (D)
6 (A)	16 (A)	26 (C)	36 (A)	46 (A)	56 (A)	66 (D)	76 (B)	86 (D)	96 (B)
7 (B)	17 (B)	27 (C)	37 (C)	47 (C)	57 (D)	67 (B)	77 (B)	87 (B)	97 (D)
8 (B)	18 (C)	28 (B)	38 (B)	48 (C)	58 (A)	68 (D)	78 (C)	88 (A)	98 (D)
9 (B)	19 (A)	29 (B)	39 (C)	49 (B)	59 (C)	69 (C)	79 (D)	89 (A)	99 (D)
10 (B)	20 (B)	30 (C)	40 (C)	50 (B)	60 (D)	70 (B)	80 (A)	90 (C)	100 (B)

TEST 08

1 (B)	11 (C)	21 (A)	31 (B)	41 (A)	51 (A)	61 (D)	71 (A)	81 (B)	91 (A)
2 (D)	12 (A)	22 (B)	32 (D)	42 (B)	52 (C)	62 (B)	72 (B)	82 (A)	92 (C)
3 (C)	13 (A)	23 (B)	33 (B)	43 (D)	53 (B)	63 (C)	73 (C)	83 (C)	93 (B)
4 (C)	14 (C)	24 (C)	34 (A)	44 (A)	54 (D)	64 (A)	74 (B)	84 (D)	94 (A)
5 (C)	15 (B)	25 (A)	35 (B)	45 (D)	55 (B)	65 (A)	75 (A)	85 (B)	95 (B)
6 (D)	16 (C)	26 (B)	36 (C)	46 (A)	56 (A)	66 (B)	76 (D)	86 (B)	96 (A)
7 (C)	17 (A)	27 (B)	37 (A)	47 (D)	57 (A)	67 (D)	77 (B)	87 (C)	97 (C)
8 (B)	18 (C)	28 (A)	38 (B)	48 (B)	58 (D)	68 (C)	78 (D)	88 (B)	98 (B)
9 (C)	19 (C)	29 (A)	39 (C)	49 (A)	59 (A)	69 (C)	79 (B)	89 (D)	99 (A)
10 (C)	20 (C)	30 (B)	40 (D)	50 (B)	60 (B)	70 (C)	80 (D)	90 (B)	100 (C)

TEST 09

1 (D)	11 (A)	21 (A)	31 (C)	41 (C)	51 (A)	61 (D)	71 (A)	81 (A)	91 (D)
2 (D)	12 (A)	22 (B)	32 (A)	42 (D)	52 (A)	62 (D)	72 (C)	82 (C)	92 (B)
3 (C)	13 (A)	23 (C)	33 (B)	43 (C)	53 (D)	63 (C)	73 (D)	83 (A)	93 (C)
4 (A)	14 (C)	24 (A)	34 (A)	44 (A)	54 (A)	64 (A)	74 (D)	84 (D)	94 (D)
5 (A)	15 (B)	25 (A)	35 (B)	45 (D)	55 (A)	65 (B)	75 (B)	85 (B)	95 (B)
6 (B)	16 (B)	26 (A)	36 (C)	46 (B)	56 (C)	66 (A)	76 (D)	86 (D)	96 (A)
7 (C)	17 (A)	27 (C)	37 (C)	47 (D)	57 (B)	67 (D)	77 (A)	87 (C)	97 (C)
8 (B)	18 (C)	28 (B)	38 (C)	48 (A)	58 (C)	68 (A)	78 (D)	88 (B)	98 (C)
9 (A)	19 (B)	29 (A)	39 (B)	49 (D)	59 (C)	69 (B)	79 (A)	89 (A)	99 (A)
10 (A)	20 (A)	30 (B)	40 (D)	50 (B)	60 (A)	70 (B)	80 (B)	90 (B)	100 (B)

TEST 10

1 (C)	11 (C)	21 (B)	31 (A)	41 (D)	51 (D)	61 (D)	71 (A)	81 (B)	91 (B)
2 (B)	12 (C)	22 (B)	32 (D)	42 (A)	52 (C)	62 (A)	72 (C)	82 (C)	92 (B)
3 (D)	13 (C)	23 (C)	33 (A)	43 (C)	53 (A)	63 (A)	73 (D)	83 (D)	93 (C)
4 (A)	14 (A)	24 (B)	34 (B)	44 (A)	54 (D)	64 (B)	74 (D)	84 (A)	94 (B)
5 (C)	15 (B)	25 (A)	35 (B)	45 (C)	55 (A)	65 (C)	75 (B)	85 (A)	95 (D)
6 (D)	16 (B)	26 (C)	36 (D)	46 (D)	56 (D)	66 (C)	76 (B)	86 (A)	96 (D)
7 (C)	17 (B)	27 (C)	37 (C)	47 (B)	57 (B)	67 (B)	77 (D)	87 (C)	97 (D)
8 (A)	18 (A)	28 (A)	38 (B)	48 (D)	58 (A)	68 (D)	78 (D)	88 (D)	98 (D)
9 (A)	19 (B)	29 (B)	39 (D)	49 (C)	59 (B)	69 (B)	79 (A)	89 (B)	99 (C)
10 (B)	20 (B)	30 (B)	40 (C)	50 (C)	60 (C)	70 (A)	80 (A)	90 (D)	100 (A)

ANSWER SHEET

TEST 02

LISTENING (Part I-IV)

파고다 끝토익 1000제 LC

ANSWER SHEET

파고다 끝토익 1000제 LC

ANSWER SHEET

ANSWER SHEET

TEST 04

LISTENING (Part I-IV)

파고다 끝토익 1000제 LC

ANSWER SHEET

파고다 끝토익 1000제 LC

ANSWER SHEET

ANSWER SHEET

TEST 05

LISTENING (Part I-IV)

NO.	ANSWER A B C D	NO.	ANSWER A B C D	NO.	ANSWER A B C D	NO.	ANSWER A B C D	NO.	ANSWER A B C D
1	Ⓐ Ⓑ Ⓒ Ⓓ	21	Ⓐ Ⓑ Ⓒ	41	Ⓐ Ⓑ Ⓒ Ⓓ	61	Ⓐ Ⓑ Ⓒ Ⓓ	81	Ⓐ Ⓑ Ⓒ Ⓓ
2	Ⓐ Ⓑ Ⓒ Ⓓ	22	Ⓐ Ⓑ Ⓒ	42	Ⓐ Ⓑ Ⓒ Ⓓ	62	Ⓐ Ⓑ Ⓒ Ⓓ	82	Ⓐ Ⓑ Ⓒ Ⓓ
3	Ⓐ Ⓑ Ⓒ Ⓓ	23	Ⓐ Ⓑ Ⓒ	43	Ⓐ Ⓑ Ⓒ Ⓓ	63	Ⓐ Ⓑ Ⓒ Ⓓ	83	Ⓐ Ⓑ Ⓒ Ⓓ
4	Ⓐ Ⓑ Ⓒ Ⓓ	24	Ⓐ Ⓑ Ⓒ	44	Ⓐ Ⓑ Ⓒ Ⓓ	64	Ⓐ Ⓑ Ⓒ Ⓓ	84	Ⓐ Ⓑ Ⓒ Ⓓ
5	Ⓐ Ⓑ Ⓒ Ⓓ	25	Ⓐ Ⓑ Ⓒ	45	Ⓐ Ⓑ Ⓒ Ⓓ	65	Ⓐ Ⓑ Ⓒ Ⓓ	85	Ⓐ Ⓑ Ⓒ Ⓓ
6	Ⓐ Ⓑ Ⓒ Ⓓ	26	Ⓐ Ⓑ Ⓒ	46	Ⓐ Ⓑ Ⓒ Ⓓ	66	Ⓐ Ⓑ Ⓒ Ⓓ	86	Ⓐ Ⓑ Ⓒ Ⓓ
7	Ⓐ Ⓑ Ⓒ	27	Ⓐ Ⓑ Ⓒ	47	Ⓐ Ⓑ Ⓒ Ⓓ	67	Ⓐ Ⓑ Ⓒ Ⓓ	87	Ⓐ Ⓑ Ⓒ Ⓓ
8	Ⓐ Ⓑ Ⓒ	28	Ⓐ Ⓑ Ⓒ	48	Ⓐ Ⓑ Ⓒ Ⓓ	68	Ⓐ Ⓑ Ⓒ Ⓓ	88	Ⓐ Ⓑ Ⓒ Ⓓ
9	Ⓐ Ⓑ Ⓒ	29	Ⓐ Ⓑ Ⓒ	49	Ⓐ Ⓑ Ⓒ Ⓓ	69	Ⓐ Ⓑ Ⓒ Ⓓ	89	Ⓐ Ⓑ Ⓒ Ⓓ
10	Ⓐ Ⓑ Ⓒ	30	Ⓐ Ⓑ Ⓒ	50	Ⓐ Ⓑ Ⓒ Ⓓ	70	Ⓐ Ⓑ Ⓒ Ⓓ	90	Ⓐ Ⓑ Ⓒ Ⓓ
11	Ⓐ Ⓑ Ⓒ	31	Ⓐ Ⓑ Ⓒ	51	Ⓐ Ⓑ Ⓒ Ⓓ	71	Ⓐ Ⓑ Ⓒ Ⓓ	91	Ⓐ Ⓑ Ⓒ Ⓓ
12	Ⓐ Ⓑ Ⓒ	32	Ⓐ Ⓑ Ⓒ Ⓓ	52	Ⓐ Ⓑ Ⓒ Ⓓ	72	Ⓐ Ⓑ Ⓒ Ⓓ	92	Ⓐ Ⓑ Ⓒ Ⓓ
13	Ⓐ Ⓑ Ⓒ	33	Ⓐ Ⓑ Ⓒ Ⓓ	53	Ⓐ Ⓑ Ⓒ Ⓓ	73	Ⓐ Ⓑ Ⓒ Ⓓ	93	Ⓐ Ⓑ Ⓒ Ⓓ
14	Ⓐ Ⓑ Ⓒ	34	Ⓐ Ⓑ Ⓒ Ⓓ	54	Ⓐ Ⓑ Ⓒ Ⓓ	74	Ⓐ Ⓑ Ⓒ Ⓓ	94	Ⓐ Ⓑ Ⓒ Ⓓ
15	Ⓐ Ⓑ Ⓒ	35	Ⓐ Ⓑ Ⓒ Ⓓ	55	Ⓐ Ⓑ Ⓒ Ⓓ	75	Ⓐ Ⓑ Ⓒ Ⓓ	95	Ⓐ Ⓑ Ⓒ Ⓓ
16	Ⓐ Ⓑ Ⓒ	36	Ⓐ Ⓑ Ⓒ Ⓓ	56	Ⓐ Ⓑ Ⓒ Ⓓ	76	Ⓐ Ⓑ Ⓒ Ⓓ	96	Ⓐ Ⓑ Ⓒ Ⓓ
17	Ⓐ Ⓑ Ⓒ	37	Ⓐ Ⓑ Ⓒ Ⓓ	57	Ⓐ Ⓑ Ⓒ Ⓓ	77	Ⓐ Ⓑ Ⓒ Ⓓ	97	Ⓐ Ⓑ Ⓒ Ⓓ
18	Ⓐ Ⓑ Ⓒ	38	Ⓐ Ⓑ Ⓒ Ⓓ	58	Ⓐ Ⓑ Ⓒ Ⓓ	78	Ⓐ Ⓑ Ⓒ Ⓓ	98	Ⓐ Ⓑ Ⓒ Ⓓ
19	Ⓐ Ⓑ Ⓒ	39	Ⓐ Ⓑ Ⓒ Ⓓ	59	Ⓐ Ⓑ Ⓒ Ⓓ	79	Ⓐ Ⓑ Ⓒ Ⓓ	99	Ⓐ Ⓑ Ⓒ Ⓓ
20	Ⓐ Ⓑ Ⓒ	40	Ⓐ Ⓑ Ⓒ Ⓓ	60	Ⓐ Ⓑ Ⓒ Ⓓ	80	Ⓐ Ⓑ Ⓒ Ⓓ	100	Ⓐ Ⓑ Ⓒ Ⓓ

ANSWER SHEET

TEST 06

LISTENING (Part I-IV)

NO.	ANSWER A B C D	NO.	ANSWER A B C D	NO.	ANSWER A B C D	NO.	ANSWER A B C D	NO.	ANSWER A B C D
1	Ⓐ Ⓑ Ⓒ Ⓓ	21	Ⓐ Ⓑ Ⓒ	41	Ⓐ Ⓑ Ⓒ Ⓓ	61	Ⓐ Ⓑ Ⓒ Ⓓ	81	Ⓐ Ⓑ Ⓒ Ⓓ
2	Ⓐ Ⓑ Ⓒ Ⓓ	22	Ⓐ Ⓑ Ⓒ	42	Ⓐ Ⓑ Ⓒ Ⓓ	62	Ⓐ Ⓑ Ⓒ Ⓓ	82	Ⓐ Ⓑ Ⓒ Ⓓ
3	Ⓐ Ⓑ Ⓒ Ⓓ	23	Ⓐ Ⓑ Ⓒ	43	Ⓐ Ⓑ Ⓒ Ⓓ	63	Ⓐ Ⓑ Ⓒ Ⓓ	83	Ⓐ Ⓑ Ⓒ Ⓓ
4	Ⓐ Ⓑ Ⓒ Ⓓ	24	Ⓐ Ⓑ Ⓒ	44	Ⓐ Ⓑ Ⓒ Ⓓ	64	Ⓐ Ⓑ Ⓒ Ⓓ	84	Ⓐ Ⓑ Ⓒ Ⓓ
5	Ⓐ Ⓑ Ⓒ Ⓓ	25	Ⓐ Ⓑ Ⓒ	45	Ⓐ Ⓑ Ⓒ Ⓓ	65	Ⓐ Ⓑ Ⓒ Ⓓ	85	Ⓐ Ⓑ Ⓒ Ⓓ
6	Ⓐ Ⓑ Ⓒ Ⓓ	26	Ⓐ Ⓑ Ⓒ	46	Ⓐ Ⓑ Ⓒ Ⓓ	66	Ⓐ Ⓑ Ⓒ Ⓓ	86	Ⓐ Ⓑ Ⓒ Ⓓ
7	Ⓐ Ⓑ Ⓒ	27	Ⓐ Ⓑ Ⓒ	47	Ⓐ Ⓑ Ⓒ Ⓓ	67	Ⓐ Ⓑ Ⓒ Ⓓ	87	Ⓐ Ⓑ Ⓒ Ⓓ
8	Ⓐ Ⓑ Ⓒ	28	Ⓐ Ⓑ Ⓒ	48	Ⓐ Ⓑ Ⓒ Ⓓ	68	Ⓐ Ⓑ Ⓒ Ⓓ	88	Ⓐ Ⓑ Ⓒ Ⓓ
9	Ⓐ Ⓑ Ⓒ	29	Ⓐ Ⓑ Ⓒ	49	Ⓐ Ⓑ Ⓒ Ⓓ	69	Ⓐ Ⓑ Ⓒ Ⓓ	89	Ⓐ Ⓑ Ⓒ Ⓓ
10	Ⓐ Ⓑ Ⓒ	30	Ⓐ Ⓑ Ⓒ	50	Ⓐ Ⓑ Ⓒ Ⓓ	70	Ⓐ Ⓑ Ⓒ Ⓓ	90	Ⓐ Ⓑ Ⓒ Ⓓ
11	Ⓐ Ⓑ Ⓒ	31	Ⓐ Ⓑ Ⓒ	51	Ⓐ Ⓑ Ⓒ Ⓓ	71	Ⓐ Ⓑ Ⓒ Ⓓ	91	Ⓐ Ⓑ Ⓒ Ⓓ
12	Ⓐ Ⓑ Ⓒ	32	Ⓐ Ⓑ Ⓒ Ⓓ	52	Ⓐ Ⓑ Ⓒ Ⓓ	72	Ⓐ Ⓑ Ⓒ Ⓓ	92	Ⓐ Ⓑ Ⓒ Ⓓ
13	Ⓐ Ⓑ Ⓒ	33	Ⓐ Ⓑ Ⓒ Ⓓ	53	Ⓐ Ⓑ Ⓒ Ⓓ	73	Ⓐ Ⓑ Ⓒ Ⓓ	93	Ⓐ Ⓑ Ⓒ Ⓓ
14	Ⓐ Ⓑ Ⓒ	34	Ⓐ Ⓑ Ⓒ Ⓓ	54	Ⓐ Ⓑ Ⓒ Ⓓ	74	Ⓐ Ⓑ Ⓒ Ⓓ	94	Ⓐ Ⓑ Ⓒ Ⓓ
15	Ⓐ Ⓑ Ⓒ	35	Ⓐ Ⓑ Ⓒ Ⓓ	55	Ⓐ Ⓑ Ⓒ Ⓓ	75	Ⓐ Ⓑ Ⓒ Ⓓ	95	Ⓐ Ⓑ Ⓒ Ⓓ
16	Ⓐ Ⓑ Ⓒ	36	Ⓐ Ⓑ Ⓒ Ⓓ	56	Ⓐ Ⓑ Ⓒ Ⓓ	76	Ⓐ Ⓑ Ⓒ Ⓓ	96	Ⓐ Ⓑ Ⓒ Ⓓ
17	Ⓐ Ⓑ Ⓒ	37	Ⓐ Ⓑ Ⓒ Ⓓ	57	Ⓐ Ⓑ Ⓒ Ⓓ	77	Ⓐ Ⓑ Ⓒ Ⓓ	97	Ⓐ Ⓑ Ⓒ Ⓓ
18	Ⓐ Ⓑ Ⓒ	38	Ⓐ Ⓑ Ⓒ Ⓓ	58	Ⓐ Ⓑ Ⓒ Ⓓ	78	Ⓐ Ⓑ Ⓒ Ⓓ	98	Ⓐ Ⓑ Ⓒ Ⓓ
19	Ⓐ Ⓑ Ⓒ	39	Ⓐ Ⓑ Ⓒ Ⓓ	59	Ⓐ Ⓑ Ⓒ Ⓓ	79	Ⓐ Ⓑ Ⓒ Ⓓ	99	Ⓐ Ⓑ Ⓒ Ⓓ
20	Ⓐ Ⓑ Ⓒ	40	Ⓐ Ⓑ Ⓒ Ⓓ	60	Ⓐ Ⓑ Ⓒ Ⓓ	80	Ⓐ Ⓑ Ⓒ Ⓓ	100	Ⓐ Ⓑ Ⓒ Ⓓ

파고다 끝토익 1000제 LC

ANSWER SHEET

파고다 끝토익 1000제 LC

ANSWER SHEET

ANSWER SHEET

TEST 08

LISTENING (Part I-IV)

ANSWER SHEET

파고다 플토익 1000제 LC

ANSWER SHEET

파고다 플토익 1000제 LC

ANSWER SHEET

TEST 10

LISTENING (Part I-IV)

ANSWER SHEET

파고다 끝토익 1000제 LC

ANSWER SHEET

파고다 끝토익 1000제 LC